Åke Hultkrantz

THE ATTRACTION OF PEYOTE

Acta Universitatis Stockholmiensis

STOCKHOLM STUDIES IN COMPARATIVE RELIGION
XXXIII

Åke Hultkrantz

THE ATTRACTION OF PEYOTE

An Inquiry into the Basic Conditions for the Diffusion of the Peyote Religion in North America

ALMQVIST & WIKSELL INTERNATIONAL
STOCKHOLM/SWEDEN
1997

This work has been published
with a grant from The Swedish Council for
Research in the Humanities and Social Sciences.

© Åke Hultkrantz

ISBN 91-22-01712-7

Norstedts Tryckeri, Stockholm 1997

ABSTRACT

Hultkrantz, Åke
The Attraction of Peyote: An Inquiry into the Basic Conditions for the Diffusion of the Peyote Religion in North America.
Institute of Comparative Religion, University of Stockholm.

The American Indian Peyote Religion is the dominating new religion on North American Indian reservations since the end of the nineteenth century. It is based on the consumption of a small type of cactus, peyote (Lophophora williamsii) which, after being consumed, causes hallucinations. Researchers, in particular anthropologists, have tried to reveal the social, economical and political prerequisites of this movement. How this religion was formed, how it came about on the basis of extant local religions ideas, new ideas from other Indian tribes and Christian Missionary influences are all problems that have scarcely been dealt with. The following work is an effort to evaluate the anthropological achievements in this connection and to construct a collected contribution to an understanding of the forming of Peyote Religion from religio-historical perspectives.

Stockholm 1997, 233 pages, monograph

ISBN 91-22-01712-7

Shoshoni Painting of a Peyote Session. Photo: the author.

Peyote Water Drum

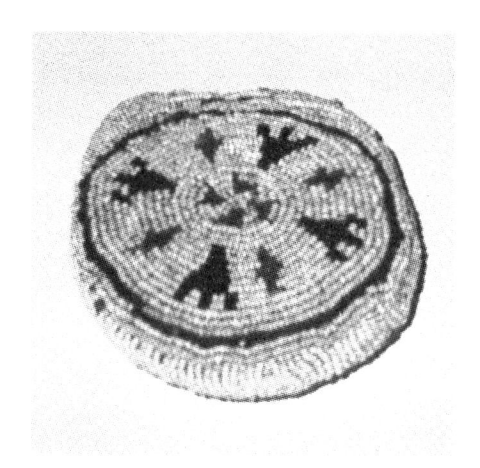

Peyote Button Pouch

Peyote Rattle

Peyote Paraphernalia from the Plains Indian Museum, Cody, Wyoming. Photos by Geraldine Hultkrantz.

PREFACE

During the past decades the use of psychoactive and narcotic drugs has swept over the industrialized world and caused both unrest and painful-joyful addiction in many circles. Occasionally we have even heard of the forming of religious groups, "cults", inspired by the common drug experiences. The expertise is unanimous that while the consummation of the drug facilitates and accentuates religious experiences the motivations for the use of the drug in a religious context must be sought in many quarters. Even where the use of the drug is the centre of religious ritual there are many underlying factors which have paved the way for its cultic realization. At the same time, the role of the religious factor as the main drive must not be overlooked.

Drugs in different forms have served as stimulants for ecstasy in shamanism since archaic times. Shamanic trance has certainly been looked upon mostly as a purely psychogenic process, but a closer study of shamanic séances often discloses an admixture of psychoactive ingredients as well. In particular has this been the case in Native America where, to quote Weston La Barre, a variety of narcotic and other drugs have been employed without comparison in other parts of the world. In some cases where hallucinogenic drugs are used the drug, or its source, the marvellous plant, is the object of veneration and divinization. We might say that the shamanic power manifested in auxiliary spirits has receded – in these cases – for the additional power inherent in certain plants and drugs. Some examples of such divinized potencies are the Ayahuasca of the Amazonas and the Peyote of North America. As we shall see, the Peyote story highlights the transmission of a psychoactive plant from being a basis of shamanic power to becoming a cult object and medicine for a group of initiated people.

The present book is a study of Peyote within a religio-scientific framing. In most anthropological publications dealing with the use of Peyote among North American Indians the "Peyote cult" is introduced as one of the standard examples of a successful acculturation between Native and white value patterns. It seems to me however that the most important aspect of the Peyote religion (as I prefer to call it) has not been treated in a satisfactory way: the problem why this religion spread so quickly over such a wide area and why it was so easily accepted in most (but not all) tribes of the Plains and Great Basin regions. This book represents an effort to solve this problem. Since the handling of Peyote operates in a religious setting religious factors have been particularly observed. They have often been strangely overlooked in comparative analyses of the Peyote religion. Other factors will be dealt with as well, but, as will be found, they do not seem to me to be of equal importance.

The necessity of discussing such an acculturated complex as the Peyote religion not only in general anthropological but also in religio-historical terms has been well formulated by Mircea Eliade:

> Few religious phenomena are more directly and more obviously connected with sociopolitical circumstances than the modern messianic and millenarian movements among colonial peoples (cargo-cults, etc.). Yet identifying and analyzing the conditions that prepared and made possible such messianic movements form only a part of the work of the historian of religions. For these movements are equally creations of the human spirit, in the sense that they have become what they are – *religious movements,* and not merely gestures of protest and revolt – through a creative act of the spririt. In short, a religious phenomenon such as primitive messianism must be studied just as the *Divina Commedia* is studied, that is, by using all the possible tools of scholarship. For, if the History of Religions is destined to further the rise of a new humanism, it is incumbent on the historian of religions to bring out the autonomous value – the value as *spiritual creation* – of all these primitive religious movements. To reduce them to sociopolitical contexts is, in the last analysis, to admit that they are not sufficiently "elevated", sufficiently "noble" to be treated as creations of human genius.
>
> (Eliade, History of Religions and a New Humanism, 1961, p. 6.)

The structure of this book may seem a bit unconventional since so much emphasis has been laid on theories which have been formed by earlier investigators, and their criticism, and so little is adduced from the empirical material on Peyotism. However, this arrangement has been necessary, for we know very little indeed of why Peyote, when it was first introduced into a tribal group, was accepted. The efforts by some scholars to follow up the individual missionaries of Peyote in the past yield very little in this connection. There is some safe data from tribes like the Winnebago, Dakota, Ute and Navajo, but very little from other groups. This situation has given rise to a wide debate on the subject.

The present investigation associates to this debate, and tries to integrate it with the sparse facts and a holistic basic view. Instead of a painstaking account of tribal Peyote histories – which in most cases would give most unsatisfactory results – it has been the author's aim to present a collected perspective on the problem. Some readers will no doubt complain that this is a shaky empirical foundation for the solution of the problem; to the author, however, who has waded through an immense amount of literature on the subject, this was the only path to tread.

In order to build up the reader's background knowledge of Peyote there is first a section on the nature of Peyote, the Peyote religion and its history. There is also a chapter on the symbolism and practice of Peyote in one particular tribe known to the author from field research. The aim is to transmit to the reader some close contact with the Peyote service as experienced by the author. Then, the various arguments which have been delivered on the spread of Peyote are discussed. Finally, the possible reasons why Peyote was so easily accepted, or accepted with hesitation, or not at all accepted, will be adduced.

Much of the literature for the present study was assembled in North America – in the field, in archives, in libraries – and in Scotland. In Aberdeen I had access to Professor H. W. Turner's great collection of reprints on new religious movements, at that time located at the Department of Religious Studies, University of Aberdeen. It was called, "Project for the Study of New Religious Movements in Primal Societies (PRONERMS)". Professors Weston La Barre and the late Omer C. Stewart have placed their numerous writings on Peyote at my disposal. Also Professor George Morgan has kindly supplied me with papers from his production on Peyote. I have enjoyed stimulating conversations with most of the scholars now mentioned, and with Professor David Aberle. To all my colleagues who have assisted me I extend my sincere thanks.

Some material is presented here for the first time: field material recorded by myself among the Wind River Shoshoni, Wyoming, and by my friend and disciple Dr. Paul Steinmetz, S. J., among the Oglala Lakota, South Dakota. I thank Dr. Steinmetz for the use of his extensive field notes. I also want to thank The Swedish Council for Research in the Humanities and Social Sciences for a generous grant to publish the work.

Last but not least I should like to thank my dear wife, Geraldine, for all her kind efforts to brush up my English into a legible form.

Åke Hultkrantz

Table of Contents

Preface 7
Table of Contents 11
Introduction 13
   I. Peyote and the Peyote Religion 21
      1. The Peyote "Herb" and Its Properties 21
      2. History and Diffusion of Peyote Religion 29
      3. Doctrine and Ritual 43
  II. The Peyote Religion: A Shoshoni Example 51
      1. Peyote among the Wind River Shoshoni 51
      2. Peyote Symbolism 59
      3. A Shoshoni Ritual Meeting 61
 III. Why Peyote Spread: the Indian Testimony 73
      1. The General Persuasion 73
      2. The Origin Legend of Peyote 74
 IV. Why Peyote Spread: the Research Opinion 79
      1. Trends of the Discussion 79
      2. The Peyote Religion as a Crisis Religion 83
      3. Peyote and the Situation of Cultural Shock 89
      4. Peyote as a Means of Personal Adjustment 97
      5. Peyote as a Medicine 99
      6. Peyote as an Expression of Religious and Ritual Continuity:
         Peyote and the "Mescal Bean Cult" 109
      7. Peyote as an Expression of Religious and Ritual Continuity:
         Peyote and the Vision Quest 113
      8. Peyotism and pan-Indianism 123
      9. The Facility of Peyote Religion 132
    10. The Role of the Peyote Proselytizer 136
    11. Peyote as an Instrument against White Domination 145
    12. Peyote Religion as an Alternative to Christianity and as
        a Form of Christianity 147
    13. Ghost Dance and Peyote 158
  V. The Religious Motivation of Peyote 163
      1. A Question of Values 163
      2. Peyote and the "Pharmacological" Theory of Religious Origins . 170
      3. The Religious Factor in the Adoption of Peyote Religion 174
 VI. The Decisive Causes: An Assessment 179
      1. A Scale of Causes 179

2. The Growth and Development of the Peyote Religion 181
  3. Factors Enhancing the Diffusion of the Peyote Religion 187
  4. Factors Restricting the Acceptance of the Peyote Religion . . . 196
  5. The Appeal of Peyote 203
Bibliography 209
Index 230

Introduction

The religion centered around the ritual consumption of the Peyote cactus variously known as the Peyote religion, the Peyote cult or – with reference to its ecclesiastic organization – the Native American Church, has stirred some attention among scholars, most of them anthropologists. There are comprehensive, now classic papers on the subject by Weston La Barre, whose knowledgeable book, *The Peyote Cult,* which opened the debate, has now been issued in the fifth revised edition, J. S. Slotkin, Omer Stewart and David Aberle.[1] Some other scholarly books have been written by Vincenzo Petrullo and Edward Anderson.[2] Among European scholars who have published studies on the Peyote religion may be mentioned Martin Gusinde, Vittorio Lanternari, Miroslawa Posern-Zielińska and Peter Gerber.[3] To these general and monographic works can be added the host of articles on special segments and problems of the Peyote religion, and some more popular books, like Alice Marriott's and Carol Rachlin's short introduction to the subject.[4] The present work thus joins an already established tradition of research, but has another emphasis.

During the past two hundred years North America has been the scene of a large number of aboriginal religious movements which have usually been labelled messianistic, prophetic, millenarian, revivalistic or nativistic.[5] All of them may in my opinion be called revivalistic since they revived (although in new forms) religious sentiments. Also La Barre's term par préférence, "crisis cults", may be used, although the word "cult" is less appropriate (cf. below). Indeed, all religions which are not "ethnic" or "national" may be characterized as originally revivalistic or crisis religions.[6] The Peyote religion naturally belongs here, but may be referred to a sub-category together with some other North American religious movements. For reasons which will soon be evident I prefer to use the term nativism, once coined by Ralph Linton.

Of all nativistic movements among present-day North American Indians the so-called Peyote cult has been the most successful: it received a rapid acceptance, it has survived the change of generation, and it has spread over a fairly

---

[1] La Barre 1938, 1975 b, Slotkin 1956 a, Stewart 1944, 1987, Aberle 1966, 1982 b, Stewart and Aberle 1984.
[2] Petrullo 1934, Anderson 1980.
[3] Gusinde 1939, Lanternari 1960, Posern-Zielińska 1972, Gerber 1980. See also Wagner 1932.
[4] Marriott and Rachlin 1972.
[5] Cf. La Barre 1971 and Turner 1978. The latter is an excellent guide for North America, including the Peyote movement.
[6] Cf. La Barre 1970 a. However, I take exception to La Barre's interpretation of religion; cf. my criticism in Hultkrantz 1971.

13

large area.[7] Although in some quarters showing signs of weakening (see Ch. I:2) it is still spreading and in several Indian communities both on the reservations and in cities like Los Angeles it is gaining an ever increasing number of adherents. The consolidation of the Peyote movement in an ecclesiastical organization, the Native American Church, creates the impression – not at all justified – that the Peyote "cult" has superseded or even replaced older religious systems. To many Indians today it stands out as a symbol of Indian unity, or pan-Indianism (cf. Ch. IV:8).

Strictly speaking the label "Peyote cult" used by several authors in the past, including La Barre and occasionally Aberle, is a misnomer as Aberle realized.[8] This "cult" is not just a cult, but a religion with prominent cultic aspects. A real cult is, to my understanding, a complex of rituals and beliefs *within* a particular religion, and revolving around one or several supernatural beings.[9] The confusion between cult and religion stems from two quarters. Firstly, A. L. Kroeber used the term cult to express movements of the Peyote type at the turn of the century.[10] The character of such movements was later defined by Kroeber when he discussed "the cults or definitely elaborated religions of California".[11] Since then it is particularly restricted religious traditions, and religions of a sectarian character, that have passed under the term "cults" in American anthropology. Paul Radin used the appellation "Peyote cult" in his pioneer work on the subject (1914), and most investigators on the subject, including Gunter Wagner and La Barre, have followed him.[12]

Secondly, sociologists have used the word cult in a specific sense, as a type of "sect". Thus, Milton Yinger characterizes the cult as a kind of sect consisting of individuals who search for mystical experiences under the guidance of a charismatic leader.[13] Such a definition is less applicable to the Peyote movement, but the very fact that "cult" has received the sociological stamp of some sort of smaller congregation has probably influenced the modern adoption of the term.

In this work I prefer to use the more adequate word "religion", but will occasionally use "Peyotism" as a synonym. (It is with regret that I admit that in an earlier, preliminary article on the subject I uncritically followed La Barre's

---

[7] Other successful movement with, however, a more restricted area of distribution are the Shakerism of the Shahaptin and Salish populations in northwestern U.S.A. and the Religion of Handsome Lake, a case of revivalism among the Iroquois. See Barnett 1957 and Deardorff 1951.
[8] Aberle 1982 b, pp. xxi f.
[9] Cf. Hultkrantz 1981 a, p. 95. See also Winick 1956, p. 143. Indeed, I hesitate to call Peyote the central supernatural figure of the Peyote cult, but it is certainly one of the supernaturals.
[10] Kroeber 1902–07, p. 398.
[11] Kroeber 1925, p. 855. It is ironical that in a later work Kroeber consistently talks about "Peyote religion": Kroeber 1948, p. 568.
[12] Radin 1914.
[13] Yinger 1957. Cf. also Marty 1960.

nomenclature.)[14] Indians, when not speaking of the Native American Church, or simply Peyote meetings, like to use the term "the Peyote way".[15]

In comparison with other revivalistic movements in North America the Peyote religion has some remarkable qualities which most of the others lack.

(1) It is displayed around a stimulating drug, the Peyote cactus, imported from the Texan-Mexican area (see below, Ch. I:1). We know of a predecessor on the Southern Plains, the Red or Mescal Bean "cult" which might have had a preforming influence on Peyote religion (see Ch. IV:6). The use of *Datura* and other psychoactive plants as parts of ritual activities is well known by ethnologists, but the Peyote religion is unique in North America as a "drug-religion".[16]

(2) There are no prophets. Fred Voget justly states that Peyotists have not received "a divine injunction", although leaders have taught and preached the new way (for instance, John Wilson, John Rave).[17] Vittorio Lanternari however calls these leaders "prophets", erroneously in my opinion, for there is no sign of any consciousness of vocation.[18] The situation reminds us rather of what Burridge has to say about the preliminary stages of religious movements.[19]

(3) Messianism, millenarism and eschatological dreams are absent. Although the afterlife plays a considerable role in Peyotist thinking the movement has definitely no "eschatological" character like, for instance, the Ghost Dance.

(4) Peyotists are organized in the Native American Church. This is an intertribal organization (of a certainly very liberal character) that has no counterpart in other North American Indian religious movements.

It is thus apparent that the Peyote religion has a very particular profile. How could we define it? It certainly has a revivalistic character, but such a statement does not say much. Some newer anthropological concepts may give us certain guidance, although primarily they try to catch the spirit of whole cultures, not just religions, and certainly not intertribal religions.

A. F. C. Wallace has introduced the term "revitalization movement" which he defines as "a deliberate, organized, conscious effort by members of a society to construct a more satisfying culture".[20] In a broad sense the Peyote religion represents a revitalization of culture, but it is scarcely a deliberate effort to reform the culture. A similar criticism can be directed against Ralph Linton's presenta-

---

[14] Hultkrantz 1975, reprinted in Hultkrantz 1981 a, pp. 282–293.
[15] Slotkin 1956 b, p. 64.
[16] It is however possible that the so-called Chungichnish religion that originated among the Gabrielino (either on the Catalina Island, California, or near Long Beach) and later, possibly around 1800, spread to some mainland groups (primarily the Gabrielino of the Los Angeles area, the Juaneño, Luiseño and Chumash), was centered around the consumption of "toloache" or *Datura* (formerly called *D. meteloides,* now *D. inoxia*). See Kroeber 1925, pp. 621 ff., and Bean and Vane 1978, p. 669.
[17] Voget 1956, p. 254.
[18] Lanternari 1960, pp. 72 ff.
[19] Burridge 1969, p. 12.
[20] Wallace 1956, pp. 265, 279.

tion of his concept of "nativism" as "any conscious, organized attempt on the part of a society's members to revive or perpetuate selected aspects of its culture".[21] However, the term Nativism is meaningful here if there is a slight widening of the definition, allowing for subconscious action. The Peyote religion is then nativistic in a sense that corresponds to Voget's "reformative nativism", a term which presupposes a synthesis of traditional and alien cultural components.[22] "Traditional" would then include not only tribal but also general Indian traits (cf. Ch. IV:8). Even with the limitation proposed here Nativism is a very comprehensive concept, and Omer Stewart regards it as a misfit when speaking of Peyote as nativistic since Peyotism is an intertribal, not a tribal movement.[23] However, Nativism may be expanded to cover supertribal feelings of "Indianness" (pan-Indianism), depending on the ideological orientation of the believer (cf. further Ch. IV:8).

For the purposes of this study, I have not seen any reason to comment upon David Aberle's interesting classification of social movements in their relation to Peyotism.[24] Otherwise his differentiation between movements aiming at changes in supra-individual systems and movements aiming at changes in individuals is rewarding. Aberle concludes that Peyotism is an individual-centered, that is, redemptive movement.

Another way of approaching the matter is to regard the Peyote movement as a case of religious acculturation, actualized by Voget's definition.[25] There is as we shall see in Peyotism a strong impact of Christian ideas and Christian Church organization, and a diffusion of Mexican Indian cultural traits has no doubt taken place: the cult of a cactus and important parts of the ritual are examples. It is obvious that Peyote Indians – if this expression is allowed – have dismissed Christian missionary programs but at the same time incorporated salient features of Christian thought and ritual in their own religion. Referring to the systematization I have presented in an earlier book I suggest that this acculturation testifies to a "manifestly negative, latently positive response" to Christianity through which traditional and imported religious elements have been integrated into a new holistic religion.[26] Now, such a type of religious acculturation may include many forms of expression. The Peyote religion is clearly one of them.

---

[21] Linton 1943, p. 230.
[22] Voget 1956, p. 250. Guglielmo Guariglia (1959, p. 173) finds Voget's characterization of the Peyote religion as reformative Nativism only partly justified.
[23] Cf. Stewart's account, Testing Anthropological Theories about Peyotism with Ethnohistorical Data, as reviewed in Lynch 1984, p. 180.
[24] Aberle 1982 b, pp. 315 ff.
[25] Voget defines reformative Nativism as "a relatively conscious attempt on the part of a subordinated group to attain a personal and social reintegration through a selective rejection, modification, and synthesis of both traditional and alien (dominant) cultural components": Voget 1956, p. 250. Some would perhaps characterize the Peyote religion as "transitional", cf. Vogt 1957.
[26] Hultkrantz 1973 b, p. 217.

Similar diversification surrounds another concept that has been central in the scientific debate on Peyote, cultural deprivation. As Bernhard Barber has pointed out, there are several alternative responses to such deprivation. The violent Ghost Dance and its messianism represents one, the peaceful Peyotism another.[27]

There will be further discussions of the concepts of acculturation (Ch. IV:2) and deprivation (Ch. IV:3) in the sequence.

The foregoing discussion ought to have clarified the religious character and uniqueness of the Peyote religion. We are here facing a basically Mexican Indian religious complex that has become integrated with North American ritual elements, absorbed some important European ideas and been transformed into a sectarian movement.[28] It is not, however, as has been suggested, a "community religion" that, through contact with a "religion of faction" (Christianity), has turned into some kind of religion of faction.[29] Inspired by the divine cactus rather than the divine word revealed by prophets, Indians have built up an intertribal nativistic movement finally organized in a church.

As stated the subject of the present book is to look for the basic motives behind the rapid spread of Peyotism.[30] The diffusion itself has been thoroughly analyzed in several works (by Shonle, La Barre, Gusinde, Slotkin, Stewart and others). New data and new dates appear all the time as the ethnohistorical study of documents proceeds. Only a cursory review of the main diffusional data will be presented here (Ch. I:2). The main perspective is historical and functionalistic: why was this religion so readily accepted in some places, but rejected in others; why did it spread so rapidly, and why did it spread as it did? In other words, we have to single out the conditions for the attraction of Peyote, the driving forces behind the diffusion, and the specific factors and obstacles that channelized and limited this diffusion. In doing this we have to rely on historical investigations, published field data and on some constructive theories on Peyote proposed by well-informed colleagues.

There have been some approaches to the same range of problems in the past, partly in the standard works on Peyotism, quoted above, partly in specific papers. In this connection I would like to particularly mention an instructive and systematic paper by Robert Bee which offers different possibilities of explanations.[31]

---

[27] Barber 1941 a. In Wallace's typology we could relegate the Ghost Dance to the revivalistic and the Peyote religion to the assimilative movements. When, however, Wallace claims that the Ghost Dance offered salvation by possession and the Peyote religion turned its devotees to mysticism he plays havoc with the concepts. See Wallace 1966, pp. 164 f.

[28] Sectarian in the sense Bryan Wilson (1969, p. 362) recommends: "Sects are ideological movements having as their explicit and declared aim the maintenance, and perhaps even the propagation of certain ideological positions."

[29] Cf. van Baaren 1975, p. 27.

[30] Cf. my preliminary paper on the subject, Hultkrantz 1975 (also in Hultkrantz 1981 a, pp. 282 ff.).

[31] Bee 1965. See in particular the section "Factors in the Diffusion of Peyote", pp. 24–32.

General statements on the causes of Peyote diffusion may be found in some older publications, but they were never much elaborated. Summary evaluations were offered as late as 1937 by a team of distinguished anthropologists in a collection of documents accompanying a Senate Bill (statements by, i.a., Franz Boas, John P. Harrington, A. L. Kroeber, Weston La Barre, Vincenzo Petrullo and R. E. Schultes, the latter no anthropologist but a well-known biologist).[32] Otherwise American anthropologists refrained from more sweeping statements. After World War II most American anthropologists have applied a more careful approach, mostly restricting the scope to individual tribes or reservations, or even local groups on reservations, as among the Navajo and Lakota. Using instensive field work, interviews and statistical operations students like Aberle, Slotkin, Stewart and Louise and George Spindler have tried to reveal the differential appeal of Peyote in particular social groups, Navajo, Menomini and Ute.[33] Comparative analyses have been less frequent. Weston La Barre who is one of our foremost experts on the Peyote religion in all its aspects has presented the main lines of authors' interpretations in his bibliographical report of 1960 and in his additions to later editions of his *The Peyote Cult,* but without making a systematic analysis.[34]

An exhaustive survey of the factors behind acceptance and diffusion would have to follow up the intricate threads of diffusion through time and place. It would also have to study the single developments in individual tribes as expressed in people's reactions and evaluations. However, such an undertaking is less realistic. Not only would it consume the time of a large number of students for many years,[35] there does not seem to exist enough tangible materials for such a procedure. First of all, there are too many lacunas in our general knowledge of individual tribes. We have a rather exhaustive material from tribes which have been won for Peyote in fairly recent times, such as the Navajo and Ute.[36] On the other hand, from other tribes there is very little or no information at all. Secondly, there is no unanimous interpretation of the old documents.[37] Thirdly, among tribes having accepted Peyote long ago the known patterns of reaction to Peyote refer to fairly recent times; a good example is Wesley Hurt's investigations among the Lakota.[38] It is only with great caution that present-day

---

[32] Documents on Peyote, Part 1 (following Senate Bill 1399, 1937), mimeographed publication, Government Printing Office, Washington, D.C., 1937.

[33] Aberle 1982 b, Slotkin 1952, Stewart 1948, L. S. Spindler 1952, G. Spindler 1955. Cf. also Wesley R. Hurt's analysis of Peyotism in the Dakotas (Hurt 1960) and Driver's quantitative investigations of distribution (Driver 1939).

[34] La Barre 1960, 1975 b.

[35] A program which however appeals to Peter Gerber, see the report on his paper, Theoretical Explanations of the Peyote Religion in Lynch 1984, p. 179.

[36] Aberle and Stewart 1957.

[37] Cf. the criticism in La Barre 1960, pp. 53 f., of Slotkin 1955.

[38] Hurt 1960.

reactions may be adduced to account for initial reactions, a point that we shall return to again and again. Discussing the acceptance and growth of Peyotism George Spindler points out that "Menomini peyotism started with an historical accident, got under way because a few individuals were in a ready state, and finally became firmly established not from any single cause but from a combination of factors".[39] This quotation shows that factors effective at one time in the history of Peyote are not necessarily operative at a later date.

The nature of the materials thus forces us to make a selective analysis. We can learn someting from the *diffusion* of Peyote – the roads of communication, the restriction of the area, the transmission of ideology –, the cultural *situation* at the adoption of Peyotism, the human *reactions* to Peyote as known to us,[40] and the *functions* of Peyote as related by the documents (some of them being quite ancient). All this evidence, and much more data, can be used to disclose the factors at work behind the acceptance and diffusion of Peyotism.

At least we may arrive at a set of resaonable hypotheses concerning the spread of that "diabolic root"[41] or "wonderful herb".[42] I have tried to pinpoint what seems to me to be the decisive factors for the adoption of Peyote. In so doing I have paid particular attention to the religious values and religious causes which, to my understanding, have not been duly observed.

---

[39] Spindler in La Barre 1960, p. 57.
[40] As far as I know the first reliable detailed account of a Peyote meeting was given by the famous reporter on the Ghost Dance, James Mooney (1897). See also his short summary in an earlier article, The Kiowa Mescal Rite, in the Washington Evening Star, Nov. 4, 1891. (The appellation "mescal" here is wrong.)
[41] Cf. the title of Petrullo 1934. The expression "diabolic root" was first used by J. Ortega in 1754, cf. Safford 1915, p. 295.
[42] Hoebel 1949.

I. Peyote and the Peyote Religion

1. The Peyote "Herb" and Its Properties

Peyote, the *peyotl* of the Aztecs (*Lophophora williamsii* Lemaire), is a spineless cactus that grows on both sides of the Rio Grande and in large parts of northern Mexico.[1] It contains over thirty alkaloids of which one, the morphine-like mescaline,[2] produces mental and emotional changes as well as certain perceptual effects. The latter are of a type usually labelled hallucinatory. The psychic impact of Peyote on the mind of the human being is the compulsive force behind the Peyote religion.[3]

It should be noticed that "hallucinatory" is a key-word which here will have a particular meaning. This term, in medical and psychological circles used today for a sensorial experience without external stimulus, will be applied here in a more extensive way to denote all visual and auditive phenomena which do not seem to have a naturally explicable source.[4] With the well-known psychologist and philosopher C. D. Broad I question the description of hallucinations as delusive and pathological in every case. As Broad has assumed, many hallucinations may be characterized as "veridical".[5] They may present in more or less distorted form impressions from a reality we normally only partly perceive with our senses. Hallucinations then say something about the limits of our sense perceptions.[6] This use of the term which, incidentally, comes closer to the Latin

---

[1] Cf. Anderson 1969, 1970. See also the maps in Stewart 1987, pp. 6, 10.

[2] Although mescaline is a Peyote ingredient and the Peyote is often referred to as the "mescal button" there is no identity of Peyote with the so-called "mescal bean" (to be mentioned in Ch. IV:6) or the "red bean" springing from the plant *Sophora secundiflora*. "Mescal" is an (originally Indian) term for the Agave plant or the food from this plant and the liquor (pulque) prepared from fermented Agave sap. See La Barre 1975 b, pp. 15, 17, 126 f., and Slotkin 1955, p. 202.

[3] Leary *et alii* consider that the drug as such does not produce these anormal experiences but "merely acts as a chemical key". "It opens the mind, frees the nervous system of its ordinary patterns and structures." The content of the experience is referred to personality factors and cultural conditions ("set and setting"). See Leary, Metzner and Alpert 1964, p. 11. Now Leary was of course the priest of LSD, but his kind of perceptions were actually once defended by William James (James 1902, p. 388). Cf. also Reichel-Dolmatoff 1972 (on Banisteriopsis).

[4] To dispel misunderstanding, this does not mean that we should investigate these phenomena with other than natural scientific means.

[5] Broad 1962, pp. 190 ff., 195 f.

[6] I thank Dr. Dan Merkur for this suggestion. Broad, with Bergson, considered that the brain is responsible for the selection of our perceptions. For American Indian examples of such hallucinations, see Kensinger 1973, p. 12 note 4.

basic meaning, soul-wandering *(alucinari),* approaches the hallucinatory phenomenon in a less preconceived way.[7]

Although I very much doubt that medical specialists will change their definitions of hallucinations this "neutralization" of what a hallucination may mean is of importance in the study of the Peyote religion.

Peyote is thus a hallucinogen, belonging to one of the psychoactive substances. If we here disregard the psychic sedatives (to which the narcotics belong, see also below) and stimulants, the group of hallucinogens includes the most well-known psychoactive drugs, mescaline (in the *Cactaceae*), psilocybin (in mushrooms)[8] and LSD which is, of course, a synthetic product.[9]

The consumption of Peyote – it may be eaten, drunk (the drink being a concoction of the plant) or smoked – induces a euphoric state of mind followed by weariness, but also a tense vigilance and power of observation. Vivid hallucinations appear, colourful visions (corporeal as well as interior), mobile illusions, and sometimes auditions.[10] Sentiments of fraternity and togetherness prevail. These qualities of Peyote have no doubt paved the path for its use as a means of religious self-realization and as a centre of a religious cult.

The hallucinogenic properties of Peyote (which thus may also be found in South American cacti containing mescaline)[11] fit very well into the visionary religious patterns of the North American Indians (cf. Ch. IV:7). La Barre even contrasts European epistemology, centering on intersubjective experience, with Amerindian epistemology whose "touchstone for truth" since ancient times has been the visionary experience of medicine power.[12] This is however too wide a generalization: European religious denominations allow for visionary experience to a varying degree, and American Indians build their actions on rationalism and intersubjective experience also to a varying degree. However, La Barre is right when he insists that much of American Indian religion is based on "direct psychodynamic and pharmacological experience" of the supernatural. Likewise, he is right when he claims that this fact motivated the Indians to explore their hallucinogenic plant world.[13] It is, for example, obvious that in-

---

[7] I am aware that this interpretation to some extent may meet the demands of certain drug-addicted apostles who talk about automatic "brain-expanding" effects of narcotic substances. In my opinion their inference is only partly true. However, it is well known that in their forms hallucinations are the products of personality and culture. Only in their general design, and corresponding to their anormal character, could some hallucinations betray potentially metaphysical tendencies.

[8] Not in all psychoactive mushrooms, however: the potent agent in the fly agaric *(Amanita muscaria)* is muscimole.

[9] The hallucinogens are, although not always habit-forming (cf. below), sometimes very powerful. LSD is exceptionally strong, and mescaline is related to the drug amphetamine.

[10] Cf. the excellent, detailed discussion in La Barre 1975 b, pp. 10 ff., 17 ff., 138 ff., 251 ff.

[11] Cf. La Barre 1975 b, p. 256, Alvarson and Hultkrantz 1975.

[12] La Barre 1975 b, pp. xv f.

[13] La Barre 1975 b, p. xv.

dulging in tobacco *(Nicotiana rustica)* afforded such subjective experiences that they could be interpreted within a religious framework.[14] The use of Peyote mediates an even stronger connection with the supernatural.

So far we have stated that the power of Peyote lies in its hallucinogenic qualities. Peyote belongs to the psychoactive drugs which, like for instance LSD, psilocybin and harmine, have been classified as hallucinogens.[15] Its attractiveness lies in its effects on the mind, but certainly not in its flavour. It is definitely not tasty, but rather feels like mud in the mouth. As a stimulant it is ambiguous, granting hallucinations and feelings of brotherhood, but also sensations of discomfort and sickness (in particular caused through the alkaloid lophophorine). Has it, then, any compulsive, habit-forming effect? Is the Peyote a drug, a narcotic?

There is a certain difficulty in discussing this subject because anthropologists do not agree as to what constitutes a narcotic drug[16] – in contradistinction to biologists and medical scientists. The root of this disagreement is, in fact, the difference of opinion as regards the physiology of Peyote. Carroll Barber defies the idea that addiction should be used as the most important single criterion for determining a substance as narcotic, for, he argues, addiction may be defined primarily as a psychological and social phenomenon, rather than as a pharmacological and physiological one.[17] Barber suggests instead that "a narcotic is a substance which can alter or distort the user's perception of himself and of the external world".[18] Barber here supplies an "anthropological" definition of narcotic to replace the medical definition.

In a comparative investigation D. W. Maurer and V. H. Vogel have demonstrated that there is no proof whatsoever that American Indians or other Peyote users should evince an habitual or addictive dependence on Peyote.[19] Also other investigations have reached the same result. Barber considers however that the anthropological position taken against calling Peyote a narcotic – possibly in order to save Peyotism from being banned by legal and political authorities – is most unfortunate. He thinks it removes Peyote from the general drug-using context to which it belongs.[20] Oliver La Farge, well-known author of North American Indian life, produced the counter-argument that Barber's definition might be exploited by anti-Peyotists in support of legislation against the use of Peyote.[21] Barber's defense was that there are so many other qualities than just

---

[14] Tobacco contains harmine alkaloids that possess hallucinogenic properties, cf. Janiger and Dobkin de Rios 1976.
[15] Delay 1967.
[16] Barber 1959, p. 641.
[17] Barber 1959, pp. 642 f.
[18] Barber 1959, p. 644.
[19] Maurer and Vogel 1954, p. 114. Cf. also below, note 20.
[20] Barber 1959, pp. 644 f.
[21] La Farge 1960, p. 688.

addiction that determine a drug's placing among the narcotics. However, the psychiatrist and neurologist Bernard E. Gorton categorically states that, from a medical and psychiatric point of view, "the decisive question is whether a drug creates physical dependency, and only if this occurs is it to be regarded as a narcotic".[22] It scarcely justifies confusing the issue by introducing a particular "anthropological" definition of narcotics, so much less since it is challenged by the majority of anthropologists.

In this presentation I shall comply with traditional interpretations of narcotics as meaning a substance which induces drowsiness and, at the same time, addiction. (In recent debate the soporific state has been deleted and main emphasis laid on addiction.) Dr. Gorton writes that Peyote "is definitely not a narcotic", that is, it is not physically addicting, creating no dependency after prolonged use.[23]

Anthropologists tend to agree that Peyote has no habit-forming effect, and psychiatrists and toxicologists are apparently of the same opinion.[24] Maurer, for instance, assures us that while Peyote is a stimulant and intoxicant, it should be distinguished from commonly accepted drugs of addiction.[25] The pharmacologist Paul Hoch denies that mescaline is a narcotic.[26] Although some older authorities in their time allowed for the possibility that Peyote may have a narcotic effect if taken in great quantities and used intensely, there is today no proof that the use of Peyote has any addictive consequences. Actually, it appears that on the whole hallucinogens do not cause physical addiction.

If the term "narcotic" is less appropriate, what term could we use for ethnographic purposes? La Barre has suggested *psychotropic,* a word which points at the mind-turning effects.[27] This term has the advantage that it is devoid of all associations of addiction and soporiferousness that weighs down the word "narcotic". When first used it was vividly supported by Oliver La Farge.[28] Psychotropic is certainly a good, descriptive word, and will be used here.

Another, alternative term is *psychedelic,* which could be rendered "mind-expanding".[29] Its drawback is, of course, that in many quarters it has become a

---

[22] Letter reproduced in Stewart 1961 a, pp. 1334 f. La Barre has summed up the discussion, see La Barre 1975 b, p. 222. I am, however, not in complete agreement with La Barre's interpretation of Barber's views.

Aberle, quoting Alfred Lindesmith, makes a distinction between physical dependence, addiction, tolerance and craving (Aberle 1982 b, pp. 9–10). On the basis of extant experimental, observational and field data he concludes that Peyote does not create physiological dependence, is not addicting, and is not the subject of compelling craving. It only promotes "some mild tolerance" (Aberle 1982 b, p. 11).

[23] Stewart 1961 a, ibidem.
[24] Cf. La Barre 1975 b, pp. 148 ff.
[25] Maurer 1960, p. 684.
[26] La Barre 1975 b, p. 223. Cf. La Barre's position, p. xiv.
[27] La Barre 1960, p. 54. *Tropé* (Gr.) means turning, psychotropic thus = the turning of the psyche.
[28] La Farge 1960, p. 689.
[29] *Delos* (Gr.) means clear, visible, psychedelic thus = mind-revealing.

degrading indication of injurious drugs. However, it was created (by the psychiatrist Humphry Osmond, in 1956) as a convenient term to characterize all drugs without specification. Unfortunately, it became popularized in connection with the drug culture of the 1960s.[30] The word will be occasionally, but carefully, used here.

There is, finally, a third term, *psychoactive,* which has been used in the foregoing and certainly is appropriate although it is perhaps less indicative than the other two.

Correlated with the fact that Peyote cannot be regarded as a narcotic, habit-forming drug is its present legal interpretation. In the United States federal legislation there is not, and never has been, any prohibition against Indian religious use of Peyote, although there are some anti-Peyote State laws.[31] According to the *Comprehensive Drug Abuse Prevention and Control Act* of 1970 there is an exemption for "the nondrug use of Peyote in bona fide religious ceremonies" of the American Indian Peyote ceremonial community, that is, the so-called Native American Church. Time and again there have certainly been convictions of Indians for the illegal possession of Peyote, and the bona fide has sometimes been difficult to prove even when these Indians have belonged to the Native American Church. As Robert Michaelsen has remarked, case law has upheld the exempt status "for use but not generally for possession outside an obvious religious ceremony."[32] However, as the same author concludes, with the Whitehorn case of 1977 a move in the direction of exempt status for mere possession has taken place.[33]

Curiously enough, in the Navajo country the anti-Peyote sentiments were so strong in 1940 that in an ordinance the tribal council ruled that the possession or usage of Peyote was forbidden.[34] This ordinance was for a long time challenged by the Native American Church, but without result. However, opinion slowly changed, and in 1967 tribal legislation changed in favour of Peyote. The next year a federal law was passed which denied tribes the right to prohibit the free exercise of religion.[35]

In all this battle for Peyote anthropologists had played a conspicuous role.[36] In a statement of November, 1951, some leading Peyote scholars addressed the

---

[30] Introduction, in Grinspoon and Bakalar 1983, p. 12.
[31] Cf. the general surveys in Slotkin 1956 a, pp. 50 ff., La Barre 1975 b, pp. 223 ff., and Stewart 1961 b, 1973 and 1987. There are now good summaries in Michaelsen 1983, pp. 121 ff. and in Stewart 1991.
[32] Michaelsen 1983, p. 127.
[33] Michaelsen 1983, ibidem.
[34] Aberle 1982, pp. xxxvii f., 109 ff., Stewart 1961 b, pp. 22 ff. The instigators were Christian members of the tribal council whose chairman, Jacob C. Morgan, was a Christian missionary (Aberle 1982 b, p. 110).
[35] I refer here to a personal communication (October, 1977) from Dr. Michaelsen.
[36] Stewart 1973.

general public with sober information on Peyote. They pointed out, among other things, that, on the basis of their experience, there are no symptoms of drug addiction, such as increased tolerance and dependence.[37]

If, then, Peyote is devoid of narcotic, habit-forming effects, this is important for our main purpose in this book: the appeal of Peyote can in no sense be reduced to a case of enforced addiction, but may reside in its hallucinogenic properties and emotional effects. Or rather, in the reciprocity between these qualities and specific cultural presuppositions.[38]

Before we turn to a closer scrutiny of these interrelations some words should be said about the purely pharmacological effects of Peyote consumption.[39] An experienced Peyote consumer like Weston La Barre finds that the most conspicuous consequences of Peyote eating are "perhaps" the visual phenomena. He notices that they are culturally reproduced in Indian symbolism and beliefs. He refers to the frequent occurrence of red and yellow birds and feathers in Mexican and Plains Peyote symbolism as consonant with the coloured vision explosions. Plains Indians often believe, he continues, that the consumption of Peyote makes their sight better, a belief that he derives from pupil-dilation. He notes that white observers have experienced more acute vision in Peyote intoxication from the same cause.[40] Of particular interest in this connection is C. R. Marshall's observation, reported on by La Barre, that form constants in Peyote visions derive from the anatomy of the eye, including structures behind the retina.[41]

A graphic picture of the process of colour hallucinations caused by Peyote has been given by W. E. Dixon; what he has to say conforms closely with the present writer's own experiences. Dixon finds that the sensory hallucinations, especially visions, are the most remarkable phenomena of Peyote consumption. They arise gradually, are at first only perceived with closed eyes but rapidly become more pronounced. Finally, on closing his eyes the test subject sees "a regular kaleidoscopic play of colours". This can be seen with either eye, and Dixon therefore concludes that the condition must be central. He adds that the colours may assume all kinds of fantastic shapes and are constantly in motion, acting like a kind of pulsation.[42] Dixon wrote down his observations at the turn of the century, and they maintain their relevance today.

In this connection the hypothesis should be mentioned, proposed by Sigvald

---

[37] La Barre et al. 1951, p. 582.
[38] It is easy to agree with Howard's standpoint: "The tacit assumption, shared by the general public and many anthropologists, that the *substance* peyote is the major *raison d'être* for peyotism, in our own opinion falls short of the mark" (Howard 1967, p. 21). See also below, Ch. V:2.
[39] It is important to realize that in causing most of these effects Peyote joins with several other psychoactive drugs, cf. Grinspoon and Bakalar 1983, pp. 13 f.
[40] La Barre 1975 b, p. 20.
[41] Marshall 1937, cf. La Barre 1975 b, p. 256.
[42] Dixon 1899/1900, pp. 80 f., cf. La Barre 1975 b, pp. 141 f.

Linné and others, that the colourful Aztec pantheon could have derived its brilliancy from the constructive imagination of Peyote eaters.[43] It is well known that drug addition may influence an artist's creations. Mervyn Levy writes concerning Modigliani that he, although an Expressionist painter, employed "the technique of emotive distortion". His distortions were to some extent, at least, due to his smoking of marihuana. Levy thinks that this addiction might account for the intensity and splendour of his colour.[44]

The Swedish Professor of Comparative Religion, Ernst Arbman, considered that Peyote visions have a decidedly "neurological" character, and pointed out that their occurrence "is evidently exclusively due to certain abnormal cerebral processes biochemically brought about by the drug"; these visions thus offer a contradistinction to the suggestively provoked ecstatic visions.[45] They are nevertheless genuine examples of religious ecstasy in religious contexts.[46] Arbman observed that they occur both as external hallucinations and as pseudo-hallucinations, and that there are visual illusions of a hallucinatory nature as well.[47] Arbman was of course aware that the religious interpretation is dictated by religious belief and not by the nature of the visions as such. However, the effects of Peyote naturally place these experiences in a religious frame whenever the structure of religion allows it (cf. Ch. V:2).

Another effect of Peyote consumption is auditory hallucinations. They are mentioned by several authors. La Barre remarks that not least white partakers in the Peyote rite have heard mysterious voices.[48] He has noted that in the Plains area the Peyote goddess joins in with the singing cult members.[49]

A third characteristic effect is the synesthetic experiences, that is, visions are coupled to auditory phenomena, and vice versa. For instance, a Menomini Indian who is singing sees a long hollow tube, and observes how his voice goes down the tube.[50] La Barre tells us that one Indian heard the sun coming up with a roar. Another Indian had kinesthetic sensations: he felt that he was lifted up into the air by the sound of the drumming.[51]

There is finally one peculiar experience with, sometimes, far-reaching consequences. La Barre points out that, like psilocybin and perhaps other hallucinogens as well, Peyote produces what he calls a "double consciousness": at the same time as the Peyotist experiences hallucinations and is convinced of their

---

[43] Hultkrantz 1979, p. 246.
[44] Levy 1961, p. 209.
[45] Arbman 1963/70 I, p. 201.
[46] Arbman 1963/70 II, p. 102.
[47] Arbman 1963/70 I, pp. 192 f., 199.
[48] La Barre 1975 b, p. 13 n. 18. The present author had such auditions, interpreted by Indians as the Peyote woman.
[49] La Barre 1975 b, p. 18.
[50] G. D. Spindler 1952.
[51] La Barre 1979, p. 35.

truth he knows quite well that he is hallucinating.[52] And he knows that it is Peyote, the wonderful medicine, that makes the hallucinations.[53] Such occurrences may stimulate feelings of psychic dissociation. The individual experiences himself as two different persons, or the body seems to be leading an autonomous life of its own.[54] The will is becoming weakened,[55] even the capacity to direct one's thinking at will is impaired, like in a hashish intoxication.[56]

Summarizing the Winnebago Indian S. B.'s experiences while in Peyote rapture, as rendered in Paul Radin's recording, Arbman declares that "a clearer, more drastic and graphic expression for the completely depersonalized and automatic nature of the ecstatic activity could not have been given by the informant cited".[57] The Peyote hallucinations have their peculiar qualities, but they evince the same general pattern as other ecstatic hallucinations.[58] What has been labelled "chemical mysticism" can, at least sometimes, have a psychedelic ("brain-expanding") effect which ameliorates a religious interpretation. In the case of Peyote, it is the hallucinogenetic properties of the cactus that have paved the way for such an orientation.

Another effect of Peyote eating, the enhanced feelings of fraternity, solidarity and friendship in the ritual Peyote circle, has already been mentioned. To some investigators, notably Gerber, these feelings seem to mean more than visionary experiences. The feelings of harmony and ease figure much in Stewart's interpretations. Anybody who takes part in the Peyote rite certainly experiences sentiments of sympathy of unusual strength in view of the fact that many of those present may be total strangers. There is also, however, a feeling of detachment at times which may conflict with the feelings of togetherness.

However, the religious experience of the Peyote ritual is not just a mechanical consequence of Peyote eating. We know that the hallucinations are subject to the alterative forces of tradition and cultural milieu. Twentyfive years ago Anthony Wallace stressed that cultural context and individual personality heavily influence the hallucinatory effects of Peyote intoxication.[59] More recently Marlene Dobkin de Rios and David E. Smith defined the general effect of drugs as the result of a complex interaction between physiological, pharmacological and sociocultural preconditions.[60] Even more important is the fact that religious belief and religious tradition provides the prerequisites for a religious interpretation of Peyote hallucinations (cf. Ch. V:1–3).

---

[52] La Barre 1975 a, p. 12.
[53] Cf. Radin 1923, p. 390.
[54] La Barre 1975 b, p. 141 n. 11; Arbman 1963/70 I, pp. 198 f., 200.
[55] Arbman 1963/70 I, p. 196.
[56] Arbman 1963/70 II, p. 634.
[57] Arbman 1963/70 II, p. 150.
[58] The word ecstatic is here used as equivalent to trance, in conformity with Arbman's usage.
[59] Wallace 1959.
[60] Dobkin de Rios and Smith 1977, p. 274, Dobkin de Rios 1976, pp. 6, 9 f., 59.

2. History and Diffusion of the Peyote Religion

When today we talk about the Peyote religion (or the Peyote "cult", rite) we usually have the modern Indian Peyote meetings in mind. Perhaps we also refer to the wider organization, the Native American Church, which was created in 1918 (on the instigation of the famous anthropologist James Mooney!) to counteract the persecutions coming from white opponents and Indian conservatives alike.[1] Nevertheless, today's Peyote religion has its ideological and ritual antecedents. It would be naive to believe that a potent herb like Peyote should not have attracted the attention of medicine men and their likes in remote times (cf. Ch. V:2).

It is thus realistic to surmise that in an earlier period American Indians used Peyote in order to intensify their subjective experiences of a supernatural world. Whether we interpret archaeologists' reports on the use of Peyote about 810–1070 A.D. as indicative of its consumption or not,[2] this cactus was well known as a divinatory and vision-inducing device and as a panacea in early colonial days in this area and certainly had been resorted to here in pre-Conquest days as well. The conquistadors talk about Peyote and other drugs as "pestiferous and wicked" poisons sent by the devil.[2a] If we restrict our historical search for "origins" to the colonial days in Mexico (the country that no doubt was the homeland of Peyotism) we find the following functions of Peyote consumption listed by ancient sources:

(1) Individual, occasionally non-ritual use, to reduce fatigue and hunger, for medicine, externally and internally, to induce supernatural visions, to bring about prophecy and divination, to fight witchcraft, to attain intoxication.

(2) Collective, ritual use at tribal gatherings usually dedicated to the promotion of life-sustaining elements. In other words, Peyote was eaten at annual thanksgiving rites and agricultural ceremonies.[3]

Slotkin concludes that individual and collective uses seem equally old, but confusingly adds, "only the collective cult seems recent".[4] No wonder that a critical scholar like La Barre was taken aback at such odd reasoning.[5] The collective practice of Peyote seems to have deep roots in Northern Mexico where

---

[1] A good presentation of this organization may be found in Slotkin 1956 a, pp. 57 ff. Its predecessor was the intertribal society "Mescal Bean Eaters" on the reservations in Oklahoma, Kansas and Nebraska, which 1909 changed its name into "Union Church." The "Native American Church" was first limited to the United States, but the spread of the Peyote religion to Canada motivated the new name, "The Native American Church of North America," in 1955. See La Barre 1975 b, p. 217 (quoting C. B. Dustin), and Stewart 1961 b.
[2] La Barre 1979 a, p. 34.
[2a] Anderson 1980, p. 3.
[3] Cf. La Barre 1975 b, pp. 23 ff., 29 ff., Slotkin 1955, pp. 209 f.
[4] Slotkin 1955, p. 210. Slotkin had one reason to suppress the data on collectivism: he favoured the view that the Peyote religion is Christian and recent.
[5] La Barre 1960, p. 54.

it was known among such ethnic groups as the Huichol, Tarahumara and Tamaulipec.[6] Peyote was consumed there at tribal ceremonies in which dances and prayers for abundant corn harvests, successful deer-hunting and fortunes of war played a dominant role, and doctoring was a conspicuous part of the program.

These ancient rituals have been well preserved until the present day among the Huichol of northwestern Jalisco.[7] Their Peyotism culminates in the annual 30 days pilgrimage to their sacred land of mythic origins, Wirikúta, a desert plateau far east of their isolated homeland in the Sierra Madre Occidental.[8] During the dry season a group of Huichol, men, women and children, walk under the supervision of a medicine man the long way to the country where the Peyote grows, a country which is identified with the mythic world where the gods operated at the beginning of time. In fact, the pilgrimage reiterates the first search for Peyote which the gods undertook when they were tormented by drought, lack of game and diseases. The approach of the sacred country is marked by a reversal of speech, roles and behaviour in the pilgrim group: this is an expression of the other-worldliness of Wirikúta. All actions of the individuals repeat the actions of the gods as known from tradition: the pilgrims are now the gods, their leader Grandfather Fire who was the first shaman. Finally, they find the first Peyote. The medicine man shoots it with bow and arrows. The Peyote is namely identified with the deer, the (mythic) animal out of whose body it is supposed to have been created.[9] Corn, deer and Peyote form a unity in Huichol thought. The first Peyote that have been picked are ritually consumed on the spot.

This pilgrimage, and the mythic-ritual complex around Peyote,[10] figures largely in Huichol thinking. It has no ritual counterpart in North America, but the journeys from the Indian reservations to the Peyote growing areas around the Rio Grande are always occasions of social reunion and pleasure. Resident Hispano traders in southern Texas, *peyoteros,* supply available dried Peyote.[11]

A study of the Huichol ceremonies makes it obvious that much depended on the medicine man and his faculties. He was also the only one who, during the Peyote sacramental meal, received true visions of spirits and gods. Original shamanic components may well emerge here. Both Beals and La Barre hint that the use of Peyote revived and strengthened shamanism in the ceremony, possibly at the expense of priestly-ritual elements.[12] Of course, Peyote intoxication could very well have been an original part of ancient agricultural rituals, just as

---

[6] Cf. La Barre 1975 b, pp. 39, 54, Gerber 1980.
[7] Benzi 1972.
[8] Furst 1972, Myerhoff 1974.
[9] This is apparently a myth upon the well-known *hainuwele* theme.
[10] Attention should be called to the exceptional artistry the Huichol show in their yarn paintings whose contents often derive from their Peyote visions and their mythical Peyote world. See Berrin 1978.
[11] Morgan 1976, cf. also Morgan 1982.
[12] Beals 1932, p. 128, La Barre 1975 b, p. 109.

drinking orgies played a conspicuous role in Old World fertility feasts.[13] Nevertheless, the ultimate shamanic origins of Peyote eating are highly probable (Ch. IV:10, V:2).

There are reasons to assume that Mexican tribal Peyote ritualism constituted the transition to the Plains Peyote rite, and thereby to the modern Peyote religion. The northern neighbours of the Tamaulipec, the Coahuiltec – living on both sides of the eastern Rio Grande – are most likely to have been the transmitters. In the summer several Coahuiltec bands used to come together for a thanksgiving ceremony, a *mitote,* that lasted the whole night. Men and women danced in the open around a fire, now and then eating Peyote. It happened that someone fell in a trance.[14] This sounds somewhat like an annual thanksgiving ceremony in the Great Basin area, as described by W.Z. Park and myself, except that no stimulants other than tobacco were used.[15] Unfortunately we do not know anything about to which supernatural powers the Coahuiltec ceremony was directed. We know however that smaller mitotes were also held on other occasions, such as victory feasts. The similarity between these ceremonies and other Mexican Indian mitotes (among the Huichol, Tarahumara) is striking.

There is reason to believe, with Morris Opler and Omer Stewart, that the use of Peyote spread from the Coahuiltec (or Carrizo, as they were called in the neighbourhood of Camargo) to their northern neighbours, the Tonkawa, the Lipan Apache (if they and other Apache had reached southern Texas by the critical time), perhaps the Mescalero Apache.[16] Somewhere and at some time during its dissemination northwards the old Mexican Peyotism changed its character and became the Peyote religion of North America. It is rather fruitless to speculate when and where this change occurred. Several groups in the area around the Rio Grande may be thought of as possible inventors. A good case could be made for such Southern Plains tribes as the Comanche, Kiowa and Kiowa Apache. However, it is just as possible that the major transformation from a tribal dancing rite to a sectarian ritual of contemplation took place among other Apache or the Coahuiltecan Tonkawa.[17] In any case, a major change

---

[13] Peyote which easily induces vomiting could possibly also have been used as a katharktic instrument, an emetic, like the "black drink" made from *Ilex cassine (vomitoria)* of the Southeast. The latter was used as a means of ritual purification at the Creek annual harvest ceremony, the so-called busk (cf. for instance Hudson 1976, pp. 369, 373, and Driver 1961, p. 105 and map 14). The Pawnee drink a concoction of mescal beans which makes them vomit and thus purifies the body. See further La Barre 1975 b, pp. 26 n. 17, 133 with n. 14.

[14] Ruecking 1954, Newcomb 1961, pp. 53 ff.

[15] On the round dance as an annual thanksgiving ceremony, see Hultkrantz 1981 a, pp. 271 ff.

[16] Cf. Opler 1938, Stewart 1974, pp. 214, 216. Stewart did not believe that the Mescalero played a major role in the spread of Peyotism (Stewart 1974, pp. 218 f.). Indeed, a Mescalero origin legend attributes the beginning of the Peyote religion to the Lipan Apache, see Opler 1945.

[17] Cf. La Barre 1975 b, p. 54. La Barre possibly assigns a more important role to the Mescalero Apache than they have had. Their name, "those who use mescal," is certainly seductive. The Kiowa attribute them as being the originators of the Peyote religion (Mooney 1897, p. 330).

could have come about as Peyote spread to non-agricultural tribes, hunters and collectors, in southern Texas. In the absence of great tribal (agricultural) ceremonies the large open-air meetings were abandoned, with dancing and feasting. The medicine men and a group of followers formed a closed society of Peyote eaters. It is characteristic that among the Mescalero Apache only medicine men were granted power by Peyote. They had meetings where they cured people through Peyote. The Mescalero Apache had no true Peyote religion, and their use of Peyote was not influenced by Christianity – two criteria of their religious conservatism.[18]

While the Mescalero possibly did not further the development of Peyotism I find it probable that it was from some similar ritual setting that the modern Peyote religion originated. As also La Barre has emphasized in recent publications, shamanism is the key. We shall return to this significant point.

We cannot be certain when Peyote was first used among North American tribes, but we have some early dates telling us when it was in use. There is testimony that several Texan groups, among them the Caddo, consumed (drank) Peyote in 1709 and 1716, but it is less certain whether a regular Peyote ritual was implied.[19] Stewart finds evidence that the Lipan Apache enjoyed Peyote in the 1770s.[20] We know for sure that they did it in 1830 when the French botanist Jean Louis Berlandier visited the southern part of Texas. He reported that the Tonkawa, Lipan and "several other native groups" used this plant in their feasts.[21] In 1859 the two tribes just mentioned were removed to the present state of Oklahoma. In this way they came closer to other tribes which as time went by were drawn together by the white authorities in this territory. The consequence was of course a rapid spread of the Peyote religion. Some time between 1850 and 1880 the Lipan Apache brought Peyotism to the Comanche.[22] The Oto were taught it by the Tonkawa in 1876.[23] Stewart thinks that the Lipan were mainly responsible for the spread of Peyotism in Oklahoma.[24]

This may have been so, but also other tribes figure in this connection. An important link in the transmission was certainly the Kiowa Apache, a small Athapascan group living as a band with the Kiowa. Anthropologist Charles Brant's Kiowa Apache informant told him that his people learned to use Peyote

---

[18] Opler 1936, Boyer, Boyer and Basehart 1973, pp. 55 f.
[19] La Barre 1975 b, p. 110, Slotkin 1955, pp. 205, 214 f. (his reference to the Caddo has been doubted, cf. La Barre 1960, p. 46), Stewart 1974, p. 214. Incidentally Slotkin has adduced materials to show that Peyote was used among the Taos of New Mexico at the same time, but his conclusion has not been generally accepted (Slotkin 1951, La Barre 1960, p. 46).
[20] Stewart 1974, p. 217.
[21] Berlandier 1830, p. 62.
[22] Stewart 1974, pp. 213, 217.
[23] La Barre 1975 b, p. 117. Stewart's (1974, pp. 216 f.) information that the Sauk received Peyote at the same date is not substantiated by La Barre (1975 b, p. 119) to whom he refers. La Barre does say however that the Tonkawa introduced Peyotism among the Sauk.
[24] Stewart 1974, p. 218, 1987, pp. 58–60.

from a person who was "either a Mescalero or a Lipan. ... I guess this was about 1875."[25] Kenneth Beals, on the other hand, was informed by a Peyote chief that the Kiowa Apache had obtained Peyote from the Tonkawa prior to 1875, and perhaps before the reservation was established in 1868. It was then used as a medicine in shamanism.[26] Perhaps the Kiowa Apache were the middlemen who brought the cactus to the Kiowa (who learned Peyote in the 1870s). The Kiowa think that the Mescalero Apache were their teachers, however; some anthropologists agree, others disagree.[27]

The continued diffusion has been analyzed by all main writers on the Peyote religion, including the early theorists Ruth Shonle and Günther Wagner.[28] Leaders like the Comanche chief Quanah Parker and the Caddo visionary John Wilson were great proselytizers. They attracted people from afar, and they visited reservations in other parts of the Plains area. The endless visiting which is part and parcel of the Indian life style certainly contributed to the swift diffusion of Peyote after the 1870s, particularly among Plains Indians.

First of all the Peyote religion spread among those Plains tribes who had been confined to Oklahoma and among some of those Woodland tribes who had been relocated to this territory.[29] The earliest known dates are, for the Oklahoma Plains tribes, if we disregard the founding tribes mentioned above: for the Southern Arapaho and Southern Cheyenne 1884–85, Wichita 1889–90, Pawnee 1890, Osage 1896, Quapaw 1898, Ponca 1902, Kansa 1907. Dates for the Southeastern agriculturists collected in Oklahoma are, Caddo 1880 (provided that the earlier dates from 1709 and 1716 are wrong, which for instance La Barre thinks), Cherokee 1913, Yuchi 1919, Seminole 1922, Creek 1931. Dates for the Eastern Woodland tribes of Oklahoma are as follows, Delaware (Lenape) 1886, Shawnee 1890, Sauk and Fox, Kickapoo and Iowa 1906, Seneca 1907, Potawatomi 1908–14.

It is obvious that Peyote conquered the Oklahoma tribes regardless of their cultural affiliation. However, the late accession of Peyote by the Southeastern Indians is remarkable and may indicate a cultural blockade.[30] The one exception, the Caddo, had been transformed into plainsmen when they received the religion. My inference is that the ceremonial emetic of the Southeast, the "black drink" made from the leaves of *Ilex cassine,* had such a firm hold in Southeastern rituals that it presented an obstacle to the adoption of Peyote.

Since the Peyote movement mainly flared up after the Indian wars – with

---

[25] Brant 1950, pp. 212 f.
[26] Beals 1971, p. 45.
[27] La Barre 1975 b, pp. 111, 112; Stewart 1974, p. 219.
[28] Shonle 1925, Wagner 1932.
[29] The following list of dates is not the result of the author's independent research but is taken from available surveys, in particular La Barre 1975 b, Slotkin 1956 a and Stewart 1974, 1987.
[30] Stewart (1987, p. 97) does not consider these Indians to be true Peyotists since they had been Christians for too long.

the exception of the Apache and Ute campaigns these wars were over by 1880 in the United States – the roads of diffusion from Oklahoma went between the new reservations, and not between former tribal home lands. Also outside of Oklahoma the main tribes to accept Peyotism were the Plains tribes. The first converts were the Winnebago in Nebraska 1889–1901, closely followed by the Northern Cheyenne in Montana, about 1900, and the Northern Arapaho in Wyoming, 1903. These groups became responsible for the further spread of Peyotism to other Northern Plains Indians, the Algonkian Woodland Indians and the Basin Indian tribes. Among the Plains Indians we observe a relatively early set of Siouan-speaking peoples accepting Peyote, the Oglala 1904, Omaha 1906–07, Santee 1908, Yankton 1911 and Crow 1912. Other Plains tribes receiving Peyote were the Blackfoot 1913, Blood 1936, and the three Prairie village tribes, the Arikara 1924, Hidatsa 1955 and Mandan about 1955.[31]

Woodland Indians who have become Peyotists include three Algonkian-speaking peoples, the Menomini 1914, Chippewa (Ojibway) 1915 and Cree (before 1936). Other northern groups affected by Peyotism are the Athapaskan-speaking Chipewyan and Beaver. In the Great Basin Peyotism is widely accepted. The dates for accession of Peyote are, for the Bannock 1905–11,[32] the Northern Ute 1916, the Wind River Shoshoni about 1909, the Northern Paiute 1929, the Gosiute 1929, the Washo 1929 and the Southern Paiute 1946.

The Ute introduced the Peyote religion among the Navajo of the Southwest in the 1930s.[33] Other tribes of the Southwest which have adopted Peyotism are, the Papago 1895, Jicarilla Apache 1900, Pima 1908, Southern Ute 1910, Havasupai 1914 and Walapai 1954. The Navajo Indians, with their deep-seated fear of the dead, made for a long time resistance to a religion of such a visionary type as the Peyote.[34] However, in the long run Peyote was accepted.[35]

The story of Peyote among the Pueblo Indians is a chapter of its own. Mescalero Peyotism has already been mentioned; although apparently old, it has not affected the Pueblos. The lack of Peyotism among these Indians is remarkable in view of two circumstances: their position close to the nuclear distribution area of Peyote, and their ancient connections with pre-Columbian Mesoameri-

---

[31] On the diffusion of Peyotism north of Oklahoma, see La Barre 1975 b, pp. 109 ff., Stewart 1987, pp. 148 ff., 248 ff., 265 ff. The best figures for the Oglala will be found in Steinmetz 1980, pp. 79 ff.

[32] This date could appear to be too early. However, H. E. Wadsworth reported in 1908 to the Commissioner of Indian Affairs that there was Peyote eating among the Wind River Shoshoni (Slotkin 1956 a, p. 40) who were in regular contact with the Idaho Shoshoni and Bannock. The Wind River Shoshoni had probably been influenced by their close neighbours, the Northern Arapaho. Cf. Ch. II:1.

[33] Cf. Aberle 1982 a, p. 222, and 1982 b, p. 109. See also Stewart 1987, pp. 293 ff.

[34] Cf. Haile 1940; but see Aberle 1982 b, p. 219.

[35] For a closer description of the Peyote development among the Navajo, see Ch. IV:2.

can religions.[36] As will be shown later, there are cultural reasons why Peyote had difficulties in being adopted by the Pueblo Indians. Only Taos, the most Plains-oriented of Pueblo societies, has arranged Peyote meetings ever since 1907–10. Here again it seems that the conservative, esoteric and theocratical nature of Pueblo religions has constituted the main impediment for the acceptance of Peyote.

This survey is not complete, nor are the dates uniformly agreed upon among Peyote students. Omer Stewart in particular was reviewing the dates all the time and would probably have changed several of the years given here.[37]

Closely connected with the problem of the distribution of Peyote is the question about its persistance today. Also on this topic Stewart could have provided a better answer than the present author, since he permanently until his death in 1991 kept track of developments in Peyotism on different reservations. Although his information on this point is not always satisfactory it provides us with some glimpses of a process which, filled in with some other data, can illustrate some tendencies in present day Peyotism (see Ch. VI:5).

It was just mentioned that Peyote failed to diffuse into the Pueblo area because of cultural reasons. Both these obstacles and others on a wider scale will be discussed in Ch. VI:4.

So far we have followed the development and diffusion of the Peyote religion in North America. We shall now concentrate on two important aspects of this development, the growth of the ritual and the ascending influence of Christian ideas in the Peyote religion. A more detailed discussion of the impact of Christian religion on Peyote thought will be presented in Ch. IV:12.

There has been some disagreement among scholars about the magnitude of changes that have occurred in the ritual development. Stewart is confident that the Peyote cultural elements diffused from Mexico along with the Peyote cactus.[38] Some years ago he stated succinctly that "both plant and ritual had been imported".[39] Stewart finds numerous parallels to the Kiowa and Comanche ritual in the descriptions of the Huichol and Tarahumara rituals given by Carl Lumholtz.[40] He mentions such items as common as curing, all night ceremony, sacred food, fire kept burning, central position of a Peyote cactus, rattles and all night singing.[41] Stewart also refers to ceremonial circuits, ceremonial use of tobacco and incense, ceremonial cross and ceremonial altar as elements occurring in both Plains Indian and Tarahumara Peyote ritual.[42]

---

[36] Cf. Kelley 1966. It must be pointed out however that Peyotism was known among Pueblo Indians three hundred years ago (Slotkin 1955, p. 210).
[37] See Stewart 1987.
[38] Stewart 1974, pp. 219 f.
[39] Stewart in Lynch 1984, p. 180.
[40] Lumholtz 1902.
[41] Stewart 1974, p. 220.
[42] Stewart, ibidem. Stewart's source for these additional features is Bennett and Zingg 1935, table 1.

Also La Barre has noted that there are many common traits in Mexican and North American Peyote ceremonies, such as the ceremonial trip for Peyote collecting, meetings held at night, the Peyote button used as a fetish, feathers and bird symbolism, ceremonial fire and incensing, curing rites, ritual breakfast, singing, confession of sins, morning star symbolism, and other traits.[43] Of course, some of them are generally Indian, or basically common traits in the two main areas of diffusion, Mexico and the Plains. In some cases we know definitely that ritual elements spread from Mexico to the Plains. As evidence of this La Barre lists items like the leader's staff and the idea of dual sexuality of Peyote cacti, as well as the composition of the ritual morning meal, all reminiscences of Mexican Peyotism.[44] It seems also rather certain that the nightly vigils were introduced from the Mexican rite. Moreover, the music used at modern Peyote meetings shows close affinities not only with that of the Apache but also with musical styles among the Mexican Tarahumara.[45]

There is thus much evidence of a direct continuity between the Mexican Peyote ritual and the ritual that we find in the modern North American Peyote religion.[46] To say, however, that the latter is nothing else than the Mexican ritual taken over is to distort the picture. Anybody familiar with the facts who has attended a Peyote meeting can tell that there are other basic constituents not present in the Mexican ritual. The differences between a Mexican and a Plains Peyote ritual concern both the general aims, the setting of the ritual, and the ritual patterns and single ritual elements.

A Swiss anthropologist, Peter Gerber, has tabulated and contrasted the main elements of what he calls Mexican "Peyotism" and North American "Peyote religion".[47] I have reformulated what I consider the critical issues and present here an alternative survey:[48]

In the Mexican Peyote ritual

(1) the performance is part of a ceremonial complex interrelating hunting and agriculture, and is often part of an annual fertility ceremony;

(2) the aims of the ritual are to establish harmony with the powers, secure the health and food of the human beings for the coming year, and reveal the future of the individuals and the people;

(3) the meeting is open-air and the whole community joins in under the control of medicine men;

---

[43] La Barre 1975 b, p. 56.

[44] La Barre 1960, pp. 49, 50.

[45] La Barre 1960, p. 54.

[46] For a convenient summary of the traits, see Driver and Massey 1957, p. 270.

[47] Gerber 1975, pp. 44 f. Stewart defines Peyotism as the American Indian use of Peyote, and includes "the old Peyote complex" and the more recent form, the Peyote religion, under Peyotism (Stewart 1970, p. 790).

[48] For other similar distinctions, see Slotkin 1956 a, pp. 28 ff., Driver and Massey 1957, pp. 270 f., and Stewart 1987, p. 52. Cf. below, Ch. IV:12, note 52.

(4) the most apparent cultic activity is dancing, accompanied by the consumption of Peyote;

(5) the main ritual paraphernalia are rattles and drums.

In the North American Peyote ritual, again,

(1) the performance is usually independent of specific tribal cultic connections, and is founded on the individual's voluntary association. It has a pan-Indian reference and is typically part of the Native American Church, and a service is given when so is demanded for particular reasons, mostly every Saturday;

(2) the aims of the ritual are to strengthen the harmony between man and the powers and between the humans reciprocally, and to achieve the individual purposes for which the meeting has been arranged: restored health, help in particular undertakings, prophecy of things to come, etc.;

(3) the meeting is indoors, usually in a tipi (conical Plains tent), and participation is extended to those invited by the host, often members of other tribes. The host himself acts as leader ("road man"), or has invited a trained Peyote leader to serve in this role;

(4) ritual activity consists of singing, praying, consumption of Peyote (eating, drinking, smoking Peyote) and contemplation;

(5) ritual paraphernalia are rattles, water-drum, staff, feathers, flutes, and particular altar arrangements.

An experienced student of Mexican and Southwestern rituals, Ruth Underhill, had this to say about the modern Peyote ritual and its Mexican predecessor, "The one that has now become standard had nothing to do with any Mexican ceremony I know of. It was definitely a ritual of the Buffalo Plains and it used their equipment."[49] Underhill noted that many Peyote properties had been used by dancing and shamanic societies on the Plains, and mentioned eagle-feather fans, the leader's feather staff, white sage that was strewn on the tipi floor, incense from cedar needles and, not least, the ceremonial tipi having had an eastern entrance. While some of these paraphernalia actually occurred also in Mexico, such the leader's staff, Underhill's observation seems very much to the point.

It should surprise no one that the ritual complex surrounding the use of Peyote underwent many metamorphoses. One cannot expect that the same ritual proceedings should serve a tribal anniversary ceremony, performed for the promotion of the crops and fertility, danced out in the open,[50] and a more privately arranged, secluded prayer meeting in a Plains tipi where individual satisfactions are sought. The main features of the process can be followed. In the Mexican rite

---
[49] Underhill 1965, p. 266.
[50] It should be observed however that dancing as part of the Peyote ritual in fact continued among the (Oklahoma) Chippewa, Washo, Kiowa Apache, Kiowa, Comanche, Southern Arapaho, Tonkawa and Lipan Apache: see Slotkin 1956 a, p. 110, La Barre 1975 b, p. 17, Stewart 1944, p. 80, 1980 c, p. 189, 1986, p. 674 (illustration), 1987, pp. 173, 279.

(if we may regard it as a unit which it only partly was)[51] Peyote consumption enhanced the encounter with the supernaturals, particularly in connection with curing. The rite was conducted by medicine men. This "shamanic" emphasis was slowly dropped in the north, but survived among the Mescalero Apache. When Peyotism spread to the Southern Plains a profane leader, the road man, took over the role of the medicine man – as I see it, because on the Plains the distinction between the medicine man and other visionaries (and most men of the tribe had their guardian spirit visions) was very slight. Perhaps in this connection the curative functions of the Peyote meeting became less perspicuous (and even absent, as among the Caddo and Lakota). In accordance with the general patterns on the Plains a "democratization" of the Peyote experience found place enabling everybody to establish relations with the supernatural world without the trying vision quest. The attention was now exclusively concentrated on Peyote and its effects.

As suggested in the foregoing, this transformation was probably connected with the acquisition of Peyote by hunters and collectors. It meant that the Mexican concern about tribal welfare was supplanted by the interest in subjective experiences within a voluntary association, the Peyote group. It is also characteristic that the change found place in societies that were in the process of losing their independence and tribal cohesion.[52] In more recent times investigators have observed another change as a consequence of this detribalization, viz, the turn to pan-Indianism and nativism.[53]

In the face of these tremendous changes of aims and patterns we are forced to expect that ritual innovations came about through the agency of the tribes concerned, in particular, of course, the Southern Plains Indians. There are two main theories about the process involved.

The first theory associates the rise of the Plains Peyote ritualism to the Red Bean or Mescal Bean Complex (Ch. IV:6). As will be shown in the sequence, the Southern Plains were the home grounds of a "cult" centered on the consumption of the so-called Mescal Bean, a drug with psychoactive powers transcending those of Peyote. The ritual frame of this "cult" was decidedly of a Southern Plains type. James Howard has vindicated the Mescal Bean religion as a precursor of the Peyote religion.[54] This problem will be discussed more in detail in the following since it has bearing on the question why Peyote spread.

The second theory proceeds from the theoretical expectation that any ritual that has been adopted into a new cultural milieu will change in order to conform to local patterns. Slotkin, for instance, has emphasized the importance of local differences and adaptation processes in the diffusion of Peyotism.[55] It is indeed

---

[51] Cf. La Barre 1975 b, pp. 35 ff.
[52] The voluntary association is of course not as such a product of the reservation situation: soldier and medicine societies were common in many old times Plains tribes.
[53] See for example Aberle 1982 b, p. 17. Cf. Ch. IV:8, below.
[54] Cf. Howard 1957.
[55] Slotkin 1956 a, pp. 32 ff.

natural that on the Plains a Peyote meeting usually takes place in a Plains tipi and makes use of ritual paraphernalia common to Plains tribes. When the same traits today appear outside of the Plains area – among the Navajo for instance – this means that the Plains model has been stereotyped as the Indian model.[56] It also says something of the institutionalization of Peyotism as a church with its distinctive formalism.

Both these theories may in the long run be subsumed under one common assumption: that in its present form the Peyote ritual originated on the Southern Plains.

Although some contributions to Peyote ritual may have been made by southwestern groups like the Mescalero Apache,[57] the Peyote rite as known today received some of its forms, and much of its contents, from three neighbouring reservation tribes, the Kiowa, Comanche and Caddo.[58] La Barre aptly calls "the Kiowa the original standardizers and teachers, who have departed only in the most minute ways from earlier forms; the Comanche the proselytizers and missionaries of the new religion; and the Caddo the innovators".[59] Mutually their Peyote rituals showed differences that became pattern-forming in the Peyote religion wherever it appeared in North America: the Kiowa kept the crescent-formed altar, the Caddo and Comanche elongated it into horseshoe-form, and the Caddo John Wilson's "Big Moon" altar demonstrated what should be interpreted as an apron and a heart, and contained an elaborate symbolism.[60] With the Winnebago the Big Moon ritual version was called the Cross Fire ritual.[61] In the main, however, one may concur with Stewart that today the Peyote ceremony shows the same features as it did when Mooney visited the Kiowa and Comanche in the 1890s.[62]

It remains to discuss the dates and extent of the Christian influence, a most difficult problem.[63] Some authors like La Barre and Opler relegate it to a secondary factor of late provenience, others, like Slotkin and Stewart, believe it has been present at an early date, before the diffusion of the Peyote religion north of the Rio Grande. Already Mooney noticed that Kiowa peyotists wore crucifixes and identified the Peyote goddess with Christ.[64] Native tradition recog-

---

[56] Strangely enough today the Peyote tipi occurs outside of the Plains area, but rarely among the Lakota.
[57] The Mescalero are supposed to have invented the crescent mound altar of earth, see La Barre 1975 b, pp. 41 no. 78, 75 n. 85.
[58] All of them Plains Indians who ranged in Texas and Oklahoma in pre-reservation days.
[59] La Barre 1975 b, p. 77.
[60] La Barre 1975 b, pp. 75 ff., 151 ff. Cf. also Stewart 1987, p. 91.
[61] Stewart 1987, p. 150.
[62] Stewart 1980 c, p. 191.
[63] A more detailed discussion of some of the problems involved will be presented in Ch. IV:12. Here an effort is made to trace the general historical lines of Christian-Peyote acculturation.
[64] Mooney 1892, p. 65.

nizes that such Christian influence occurred even before, in 1887.[65] Lumholtz reports Christian ideas among the Tarahumara of Mexico.[66] Whereas La Barre talks of an "overlay of Mexican Catholicism" which is "thin and localized"[67] Stewart points at the importance of Franciscan missions in the land of the Coahuiltec tribes which is also a homeland of Peyote.[68] Both authors agree however that the Christian impact grew stronger as the Peyote religion appeared on the North American scene.

The Christian background is vaguely perceptible in several early Peyote documents from the Southern Plains Indians.[69] The early Plains Peyotists knew of Christian missions and were certainly to some extent influenced by their presence; it is however doubtful if they had integrated Christian ideas in a meaningful way. The reason for this suspicion is not only the fact that the gap was so great between Christianity and Native, culture-bound religion, but also the undeniable fact that preconceived ideas of many missionaries impeded a reasonable religious communication.[70] The tendency to condemn all Native religion as a misunderstanding of the only truth or even as the work of the devil persisted until late times among many clerics, even in spite of their occasional theoretical commitments to more modern doctrines, such as evolutionism or "social Darwinism."[71] In such conditions seeds for a propagation of Christian teaching were hard to sow. Also, the very fact that Christianity was white man's religion – the ideology of the oppressors – precluded its rapid spread and voluntary acceptance. If Christianity had adapted itself to the Indian situation during the last century it would probably have gained a solid ground among the Indians, and – perhaps – made Peyotism redundant. As it was, Peyotism and not Christianity filled the vacuum left by old tribal religions.

Until very recent times Peyotism was only marginally affected by Christianity. Take, for instance, the Caddo Peyote leader John Wilson. We are informed that he had received some Catholic instruction.[72] In his speeches he made occasional references to Christian concepts which in a superficial way could be used as Peyote symbols.[73] However, he considered that the Bible should not be consulted by the red man, for it was intended for the white man. The red man

---

[65] Slotkin 1956 a, pp. 45, 118.
[66] Lumholtz 1902 I, pp. 360 ff.
[67] La Barre 1975 b, p. 162.
[68] Stewart 1974, pp. 214, 220.
[69] Not, however, from the Southwestern Apache Indians. The Mescalero Apache lacked Christian elements, indeed, their acceptance of Peyote resulted, according to Morris Opler, in an intensification of their Native religious values. See Opler 1936.
[70] Cf. Hultkrantz 1977 a, pp. 412 ff.
[71] Hultkrantz, ibidem.
[72] Petrullo 1934, p. 45, Thurman 1973. Thurman insists that "Catholicism, the Ghost Dance, and peyotism seem to have blended into a unique religious complex among the Caddos" (Thurman op. cit., p. 283). Cf. also below, Ch. IV:10.
[73] Cf. La Barre 1975 b, pp. 151 ff.

should seek spiritual enlightenment directly through the Peyote spirit.[74] As we shall see, this attitude to Christianity was rather common among peyotists, and still is (see Ch. IV:12).

In this century a more radical Christian influence emanates from the revised Peyote religion among the Siouan Oto. The initiator was Jonathan Koshiway, a Sauk and Fox Indian whose mother was an Oto. He had been a Mormon missionary and Presbyterian minister and had also been affected by the Russellites. With the sanction of White Horn, the leader of the Oto peyotists, Koshiway turned the Peyote religion into a Christian faith, "First-born Church of Christ" (1914). Here for the first time, Protestantism made inroads into Peyote religion. Koshiway conducted weddings and funerals but also acted as a medicine man. The basic ideas and rituals of the revised religion took form already in the latter part of the 1890s. It was preached to the Omaha and Winnebago of Nebraska in 1897. It should surprise no one that Koshiway was one of the active figures who brought about the creation of the Native American Church in 1918.[75]

The Christian interpretation, with Bible-reading and thoroughing Christian symbolism troughout, bacame firmly anchored among the Winnebago, Omaha, Iowa, Menomini and Northern Cheyenne. Also the Lakota were reached by this version of Peyote religion ("the cross-fire"), through the influence of the Winnebago. It is interesting to study how in their apologetics and also in other connections these peyotists make frequent use of Bible quotations.[76] Stewart claims that the Ute evince a strong Christian character in their Peyotism.[77] Other anthropologists deny this.[78] The debate goes on.

It is La Barre's opinion that the layer of Christianity on Peyotism on the whole is thin and superficial.[79] In clear contrast to him other students, in particular Omer Stewart, count the Christian elements among the basic traits of Peyotism. As just mentioned, Stewart has developed his thesis – in clear distinction to his opponent Marvin Opler – in two papers on the Ute Peyote religion.[80] Slotkin, who makes a distinction between "the old Peyote complex" that streamed into the Plains from the Gulf and the Southwest, and "the Peyote religion" which "was probably invented in the southern Plains on the basis of the old Peyote complex",[81] considers that the religion's pantheon was syncretistic and had been so already in 1887.[82] Also Carling Malouf, writing about Gosiute Peyotism, attributes a decided Christian flavour to their Peyote religion

---

[74] Speck 1933, p. 547.
[75] La Barre 1975 b, pp. 167 ff., cf. also pp. 117 f., and Stewart 1987, p. 223.
[76] Slotkin 1956 a, pp. 65 f., La Barre 1975 b, p. 102, cf. p. 164.
[77] For what follows, cf. also La Barre 1960, pp. 51 f.
[78] See in particular Opler 1942.
[79] La Barre 1975 b, p. 165; cf. p. 93.
[80] Stewart 1941 b, 1948.
[81] Slotkin 1956 a, p. 18.
[82] Slotkin 1956 a, pp. 44, 45.

and to the Great Basin Peyotism as a whole.[83] La Barre has noted that Bryan Wilson, well-known sociologist, characterizes the Peyote religion as an essentially Christian faith adapted to Indian conditions. This is of course completely wrong, as La Barre indignantly remarks.[84]

From a perusal of documents from the last decades it is my impression that the Peyote movement has become more and more Christianized. We are here not facing an immediate outcrop of Christian mission activities, but rather a slow increase of Christian ideas inside Peyotism. Two major factors may have been responsible for this development: the general policy of the Native American Church, fighting for a status and a program bringing it in as a Christian Church, and the modernization process aiming at an erasing of the ideological barriers between whites and red. (This process seems to have been checked through the new nationalistic tendencies on the Indian reservations.)

The process of indigenous Christianization has an interesting counterpart in the West African Bwiti "cult". This movement which encompasses 10% of the Fang (Pangwe) people in Gabon originated around the turn of the century as a cult of the ancestors. To begin with, beliefs and rituals had been incorporated from other tribes of Bantu affiliation which the Fang had replaced. Catholic influences slowly penetrated the cult, and this syncretistic process was speeded up after World War II keeping time and pace with the emergence of African states.[85] Stanislaw Swiderski who has investigated this religious acculturation points out how the believers have tried to save old religious ideas and enriched them with new forms taken from Christianity, the religion of the economic and social establishment in the Western world. "Attracted by the richness of Catholic liturgy, convinced by the coherence of the ideas and by the new values that they discovered in the gospels, the spiritual guides began to 'translate' Western Christianity into the religious and historical language of the Fang."[86] This parallellism between aboriginal and Christian concepts moved the people to "a complete comprehension of Christianity".[87] Swiderski concludes that the syncretistic Bwiti religion should be less considered as a separate religious unit, but rather as an African Christianity of a Bwiti speciality (un christianisme africain 'bouitisé') or, simply, a Christianity parallel to Western Christianity".[88] The main difference between Bwitism and Christianity is, says the same author, the use of a vision-provoking drug, *eboga,* (from *Tabernenthes eboka*), in the liturgy.[89]

The similarities between this cult and the Peyote religion should not be over-

---

[83] Malouf in La Barre 1975 b, p. 217, Malouf 1942.
[84] Wilson 1973, chaper 13, La Barre 1975 b, p. 262.
[85] Fernandez 1965.
[86] Swiderski 1975, pp. 344 f.
[87] Swiderski 1975, p. 345.
[88] Swiderski 1975, p. 356.
[89] Swiderski 1975, p. 357; the botanical classification is from Fernandez' article.

stressed, but there are some general features that they share. In both cases, a reformative movement centered around a drug has become christianized by the agency of the movement's own people. In both cases the status and power of Christian religion has served as a model. In both cases the aboriginal religion has, more or less, become acknowledged as a part of Christian religion.

3. Doctrine and Ritual

Peyote religion has as we have noticed developed around the usage of the Peyote cactus. Its history is the story of a continual accretion with elements from Mexican, Catholic, Plains and divers Christian milieux. This mixture of elements characterizes both doctrine and ritual. The ethics are to a varying extent coloured by Christian ideas.

The doctrine of the Peyote religion deserves more analysis than what has hitherto been achieved. The publications on Peyote by American anthropologists like Shonle and La Barre tend to dismiss the doctrine as inessential – as La Barre has later admitted, in answer to my criticism.[1] Slotkin discusses the Peyote pantheon which however he largely identifies with the Christian supernatural beings: there is a Trinity consisting of God, Jesus and the Holy Ghost, there is a devil (or many devils, Slotkin is vague here), and there are angels. Slotkin admits however the existence of beliefs in a waterbird spirit (which he aligns with the white dove, that is, Holy Ghost in Christian faith), a Peyote spirit (which might be Jesus) and "various traditional spirits, differing from tribe to tribe". But "these are survivals, and not an integral part of Peyotism".[2] When occasionally La Barre mentions supernatural spirits the reference is to the last three types of beings. The reasons for these differences are probably different inclinations in these two authors: La Barre, although uninterested in Peyote theology, pays attention to the aboriginal heritage and Native inventions, whereas Slotkin, a partial Peyotist viewing this religion in a Christian perspective, underlines a Christian theological background.

Both views are justified, although they only contain part of the truth. The Peyote doctrine must be seen in a dynamic and pluralistic perspective. Dynamic, because it changes with time. Pluralistic, because it varies from place to place. Any effort to cover it in descriptive terms will therefore fail. However, there is a nucleus of concepts which may be identified behind the screen of disguises.

The following presentation is influenced by the Wind River Shoshoni evidence but takes into account also what I know from other reservations.

---
[1] La Barre 1975 b, p. xviii n. 1.
[2] Slotkin 1956 a, pp. 68 ff.

First of all, the Peyote religion seeks in its ethics to achieve a good life for the Indian both in this world and in the world after death. Its main goal is to establish man's harmony with his fellow-men and God, and it will promote man's general wellbeing, deliverance from diseases, and protection in times of stress and need (for instance, in wartime). "The teachings of Peyote go beyond the confines of the tipi", writes a white convert to the Peyote religion, "my experiences sitting by the sacred fireplace have helped guide my daily life".[3] The feelings of satisfaction and brotherhood, and the blessings granted by Peyote are proofs of the fulfilment of this religion. Peyote adherents are supposed to "follow the Peyote road" which is graphically symbolized on the earth altar during the ceremonial session. Peyote inspires them to follow this road which, as outlined by Slotkin, is characterized by brotherly love, care of family, self-reliance and avoidance of alcohol.[4] Such a way also prepares for a good life after death close to God and one's loved ones.

It is apparent that as presented here the ethics have largely a Christian provenience. This was pointed out by Edward S. Curtis when he reminded his readers that American Indian religion "does not of itself necessarily embody a moral code, and in this respect the Peyote [ritual] formula differs from other Indian cults".[5] Whereas Slotkin and Stewart saw a constitutive Christian element in Peyotism La Barre accepted only a superficial veneer of Christian ideas among Peyotists. A discriminating author like Christopher Vecsey makes a difference between older Peyote religion represented by the Mescalero Apache and later Comanche Peyotism as expressed by Quanah Parker; "The Apaches used peyote shamanistically, without a christianized ethic of brotherhood; it took Quanah Parker and other peyotists beginning in Indian Territory to fashion the peaceful peyote ethics that have prevailed to the present day."[6] Although the role of the Mescalero Apache is not quite certain in Peyote diffusion, it seems that this difference in ethics between older and younger Peyotism is well taken.

Secondly, there is a pantheon. Beside prayers being directed to older gods and spirits of the individual tribes – it seems mostly the names of the traditional high gods have been called upon[7] – there is a cult of gods and spirits that may be classified as Peyote supernaturals. However, as was remarked above, it is difficult to expound the pantheon on one reservation as being identical with the pantheon on the next reservation. Anthropologists' presentations are, furthermore, not always correct. For instance, Slotkin principally derives all spiritual activity from the power that the Greek New Testament calls *pneuma,* and anthropologists *mana.* This is a clever combination of Indian beliefs with Christian

---

[3] Morgan 1983, p. 91.
[4] Slotkin 1956 a, pp. 44 f., 71. On alcohol in Peyotism, cf. below, Ch. IV:5.
[5] Curtis 1930, p. 199.
[6] Vecsey 1988, p. 188; cf. pp. 185 ff. Cf. also Radin 1923, pp. 351 ff., and see below, Ch. IV:12.
[7] La Barre 1975 b, p. 166.

dogma and anthropological theory.[7a] It is, however, in conflict with various local Peyote conceptions. Among the Washo in westernmost Nevada the Peyote people have had a fierce fight with the tribal medicine men. Consequently, the concept of power is strenuously opposed by Peyote ideology, and "many Peyotists take the position that the idea of 'power' itself is alien to the true spirit of Peyote".[8] As a further stricture on Slotkin's presentation (in this case his concepts of Trinity, the devil, and so on) could be quoted the following observation by Alan Merriam and Warren d'Azevedo, also from the Washo: "Christian elements have diminished considerably; the Bible is no longer a part of the leader's paraphernalia, and biblical references in prayer and conversation are rare."[9] This was said in 1957, one year after the publication of Slotkin's work. It is obvious that the Trinity concept could not be at home in this milieu.

Although no general account of the Peyote pantheon coula be written the following supernatural personages play a great role:

(1) God, that is, the Supreme Being of aboriginal religions (where he occurred), modified by Christian teaching. For instance, in many Peyote groups he is identified as the Creator, although Native North American religions mostly invested other beings with creative powers.[10] Likewise, his central position and clear personality seem to reflect Christian teachings (cf. also the discussion in Ch. IV:12). Possibly also a more personal relationship between man and God is a result of missionary influence.

(2) Peyote, understood as a spirit. Peyotists on the Plains wear around their neck a necklace with a pouch containing a Peyote button, obviously as a talisman; and many users of Peyote have a Peyote button or plant as a fetish in their homes. La Barre maintains that Peyote is the only plant toward which the non-agricultural Plains tribes have a religious attitude, and which gives them power.[11] This is not so. As we shall see, the Wind River Shoshoni show reverence for a magic flower growing in the foothills and mountains (see Ch. IV:5). Steinmetz tells us that among the Oglala Lakota the administration of herbs is a religious act accompanied by Lakota praying. Before pulling up medicine plants the Oglala offers up tobacco and prays to the plant.[12] The religious attitude to the sacred Peyote is thus no foreign element in the Plains Indian pattern.

As a spirit Peyote is conceived in many forms. First of all it is there, visible to all, a big button on the earth altar (cf. below). It is called "Peyote chief", or "Father Peyote". It is said to be a representative of the first peyote that was discovered in mythic times.[13] Secondly, it is also represented as a goddess, "Peyote

---

[7a] Slotkin 1956 a, p. 69.
[8] Merriam and d'Azevedo 1957, p. 617.
[9] Merriam and d'Azevedo 1957, p. 618.
[10] Cf. Hultkrantz 1979 b, p. 32.
[11] La Barre 1975 b, p. 72.
[12] Steinmetz 1980, p. 48.
[13] Vecsey 1988, p. 194, quoting Robert C. Kiste; cf. below, Ch. III:2.

woman". Peyotists can hear her sing during Peyote meetings – the supernatural materialization of auditive hallucinations that many attendants, this author included, have experienced (cf. above, Ch. I:1, and below, Ch. II:3). The Wichita identify the voice with a supernatural female water being, the Kiowa with the woman who according to their myth first found Peyote, the Lakota with the mysterious Buffalo Calf woman, and the Lipan Apache with Changing woman, the goddess of the Moon, or possibly the Virgin Mary.[14] The woman who brings in the breakfast into the Peyote tipi in the morning is by some supposed to be a personification of the Peyote woman.[15]

Thirdly, as a messenger between God and mankind Peyote is sometimes, in more pronounced christianized Peyote circles, referred to as Jesus or the Holy Ghost.[16]

(3) The Waterbird, messenger spirit. Its identity is uncertain. There are indications that the waterbird has been understood as a waterturkey or any waterfowl, or as a dove – the form of manifestation of the Holy Ghost. During the midnight song in the Peyote meeting the leader blows on his eagle wing-bone whistle "to imitate the water bird".[17] Another event during the meeting is the building up of the ashes from the fire into a bird. This bird is identified as the waterbird by the Shawnee and Kickapoo, but the Comanche and Pawnee interpret it as an eagle, and the Kiowa as a hummingbird.[18] Bird symbolism seems to have surrounded the Peyote ritual since ancient Mexican days.[19] La Barre makes a suggestive reference to a Tarahumara fishing bird which is a cross between an eagle and a hawk: could it be the osprey that is, in fact, an eagle-like hawk? A Mexican Indian friend of mine, Mr. Edward Tafoya, has suggested the Roseate spoonbill, an Ibis-like bird, associated with the XIVth Aztec month (Quecholli).[20] In any case, the origin of the waterbird symbolism remains an enigma.

Beside the divinities and spirits now mentioned there are a host of other deities and spiritual powers, differing from tribe to tribe, such as Mother Earth, Thunderbird, ghosts and spirits of the vision quest. In christianized Peyote theology these powers may be compared to and identified with Christ, the Holy Ghost, the angels, etc. For instance, a peyotist told Ruth Underhill that Peyote,

---

[14] La Barre 1975 b, pp. 13 f., and p. 13, n. 18. Concerning the White Buffalo Calf woman, see Vecsey 1988, p. 169, the Kiowa mythic woman, see Mooney 1897, and Changing woman, see Opler 1938, p. 279, and 1940, p. 16. The latter is described in such a way that she comes close to the general South Athapascan idea of the goddess of the earth and vegetation.

[15] Cf. La Barre 1975 b, pp. 51 n. 113, 85, Vecsey 1988, p. 196.

[16] La Barre *et al.* 1951, Stewart 1938, p. 3, Vecsey 1988, pp. 170 f.

[17] La Barre 1975 b, pp. 50 f. The whistling is the cry of the bird in search of water, op. cit., p. 71. See also Stewart 1970, p. 790.

[18] La Barre 1975 b, p. 78.

[19] La Barre 1975 b, pp. 39, 71.

[20] The same informant called my attention to the fact that in the summer month VI (Etzalqualiztli) Aztec priests bathed imitating waterbirds, see Sahagún 1950–69, Book 2, pp. 74 f.

God, Christ and the Great spirit are all the same power.[21] Similarly, a Lakota Indian identified the Virgin Mary, the White Buffalo Calf Woman (who once brought the sacred pipe to the Lakota) and the Water woman.[22] Whether such identifications are only formal accommodations to a Christian surrounding or earnest faith depends of course upon the cult groups and the individuals.

The Peyote ideology has been discussed here in some detail because the subject has been nearly bypassed in general works on Peyote.[23] This does not mean to say that this short survey exhausts the subject, far from it. We need detailed tribal accounts and analyses. The behaviouristic emphasis of American anthropology has not been fruitful for this kind of research,[24] and students of religion have so far abstained from writing on the subject. What has been presented here affords us however with some necessary background material for our central investigation.

The ritual performances will be more summarily described here, both because there are fuller accounts in other general works and because a closer presentation of a Shoshoni ritual will be given shortly (Ch. II:3). The historical process leading up to the present-day Peyote nightly meeting in a Plains tipi was, I hope, sufficiently discussed in the preceding subchapter.

The reasons for taking Peyote in today's Indian communities differ between individuals and, seen from the perspective of the organizers, from one occasion to another. Speaking about the Pine Ridge (Oglala) Lakota George Morgan tells us that "there is no single reason that a person is drawn to the Peyote religion. Some take refuge in the church as a last resort to cure a sickness after the white man's medicine fails. Some start attending meetings out of sheer curiosity, and some want to escape the monotony of reservation life. Many come because they have heard that the Native American Church is a place where one can talk to God and feel His presence. They have heard that Peyote can change minds, habits, and lives for the better, or that Peyote can bring happiness to man in this life. The actions, words, and morals of Peyotists themselves have been positive living examples to the Indian people. Another attraction is the close fellowship of Peyote meetings."[25]

Similar multifacetted expectations predominate in the ritual Peyote circle among the Plains Cree of Montana. Here a Peyote meeting "may be held to ask for the recovery of a sick person, or it may be held as a result of a vow made if a person recovers from an illness. The person who gives the meeting always tells the others the reason for the meetings. Sometimes they have meetings to doctor a sick person who attends and the participants pray all night for him.

---

[21] Underhill 1965, p. 267.
[22] Lame Deer and Erdoes 1972, p. 223.
[23] Cf. my comments in La Barre 1960, p. 57.
[24] Cf. Hultkrantz 1977 b, pp. 84 f.
[25] Morgan 1983, p. 93.

Anyone can smoke for him or pray to the peyote to let the person get well. They can also pray for better homes, for the education of their children, for the health of the old people, and for peace. Sometimes they have birthday meetings where they pray for the luck of the child's future."[26]

These two reports summarize rather well the needs that a Peyote meeting on the Plains may be thought to fulfil. In former days other motives could be found, like weather prediction and divination for success.[27] However, the motives behind the original acceptance of the Peyote religion were different, as we shall see.

Peyote meetings are held all the year round, usually on Saturdays, but also at irregular times (for instance, when an instant curing is demanded). In typical cases they are attended by a closely knit group of people, kinsmen and friends who believe in this "medicine". Also Peyotists from far off tribes are often present; on such occasions the English language, but sometimes even sign language, may be the means of communication. Women were originally excluded from taking part in the rite, but this rule no longer holds except in some places. (Their most important function traditionally is to serve the morning meal.) As a ritual the Peyote meeting is characteristically Indian, but lacking the detailed elaboration of most Plains and Pueblo rituals. The stress is laid upon the experience of Peyote and its beneficiary consequences, not upon the right measures of ritual action (although for instance certain observances like taboos for menstruating women to attend the ceremony are adhered to). The observer who takes part in a Peyote meeting is himself a vehicle of Peyote's power.[28] It is possible that this lack of ritual intensification has given rise to the derogatory name by which the Peyote meeting is known to Wind River Shoshoni non-believers: *wogodikare'*, "eating cactus". To the believers it is known as *nani-suntɛi*, "prayer meeting".[29] Indeed, prayers and contemplation fill up most of the time at a Peyote ceremony.

The word "prayer" should here be qualified. As stated by Underhill, it covers the old Indian attitude – not begging, but talking in a friendly way.[30] It is a spiritual communication on the level of personal transfer.

As was indicated in the last subchapter, the Peyote ritual differs between tribes and groups. There are, for instance, various forms of the altar, that is, the fireplace, and now and then innovations in paraphernalia occur.[31] The main dif-

---

[26] Dusenberry 1962, pp. 177 f.
[27] Cf. Driver 1961, pp. 98 f.
[28] See for instance Hoebel 1949 and Hultkrantz 1968 b. Hoebel describes a Cheyenne, Hultkrantz a Shoshoni Peyote meeting. See also Morgan 1983 (Oglala Lakota).
[29] Hultkrantz, Wind River Shoshoni Field Notes.
[30] Underhill 1965, p. 267.
[31] It could be mentioned here that I was asked by an active Shoshoni Peyote leader, George Wesaw, to bring him a Swedish feather fan – I suppose in order to enhance his social prestige.

ferences have been listed by La Barre.[32] An average Peyote meeting takes place in a tipi between 8 PM and 8 AM. The meeting is conducted by a leader, the "road man", who has three assistants, a drummer who treats the water drum (with a drum stick), a "cedar man" who handles the bundle of sweetgrass that he strews as incense on the fire, and the "fire man" who looks after the fireplace. The road man is equipped with a staff, a fan of bird's tail feathers, and a gourd rattle – ritual instruments that otherwise are used by medicine men. Slotkin has characterized the rite as essentially consisting of "four major components: prayer, singing, eating the sacramental Peyote, and contemplation."[33]

The ceremony usually starts with a prayer and the taking of Peyote "buttons". The fire man creates an altar mound of earth, shaped in crescent form, and places a Peyote button on its top. In front of this so-called "moon" he makes a fire on sticks piled up in V-form. As the fire burns the ashes are used to form another crescent, smaller and whiter, besides the original one. Drumming, singing, praying, Peyote taking continues until midnight when the fire man outside of the lodge blows an eaglebone whistle at the four cardinal points, thus imitating the waterbird or the eagle; this is followed by the strong and vivid "midnight song" inside the tipi.[34] The rest of the night is taken up by singing, meditation, praying, consumption of Peyote in various forms (eating the cactus, drinking a decoction of Peyote, "Peyote tea", and smoking cigarrettes containing a tobacco blended with Peyote[35]), public confessions of sins (that is, transgressions of the ethical rules presented in the foregoing) and, occasionally, vomiting. It is said that a sick person becomes well if he vomits after having taken Peyote.[36] It seems possible that we are confronted here with the same medical practice – removal of disturbing disease objects – that has prevailed in aboriginal North American folk medicine. Curing through prayers, divination through visions and other truly shamanic feats may occur.

The vigil ends with the common feasting of a ritually composed morning meal: four vessels of water, corn in sugar-water, fruit and some meat. This meal is a relic of the original Mexican ritual of first fruits and thanksgiving.

---

[32] La Barre 1975 b, pp. 57 ff. The different altar forms have often come about through visionary instructions given by Peyote to some cult member, cf. for instance Stewart 1987, pp. 268 f.

[33] Slotkin 1956 a, p. 73. It is remarkable how often Peyote consumers who are also Christians, or pseudo-Christian sympathizers like Slotkin and Stewart, have referred to the eating of the sacred cactus as a sacrament. Also in the famous research report where the two scholars were involved this term recurs (see La Barre et al. 1951) . The propagandistic purpose is obvious, and scholars like La Barre and Tax seem to have given in.

[34] The midnight ceremony is performed in many variations.

[35] Each participant is supposed to start with four pieces of the Peyote dish, and then to continue eating, drinking and smoking Peyote throughout the night. In some Peyote rituals, for instance the Crossfire ritual among the Oglala Lakota, smoking as a whole is not allowed. In another Oglala Peyote ritual, the sacred pipe has been introduced, see Steinmetz 1980, pp. 80, 85 ff.

[36] Slotkin 1956 a, p. 76. Vomiting is actually a natural reaction for a beginner in Peyote eating. Cf. also what has been said above about ritual vomiting, Ch. I:2, note 13.

II. The Peyote Religion: A Shoshoni Example

1. Peyote among the Wind River Shoshoni

In order to demonstrate the appearance of the Peyote religion in an American Indian society I shall here present a summary of Wind River Shoshoni Peyotism as witnessed by myself. Other information on this Peyotism has been published by Dmitri Shimkin and Molly Peacock Stenberg.[1] My field work on the Wind River Reservation, Wyoming, was mainly performed during the years 1948 and 1955. The Shoshoni share their reservation with the Arapaho, but I have not witnessed any Peyote meeting among the latter. Miss Stenberg assures us, however, that the only Indian activity on the reservation that cuts across tribal lines and in which mutual participation is practised is the Peyote ritual.[2] It is thus an efficient means of pan-Indian understanding, for in the old days Shoshoni and Arapaho were bitter enemies.

The first Wind River Shoshoni to have tasted Peyote was Charlie Washakie, a son of the noted Chief Washakie and a Crow woman. Apparently he was invited by Arapaho Indians to participate in Peyote meetings as early as 1909.[3] After having visited Southern Arapaho Peyotists in Oklahoma during the winter 1916–17 he introduced the new religion among his tribesmen. It was however a version of the ritual that did not entirely conform to the Northern Arapaho rite, and was therefore for a while contested by the latter. Nevertheless, about 1919 the Peyote religion was an established creed among the Wind River Shoshoni. Charlie Washakie was still a leading Peyote man when I saw him in 1948; he was then seventy-five. He died from an automobile accident a few years later, in September, 1953.

One very important feature in Peyotism is the authorization of the ceremony through tradition. Each Peyote leader is thought to represent such a tradition, and forcefully claims it, just like a Muslim lawyer adduces his *isnâd* or chain of authorities. For Charlie Washakie, the Southern Arapaho medicine man Jock Bull Bear was the teacher. Molly Stenberg has published a very interesting letter from Bull Bear to Washakie in which he gives rules for the use of incense.[4] It appears from the letter that Bull Bear had taken Peyote already in 1883; he

---

[1] Shimkin's notes on Wind River Shoshoni Peyotism in Stewart 1944, pp. 105–120; Stenberg 1946. See also Hultkrantz 1968 b.
[2] Stenberg 1946, p. 93.
[3] Stenberg 1946, p. 146.
[4] Stenberg 1946, p. 147.

would then, if our previous historical analysis is correct (Ch. I:2, above), have been amongst the first group of Peyote eaters in the Arapaho tribe. According to my information all the later members of the Washakie family – a family known for its previous agnosticism – embraced the Peyote religion.

It is however doubtful whether Charlie Washakie was the sole inspirator. Take for instance his nephew Marshall Washakie (nominal "chief" of the tribe after his father's, Dick Washakie's, decease in 1944). Peyote theologians found it remarkable that he constructed an altar of red earth.[5] Now, Marshall was friendly with a Northern Arapaho, John Goggles, who had used Peyote since 1897.[6] Goggles, who was a medicine man as well, had introduced Peyote to several Shoshoni. According to my informant Tom Wesaw, himself a peyotist, Marshall Washakie received the Peyote way from John Goggles and handed it on, in his turn, to Tom's son, George Wesaw (cf. below).

This discussion may seem to be a petty thing, but it is not to the believers. For instance, father and son Wesaw belonged to two different Peyote traditions, Tom to the "Comanche way" with its altar in a horseshoe form, and George to the "Kiowa way" with a crescent-formed altar. The differences are dogmatically important, just as the differences between homoiousians and homousians were in early Christianity.

It is difficult to trace the spread of Peyote within the Shoshoni tribe. Some people joined and fell out again, others visited Peyote meetings occasionally, still others became stern adherents or antagonists. If we say that approximately 75% of the Shoshoni could appear now and then at such meetings during the 1940s and 1950s[7] this does not mean that they all "followed the Peyote way". However, Peyotism has been most active, and the quick beating of Peyote drums may be heard from different parts of the reservation.

Indeed, meetings sometimes take place two or three times a week. Tom Wesaw told me that they may be held "any time", and that sometimes there could elapse one to two months before he joined a meeting or arranged one himself. Although there has never been any Government sanction against Peyotists Shoshoni Peyote leaders were worried of possible reactions from authorities at the time of my field work. Actually, the reservation superintendent – who once picked me up from a Peyote meeting – declined to listen to my account of what I had experienced. As we shall see, the Indians implored me to tell the authorities of the harmlessness of the Peyote drug (see Ch. II:3).

---

[5] I was told that the red crescent is a modern feature, borrowed from the Arapaho, and part of the so-called Kiowa way (see below). It was at that time used by Marshall Washakie and Jasper Wadi.

[6] Stenberg 1946, p. 139.

[7] This was the impression of the agency interpreter Tom Compton and of Wallace St. Clair, a most able Shoshoni of a prominent family. Some peyotists thought in 1948 that most Shoshoni actually used Peyote, and more than half of the tribe recgularly. They also asserted that at that time more people took Peyote than ten years earlier. Molly Stenberg's estimation (1946, p. 116) agrees with my own.

What kind of people engage in the religion? The answer is, all kinds of people, and usually whole families. It is difficult to judge if the "aristocratic" Washakie family set an example; many of the descendants of old Chief Washakie, deceased in 1900, were not so highly regarded. One remarkable fact is that the Peyote people are often defendants of tradition and of old ingrained ways. Some are medicine men, others excellent story-tellers. They set up Sun Dances. Usually there are two or even more Sun Dances each summer season, and it happens that one of them is organized by members of the Peyote religion. Such a Sun Dance is arranged if the Peyote men have not taken part in the preceding ordinary Sun Dance. There is no difference between the Sun Dances, and no Peyote is consumed when the Peyote leaders institute the Dance. Observers will notice however that in all Sun Dances Peyotists differ from ordinary dancers in having a necklace with a pouch containing a Peyote button.

Miss Stenberg thinks the Peyote religion is a factor influencing the return of old Indian crafts.[8] I am not sure that Peyotists are more outstanding in this field than others.

There is also the reverse side. During my visits to the Shoshoni the Peyote eaters, with the exception of the relatively wealthy members of the Washakie family, all lived in the most awful, delapidated shacks, wanting in every respect. Although housing conditions were poor all over the reservation at that time those of my Peyote friends were alarmingly so. Moreover, two of these acquaintances, Tom Wesaw and Gilbert Day, were on relief-pay. Since then things have partly improved, however, and it would be difficult to pass the same categorical judgment today.

My chief informants on Peyote were Tom Wesaw and his son, George, now both deceased. Tom Alec Wesaw, born in 1886, was the grandson of an intelligent old Indian, Wesaw (*wišo:'*, "(eats) too much grease"), who acted as a guide for early white expeditions travelling through the mountaineous area of northwestern Wyoming.[9] Tom's father was George Wesaw or *naŋgitu:rna'*, "too many lobes of the ear", or *a:zux*, "old Crow Indian man". Tom held the reputation of being a medicine man. At about fourteen years of age he had received a guardian spirit from his grandfather, a spirit that had been inherited from one generation to the next. It was the ghost of a deceased ancestor and consequently looked human (which is rather exceptional among the Shoshoni). This guardian spirit appeared to Tom Wesaw in a dream in 1957 and ordered him to set up a Sun Dance. (Tom had arranged many Sun Dances before, but I do not know with what spiritual authority).[10] In spite of his prestige as a medicine man Tom Wesaw was won for the Peyote movement about 1918. He told me that he tried

---

[8] Stenberg 1946, p. 99.
[9] Norris 1882, p. 38.
[10] One of my informants claimed that Tom had lost his guardian spirit; but this was denied by the Wesaw family.

the new medicine, found it good, and joined the Peyote church. He did so without giving up his activity as a medicine man and Sun Dance leader.

Tom Wesaw later received the Comanche way, like many other prominent Shoshoni Peyotists (such as Percy McCloud and Gilbert Day). His teacher was Gilbert Day, who in his turn had received Peyote instruction from the Comanche, Shanom Wahnee. According to Tom Wesaw's understanding the Comanche Indians, a Shoshoni-speaking people in Oklahoma, had been blessed with Peyote from the Apache, the "bearfeet". Already at the turn of the century Tom had heard that these bearfeet were the first to own "the medicine called Peyote". It seems however that Peyote did not give him and his family all the blessing he hoped for. In the year of my first acquaintance with Peyote in the company of Tom Wesaw, he had suffered several deaths in his family. He lost a son and a daughter earlier in the year, and when he served as ceremonial leader in the August Sun Dance one of his grandchildren died, so he had to break off his dancing that night.

Tom Wesaw was a knowledgeable man, modest and truthful. Shimkin's judgement – that he was intelligent and well-informed, not always in good health, taciturn at first, and always a little suspicious, fits the picture well.[11]

With his wife, Helen Hill, Tom Wesaw had the son George Wesaw, born in 1915. He was an energetic Peyote man, more occupied with Peyotism than any other Shoshoni I knew of. He received the Kiowa way from Marshall Washakie. A meeting under George's leadership will be presented in the following (Ch. II:3). Every third year he used to visit the Comanche in Oklahoma, where his brother-in-law lived, to discuss spiritual experiences with his kinsmen there. It is remarkable that his close peyotist partners were Comanche, although he held the Kiowa way! George was a good connaisseur on Peyote, but also embraced empathically the old Shoshoni beliefs and values. I heard him talk lyrically about the old buffalo days when Shoshoni tipis dotted the wide plains and the green mountain meadows. However, he knew less traditional lore than he thought.

Some time after 1958 (when I saw him last time) George Wesaw moved to Fort Hall reservation in Idaho. From here he made annual excursions to the Rocky Boy Cree in Montana, to conduct Peyote meetings there.[12] According to Dr. Joanna Scherer of the Smithsonian Institution he died before his father.[13] George was married to Isabel Tindall, a Shoshoni whose great-great-grandmother on the paternal line was Sacajawea, the famous guide of Lewis and Clark. The couple had a number of children, but had lost most of them before the time of my visit.[14]

---

[11] Shimkin 1953, p. 476.
[12] Stewart 1979, pp. 153, 154.
[13] Letter from Dr. Joanna Scherer, Smithsonian Institution, May, 1985.
[14] Cf. Stenberg 1946, p. 108.

The situation on the Wind River Reservation among the Shoshoni may be characterized as a peaceful coexistence between Peyotists and traditionalists, where many traditionalists are also Peyotists or people who may take intermittently Peyote. There is however, generally speaking, a mutual distrust between the two camps, as revealed in verbal comments on different occasions. It is difficult however to pinpoint the shades of this antagonism. The Shoshoni are factionalists and have always been, except when some great personality, such as Chief Washakie in the last century, has kept them together. Reservation life has, it seems, sharpened former oppositions and created new ones. Peyotism has certainly contributed to this process, and made it more complicated.

In the main, the following picture emerged during my field research in the 1940s and 1950s.

The non-Peyotists reacted differently to the Peyote religion. In part they resented it, in part they feared its supertribal character, in part they accepted it tacitly. When Tom Wesaw told me that he and his fellow-believers had more friendship with Arapaho peyotists than with non-Peyotist Shoshoni this was an indication of the Shoshoni bent for factionalism. The non-Peyotists answered by ignoring the Peyote people. One informant told me that the famous medicine man Morgan Moon, or Moogutsie (1873–1944), had a vision in which the spirit told him not to deal with people who "mixed medicines". When Peyote had come into use some Peyote men came and asked for his help in curing. Against the spirit's instructions Morgan helped them out. But then he fell sick and was ill for a long time until he died. "He would have lived even this day if he hadn't acted the way he did", commented his sister.[15] Another prominent medicine man, White Colt (1853–1936), who used to sponsor ghost dances, taught that the path to the beyond has a fork from where there are two ways. A person is standing there, trying to seduce you to take the wrong path and saying that it leads to a beautiful place. Some people want to walk that path, for instance, the Peyote people. However, Our Father [= the Supreme Being] brings them all back and places them on the straight path that leads to the blessed country.[16]

The disapproval of the non-peyotists is violently reciprocated by Peyotists. Tom Wesaw charged non-peyotist medicine men of being no good, no medicine men, and even being liars. He also accused one, well-established medicine man for not knowing how to pray. The mutual distrust never turned into open animosity, however. The case of the medicine man John Trehero, belonging to the non-peyotist camp, is illustrative of the feelings and reactions of an interested outsider.

John Trehero emphatically declared that he did not understand Peyote and did not take it. He was aware of that the Peyote cactus, $wogwei^{wi}$, has a place similar to the Christian sacraments: "The Peyote people say that the white man has

---

[15] Information volunteered in 1948 by Morgan's sister, Nadzaip.
[16] Information in 1948 by Lynn St. Clair.

wine in his church for holy communion, whilst the Indians have Peyote in their church for holy communion." This statement reflects the Peyotist ideology of making Peyote religion and Christianity racial alternatives in North America (cf. Ch. IV:12). Long ago John went to Peyote meetings, but he did not like them; as a medicine man he found that the leaders were insufficient, and that the drug was impotent. "When you drink Peyote you imagine that you see things", was his sceptical remark. He did not think, he said, that the spirits you imagine you see are real. He did not himself see any vision when he took Peyote. "I only felt like after two to three shots of whiskey." Finally, he criticized the Peyote people for not believing in guardian spirits.

It is obvious that John Trehero's reactions were dependent on his self-consciousness as a traditional medicine man. His objections to the Peyote leadership and the subordinate role of spirits and spirit-visions are telling. The surprising statement that Peyote visions are weaker than other visions of the more traditional vision-quest type reflects the experiences of the well-trained medicine man.

The arguments of the Peyote people were of course quite different. They would tell you that the Peyote religion is ancient and powerful, and works for the good. An ingrained Peyotist like Tom Wesaw declared that he had never had any visions during Peyote meetings, but he felt power.[17] The important thing, he told me, is not the vision, but this feeling of power. "You feel the power, you know that God or Jesus exist, but you do not know where." This sounds like an intuitive cognition. Tom considered Peyote more powerful than the Sun Dance, a remarkable statement from a man who during my visits to the Shoshoni set up several Sun Dances.

Although Tom, like many other Peyotists, may be judged a traditionalist he contrasted the present Peyote age with the time before Peyote. "The old Indians had no religion, they walked around looking for fight and war. The Peyote people don't like fighting." His son George, sharing his father's ideological position, assured me, "Before they believed in God they prayed to the sun, the moose, the buffalo, the mountain lion, the rock. Before Peyote came there was no creed in God, but they learned to know God before the whites arrived." Such statements are of course of no historical value,[18] but they say a good deal for the convictions of a Peyotist. Like his father George had an aversion against warfare: "If I kill I get killed, [then] I can never return, and I have to roam around." Here the idea of the revenant has been extended to all fallen in combat – an

---

[17] Since this negative evidence may reflect on the theme of this work it seems urgent to point out that, as Tom told me, neither had he received any visions in the Sun Dance. This is exceptional for a Sun Dance leader.

[18] In fact, on another occasion the same informant said, "Before Peyote came here we didn't pray to anything, not even to God. We didn't believe in God until [the Episcopal missionary] Roberts came here – but I don't know this well." Dr. John Roberts arrived in 1883. Similar declarations were formulated by other Plains Indians, see Vecsey 1988, p. 160.

expression of the Peyote philosophy that made this religion survive the militant Plains culture of the last century.

This lack of fighting spirit is in line with the Peyotist efforts to come to a *modus vivendi* with the whites. Said Tom Wesaw, "This is an Indian religion, it is not for the whites, but each white man is welcome to come in. No white man can start a Peyote meeting. There is something powerful here. They [= the whites] can't do it." It is possible that the instructions of the legislation – Peyote only allowed for Indian rituals – echo here. Perhaps there was also a feeling of the white man's incapacity to handle Peyote. I suppose the same idea lay behind George Wesaw's refusal to give me a packet of Peyote buttons.[19] He said, "Peyote may only be kept consumed[!]. You lose it if you keep it in a packet, for it is too powerful. I have myself lost Peyote by having it in my pocket." Maybe also the consideration contributed that the Shoshoni have to make long journeys to find their Peyote buttons, "better than 2000 miles from here", as Tom Wesaw expressed it.[20]

It is difficult to answer the question, related to our main theme, why Peyote spread to the Shoshoni. There was certainly no particular reason over and above the ones which can be adduced to the Peyote movement as a whole. The Shoshoni were part of the general Peyote wind that swept over the Plains during the first two decades of the present century. Their mental and cultural conditions in no way deviated from the other Plains groups at this time. There is little need here to speculate to what extent political and cultural loss, difficult acculturation with white culture, bad housing conditions, diseases and mental depression paved the way for Peyote. The stress on the chain of Peyote traditions and Peyote teachers may seem to favour Stewart's argument of the importance of proselytizers (see below, Ch. IV:10). However, there are other, more latent motivations.

The pioneering efforts of the Washakie family through Charles Washakie may give a hint. Peyotism offered a religious anchorage for the agnostic members of this family; but it is difficult to know to what extent Charlie Washakie was an agnostic before his conversion to Peyote, if he ever was one – he gave the same standard replies as the Wesaws.[21] It is certain that this distinguished family set a precedence for some other Shoshoni. However, the Shoshoni In-

---

[19] In retrospect I find my demand most inappropriate since it conflicted with the law and endangered Shoshoni Peyotism. At that time I was not quite acqainted with the legislation around Peyote.

[20] Sometimes Tom went by car all the way down to Texas by himself to procure the cactus. As was said earlier, his son George visited the Comanche of Oklahoma each third year, partly for the same purpose.

[21] Eloise Sonnicant (Mrs. Lynn St. Clair) whose mother was a daughter of Dick Washakie told me that the whole Washakie family, including her own mother, disbelieved in guardian spirits and afterlife and did not follow the rule of shutting up women in particular huts at the time of their menstruation. She ascribed their indifference to traditional Shoshoni religion to their Flathead heritage (Chief Washakie was half Flathead). Still, the old Chief Washakie's grandson John was on the verge of becoming a medicine man when he lost his life in World War I.

dians are very individualistic and, as we have seen, their Peyote traditions do not necessarily go back to Charlie Washakie.

Although it is dangerous to compare latter-day responses to Peyote with those current at the time of the first acceptance of the Peyote religion some motives for its hold on the Shoshoni may be found in the following words uttered by Tom Wesaw: "I have been on Peyote meetings among the Southern Cheyenne in Oklahoma, the Ute and the Shoshoni-Bannock of Fort Hall. I have become more happy and healthy through Peyote. In the next life we will have it good. We always pray to Peyote to protect us so that there will be no troubles. I have lost many relatives. When my time is out that can't be helped, we all go that road. But Peyote helps a lot of times. In the next life there is probably no Peyote, but I don't know... Sometimes the dreams come true, sometimes they don't." Happiness, health, lack of worries, a good existence after death, this was what Peyote would bring. But did it? Tom had been afflicted by the deaths of many close relatives. This was not what Peyote should allow. The disappointment was there, but also the dreams.

The hopes cherished by Tom Wesaw are the hopes that all charismatic religions aspire to fulfil, they are not peculiar to Peyotism. If we are eager to find out what the first peyotists felt, why they went over to the new religion, we shall learn nothing through the Shoshoni materials. Peyotism was an institutional religion when it reached Charlie Washakie, a religion of the Plains. We can guess, in the case of Charlie Washakie, that it implanted religious certainty where there was none before.

It is natural if in the beginning, a hundred years ago, Peyote spread because of its vision-producing capacity. It could here fit in with the visionary patterns in Plains religions. However, other factors were imperative at the beginning of this century.[22] Peyote offered help in the new reservation situation. It became resorted to in situations of stress. Today, it may be taken as a medicine for practically everything.[23] A person who feels sick from Peyote is urged to take more, "it helps". An ill person who participates in a Peyote meeting perceives the drumming, wakes up and becomes healthy again, "that's what they claim" (Tom Wesaw). Many Peyote meetings are prayer meetings *(nanisuntɛi)* for some person afflicted by a disease. Tom Wesaw cured pneumonia – the only disease he could handle – by praying and giving Peyote to the sick person. Sometimes, said George Wesaw, when a member of one's family falls ill some person – be it a man, be it a woman – makes a vow to set up a Peyote meeting in a tipi, or in a house, just as he decides, if that relative regains his health. Such a vow must be kept.[24]

---

[22] Besides, there was a reaction against the old vision quest as an acquisition of evil powers at the beginning of this century; spontaneous dreams took the place of the visions. In this connection Peyote visions were less desirable.

[23] My informants told me however that Peyote has no effect on an alcoholic.

[24] This should be compared with the custom to put up a Sun Dance after a similar vow.

Peyote meetings are also arranged so that people may pray for those who have been drafted – just as Sun Dances are set up for the same reason.

Peyote rituals can also be used for occasional aims. Thus, according to George Wesaw, "when we quit [the Peyote tipi] we take the water out of the drum, make a little prayer and pray that water may rain over us; then we pour the water over the whole moon [altar]." Rain-making is part of traditional Shoshoni religion, but certainly not in this form.

To practise Peyote religion is, as one believer told me, "to sit up suffering and praying one night". Like any other prayer meeting a Peyote night is a seeking of blessings of all kinds. The participants feel, under the influence of Peyote, an exalted unity of mind, a harmony amongst them and with the Spirit, a oneness with the world. This feeling is typically Indian, it is a realization of tendencies that are present in Indian religious representations and symbolism all over North America. To the Shoshoni, Peyote religion equals Christianity in all respects. It is of course, at the same time, more Indian.

2. Peyote Symbolism

To those Shoshoni who believe in Peyote it is the oldest of all religions. One Peyote man told me it is the Old Testament, therefore very ancient, existing long before we were born; another meant that with all its accessories it is older than all our churches. Because of this it is a sacred creed, and its followers ornate themselves with necklaces carrying Peyote pouches, or with buttons made from silver by Peyote people in Oklahoma. This is a kind of an outward sign that they belong to the Peyote church.

Like the Sun Dance the Peyote lodge and the paraphernalia used in the Shoshoni Peyote meeting have symbolic implications.[1] The Peyote lodge is in a way, like the Sun Dance room, a cosmic model, but as far as I could find without the spatial interpretation typical for the Sun Dance lodge. I was told that the poles of the Peyote tipi stand for the disciples of Christ (it is then presupposed that only twelve tipi poles are used). The fire in the middle of the tent represents God, for God is light. God answers our prayers through the fire. The Christian origin of this symbolism is obvious.

The moon crescent altar is made from earth or, as one informant said, it is "the dirt itself". He was implying that it represents Mother Earth, "not Jesus' mother, but the mother of us all".[2] A score is drawn on the top of the crescent, from one end to the other. This is "the good Peyote road, a highway in our life".

---
[1] On the Shoshoni Sun Dance symbolism, cf. Hultkrantz 1981a, pp. 235 ff.
[2] The otherwise so well-informed Tom Wesaw said that the crescent should be there because it belongs to the ceremony; but he did not know why.

It is the path we have to follow in this life, said Tom Wesaw, adding, "the next life I don't know". In the middle of the score a Peyote button is placed. This was explained to me as the point on the path of life where man is middle-aged. The end of the score that runs towards the north is supposed to be "the old age road".[3]

The Peyote button is said to be "God's power", or, alternatively, "God's will-power, his spirit". Both expressions were given to me in English; however, the Shoshoni word used was *puha* which stands for both spirit and power. You pray to the Peyote button during the meeting. "Peyote is a fruit of the earth, our mother, who makes such wonderful things." "Peyote is power."

In front of the concave part of the crescent there is another crescent, made from ashes, which is often formed into the likeness of a bird during the nightly vigils.[4] This bird, an eagle, is there "because it belongs to the Peyote". I was also told that the eagle offers protection. In a prayer offered by Tom Wesaw (see below, Ch II:3) the eagle is mentioned as a guard put there by God. It was emphatically stressed, however, that the eagle's old associations with the sun and sunset are not recognized. The scores made on the wings of the ash eagle represent, according to George Wesaw, Jesus and his twelve disciples.

Three musical instruments are used, the drum, the rattle and the flute. The drum is a kettledrum, made from iron. Its membrane is made from buckskin, its sides are decorated with seven stones joined by cords hanging in bow-patterns (and lacing the drum-skin). The reason is, I was told, that there are seven days in the week. The inside of the drum is filled with water, a stone and four pieces of charcoal. The lone stone is supposed to represent the rock in the river that "protects the purity of the river".

The rattle, which is a gourd with small stones inside, and the flute, an eagle-bone whistle with one hole, and no feathers, are not surrounded by any particular symbolism as far as I know.[5]

A particular power is invested in feathers. "In the Peyote ceremony I pray to God through the feathers", said George Wesaw. "I collect feathers of all kinds of birds to get many colours. Multi-coloured feathers give more power. I dare not have eagle feathers in the Peyote ceremony, although I own such feathers. They have too much power, and that is dangerous for me. When I am sixty-five I may dare to use them." George was apparently deeply influenced by the old tribal religion in which eagle worship was a powerful component. Otherwise we

---

[3] I also heard that the score on the crescent is sometimes thought of as God's road, sometimes as Peyote's road. As a symbol of the path of life the earth crescent score has its counterpart in the eagle rafter in the Sun Dance lodge.

[4] The ash eagle was introduced by the Arapaho John Goggles (Stenberg 1946, p. 118 n. 3) and has, via Marshall Washakie, passed to George Wesaw (see Ch. II:3). Goggles received it from a Southern Arapaho who, during a Peyote meeting, in a vision saw an eagle taking form in the ashes (Stenberg 1946, p. 118). On this bird, see Ch. 1:3.

[5] Shimkin's statement (in Stewart 1944, p. 115) that the leader allows others to blow a whistle as a thanksoffering to God is not corroborated by my own experiences, but may of course be correct for the cases observed by Shimkin.

learn that whosoever wants may make himself a fan of (usually twelve) feathers, even one of eagle feathers. The road man is always equipped with a fan of feathers. Feathers have protective power.

Besides the feathers, often arranged as a fan, the Peyote singer has at his disposal a rattle and a drum, four bunches of sweetgrass and a staff, "the staff of Peyote", which is said to have received its power from Peyote. The staff, which is kept in the left hand together with the feathers and sweetgrass, is about one meter high and has at its top some hanging tufts of hair and grass (or sage). It is held vertically, its lower end placed on the ground, the singer's hand grasping it at the middle. The staff warrants its owner a high age, for old men walk with staffs.

Also the sacred morning meal has symbolical implications. There are four dishes, because four is a sacred number: water, corn, fruit and meat, representing all the products of the earth. The order of their being served is fixed, for the Creator sent first the water to the earth, then the maize, then the fruit, and lastly the meat, for the animals were the last ones to be created (and the buffalo was the first created animal). This symbolism refers, of course, to an Indianized version of the Christian tradition of creation. As pointed out earlier, the original Indian high god was usually no creator, and certainly not the Shoshoni god; at least no creation myth was associated with him.

Something should finally be said about the symbolism of smoking in the Peyote tipi. During the meeting the participants smoke a particular kind of cigarrette as "prayer smoking". According to my informants their tobacco is a mixture that "makes them taste nice".[6] The cigarettes are rolled in paper or maize husks in the tipi, and at midnight the fire man i supposed to be the first one to smoke them. The prayer goes upwards with the smoke.

Also actions during the tipi meeting have a symbolic value. This will be evident from the following description of a Peyote ritual.

3. A Shoshoni Ritual Meeting

The Peyote religion cannot be caught in theoretical terms only, it must be studied in action. There are a few eyewitness reports from the Wind River Shoshoni, including Molly Stenberg, Joe Moore and Blanche Schroer.[1] The following account refers to a meeting in which I partook, and at which I made rather detailed notes on what was going on, and at what time in the night. The prayers of my next neighbour which I wrote down were controlled with him the next day;

---
[6] The tobacco is mixed "with some herb that reminds of sweetgrass, but is smaller". I was unable to identify it.
[1] Stenberg 1946, pp. 119–27, Moore and Schroer 1950.

his emendations of the text on this occasion brought on a certain elaboration. My own personal experiences from taking the drug while not totally ignored have been played down in this report.[2]

A Shoshoni Peyote meeting is initiated by the person "who puts up the lodge" and who also bears the expenses. He appoints the leader, or road man. The latter cannot refuse; if he does he commits a wrong. People who hear about the meeting join it if they want to. The road man appoints a fire man, a cedar man and a drummer. The fire man in his turn calls for an assistant. These functionaries are usually responsible for the singing. People practise Peyote songs together. It usually takes a person some three months to pick up the songs and learn them.[3]

The meeting to be described here was a curing ceremony, although the patient was not present. A young boy had been ill for a long time, his legs had become paralyzed, and his father, Ray Wichy, implored George Wesaw to help him out. There are particular rules at a curing ceremony. Whereas on other occasions many volunteers want to beat the drum, this cannot be done when curing is implied, except if the drum chief so declares. Furthermore, the doctoring is always handled by somebody who should have some experiences from curing activity, and ought to be a medicine man. The curing Peyote rite is thus tantamount to a shamanic séance, except that the mental state of the practitioner rarely transcends light meditation. At this meeting Tom Wesaw was the medicine and cedar man. Although Tom denied that he had supernatural powers and only admitted he could cure pneumonia he was generally considered a medicine man, albeit no strong one.

The Peyote meeting was held during the night of the 10th of September, 1948. It was put up by Ray Wichy. The scene was a lodge close to George Wesaw's home. Peyote meetings are usually held in a tipi in the summer, but inside a house in the winter. On this occasion it took place in a spacious, oblong tent with a small, round iron stove as the fire-place. This was less "typical" but was motivated by the chilly night air at this time of the year, the family Wesaw having suffered much loss from TB. The use of the iron stove forced the cedar man to arrange a particular place nearby for the coals over which juniper leaves could be strewn.

The following persons appeared as functionaries: Road man, also called chief *(tegwahin)* was George Wesaw, cedar man Tom Wesaw, drum chief Percy McCloud, fireman Lynn Perry, and fireman's assistant Willy Tornese. A privileged position was also granted Gilbert Day, a prominent member of the Shoshoni Peyote community who initiated several of the ritual moves, and Mrs. George Wesaw who acted as the bringer of the "morning water". Altogether ten

---

[2] My own personal experiences have been noted down in Hultkrantz 1968 b, 1975, 1995, pp. 58–61.
[3] It was pointed out by the Shoshoni that I could learn them, just as the Blacks of Oklahoma sing Peyote songs they learnt from the Indians there.

persons took part in the meeting. No woman was present until the serving of the morning meal.[4]

The account now follows my diary.

9.30 PM. The participants enter the lodge (in no particular order) and take their seats on blankets. Some wrap themselves in the blankets. The road man is however seated on a cushion. He opens a satchel and exposes its contents – his ritual paraphernalia – on a cloth. The fire man and his assistant have their places close to the eastern entrance, on the northern side; the road man, with the drummer on his right and the cedar man on his left side, are seated opposite the fire, facing the east. In front of the leader is a bowl with Peyote buttons and the earth crescent, with its concave base towards the fire and the east.

In the light of a paraffin-lamp the fireman kindles the fire, puts down a firestick (used for lighting cigarettes) and arranges a heap of burning coals, taken from the stove. The cedar man places "cedar" leaves (that is, juniper needles) on the coals, thus making incense. The drummer opens a packet of tobacco which then, together with cigarette-paper and the fire-stick, circulate clockwise among those present. The road man says a prayer as he places a Peyote button on a bed of sage in the middle of the crescent. Like all the others he prays with closed eyes, head bowed down to the ground, the cigarette in his hand. This is the first of the four prayers offered during the night. I was not able to take down George Wesaw's prayer, but here is his father's, Tom Wresaw's:[5]

> Almighty God, you have made the earth which we are living on, and it is a wonderful thing that you have made for us Indians and other nations. I am thanking you because I am living still tonight. I also want to ask you to bless us so that we can live a long time. And I want you to look down on us so that there will be no sickness to bother us. We like to live in a good healthy way. Please bless us in the way I ask you for.
>
> And here is your holy spirit, powerful Peyote, which you have given us. It is a wonderful thing that you gave us to protect us. So that is why I am asking you for a good blessing, because you have made the earth and you have created the water and the timbers, rock, mountains, and all kinds of big and little insects. Also, you have created all kinds of animals and birds, and you have made the eagle. The eagle is your watchman, and I can say that this bird is next to you.
>
> We have all had these "smokes" which the fireman gave us, and now we are cooperating through the "smokes" that you have made. I am praying to you the way the old-timers back in the south, the tribes of Indians called Apache, Kiowa and Comanche have told us to pray. Now I am smoking to the Peyote, asking the Peyote to take care of us through the night, and I want you to bless us in a good way, so that we can sit up with you all through the night.
>
> I am asking you again, Our Father,[6] that this one night when we are all sup-

---

[4] Several of the functionaries mentioned here were photographed together in Stenberg 1946, p. 120.
[5] As he repeated it for me the next day he told me that this is the prayer he always used during the Peyote ceremonies.
[6] Our Father, *tam apö,* is the traditional name of the high god.

posed to rest [you will bless us]. We are praying for this one night, that you Peyote leaders will be in a good way. Please take care of us. Please, I want to see all of my children grow up, boys to become men, girls to become women. May babies not yet born be born in a good way so that the mothers won't have a hard time having them. We want our people here to grow big, instead of us losing too many of them. And those who are living, I want them to live a long time, and without hardship.

Again, Our Friend Peyote, I am going to ask you again for a blessing. I want you to take care of the prayers I offer you. What I want to say is this: I want you to be with us every day and night, and also be with us this fall until Thanksgiving day, Christmas, the New Year and Easter. We like to live to all these events, and on to more summers and winters, and up to the end of the world. Wherever we go, to different places, I want you to be with us. Our father has put you far away in the south, so you are a long way away from here, and you are hard to get. But I want you to take care of all of us, even the whites and other nations. Be our brother! I thank you for listening to the prayers I am offering you. You know that I am poor and humble, and I don't know much of prayers. Please see to me as I am asking you for a good blessing.

Now I am going to call upon our brother, Jesus, Our Saviour. Please, I want you to look upon us and give us life every day. Since your father God created you to be Our Saviour, please save us so that we may live a long time. Be with us like you said you would when you went back to Our Father. You said that whenever we want help we should call upon you. Therefore I may answer your offer in a humble way. Because you are the only son of God, because when you were living in Jerusalem, you were praying for your people, and because you used to cure a blind man or a person who was so ill that he couldn't walk – that's why I say you are a powerful man. So, please bless us the way you used to do, I thank you. Please take care of us because I am poor and humble. Because I have gotten no power like you have, that's the reason why I am asking the blessing from you. Please don't forget your brothers and sisters.

Again I ask yrou, Our Father, for Mother Earth, whom you have made for us to live on. Here we are in our ceremony-tipi, sitting on Our Mother Earth. And I want you to see to it that Our Mother Earth listens good. I pray to you, Our Mother Earth. I want us all to live on you in good health. Whatever we do on you, if we do wrong please forgive us for what mistakes we have made on you. And whatever we raise, crops or gardening, I want you to take care of it for us so that we'll have vegetables to eat so that we never get short of living. We like to have plenty of groceries considering the way groceries cost. We don't like to see them be too expensive; you know that we Indians are awfully poor. That's why I ask you to find an easy way for us. Also I want you to allow children to grow up on you. I ask you again, whenever we travel on you where the highway roads have been built, take care of us as we are going visiting other tribes. Take care of us so that we won't have any accident or get hurt. Please, take my poor, humble prayer so that we can all return back home, and please, I am asking you for a good blessing. We like to live on you up to the end of the world.[7]

---

[7] We notice that the prayers were directed to the Supreme Being, Peyote, Jesus ("Brother Jesus") and Mother Earth, in this order. Tom Wesaw made the remark that as a Sun Dance leader he prayed to God, Jesus and Mother Earth, but not to Peyote. As emerges from the prayer its focus is on individual and collective survival.

Tom Wesaw repeated this long prayer several times during the nightly ritual – at the Midnight rite, when the morning water was served, and when leaving the Peyote tipi. The prayer was thus used four times. What may surprise us is that the sick boy for whose regaining of health the ritual was arranged was never mentioned in the prayer. Being so often afflicted by diseases and deaths in his family Tom's attention was constantly paid to his own troubles. The prayer thus reflected his innermost worries.

After the first prayer the cigarrette-butts are placed at the southern end of the crescent horn. New coals are put down, new "cedar" laid on them. Three times the cedar man moves the dish with Peyote buttons over the incense. A bunch of sweetgrass is passing clockwise between the people. Each one of us breaks off some tops and rubs his hands, arms and face with them.

10 p.m. The bowl with the Peyote buttons passes clockwise among those present. Each of us makes use of a spoon to put a part of the earthlike drug in his right hand, divides it into two parts, and swallows it. Out of a box the road man takes his feathers and the staff which he holds in his left hand, together with a bunch of sweetgrass, whilst he shakes his rattle with the right hand, and sings to the beating of the drum. This is the so-called Starting Song. It is repeated four times. In the pauses between the singing the drumming and rattling continue. When the road man has finished his fourth song he changes roles with the drummer, who now takes over the leader's paraphernalia and sings four songs, whilst the leader handles the drum. All the time the fireman tends to the fire. His assistant sits with a lone feather – a feather of meditation – in his hand.

The turn to sing has now come to the cedar man, who thus takes over the road man's instruments. The road man is drumming while the ordinary drummer pours hot water into the Peyote bowl and stirs around with a spoon. The drum and regalia then pass from man to man, one is drumming, the other singing. Each singer performs his song four times.

10.25 p.m. Paper cups[8] and the bowl with hot water pass around. Everybody drinks from the water which turns out to be a decoction of Peyote. "Peyote water purifies your body, that is what I was told", says Tom Wesaw. The road man has a fan of twentyfour eagle feathers spread out in front of his face.

10.40 p.m. The Peyote bulbs and the Peyote drink pass around for the second time. Some Peyote decoction has been poured on the drum-skin, and now and then somebody drinks from it. The fireman forms a crescent of the ashes in front of the earth moon. Tom Wesaw implores me to tell the authorities that this Peyote is quite harmless, but works for good. I shall bear witness to that so that they do not stop the ceremony. That is why I have been invited to the meeting.

11.05 p.m. Drum and accessories pass me again. It is essential that I touch them and send them on to the next person who is able to handle them. Cigar-

---

[8] Paper cups are used all through the ceremony, also in the morning meal. Formerly, Tom Wesaw told me, the participants drank from the same bowl.

rettes also go around the circle. Everybody who wants a smoke must use the firestick which has been lit at the fire. The butts are placed at either end of the earth crescent.

11.15 p.m. The leaders leave the lodge for a minute or two, apparently for a nature call. When Tom Wesaw has returned he sits smiling with eyes closed, an eagle feather in his left hand. The fireman now and then adds more ashes to the ash crescent.

11.25 p.m. The road man takes a little flute that until now has been lying in front of him, and places it leaning on the earth crescent with one end pointing to the Peyote button there, and the other end pointing to the road man. The changing positions of the flute form a cross (according to what Tom Wesaw tells me).

11.30 p.m. Some people leave again for a minute or two.

11.35 p.m. The Peyote bowl passes around again.

11.40 p.m. Introduction to the Midnight rite. The road man blows four times on the flute that the drummer has passed him, and then quickly six times more. This means that he is "calling for water". The cedar man lays down the flute alongside the earth crescent.

11.45 p.m. Cautiously all paraphernalia are laid down in front of the cedar man. The fireman's assistant continues to build on to the ash crescent. Singing and drumming have ceased. New coals are collected, and cedar is strewn out over them. I am exhorted to wave in the scent with my hand and to inhale it. The midnight water is brought in by the fireman and placed at the fireplace. The fireman prays over it. He kneels in front of the water bucket, and the others put their heads in their hands. The fireman thanks George Wesaw for the fine task that has been entrusted to him and he says that he has asked George to support his prayer. He then prays for the sick boy in the hospital who is going to be operated upon. He prays that the boy will grow up to be a big man, and that he will stay alive. (The details of the prayer escape me.) He finishes the prayer in the names of God and Jesus. All through the prayer the fireman has had a lit cigarrette in his hand, and tears have come into his eyes.

12 p.m. The road man prays, also with a cigarette in his hand. It is difficult to hear what he says, but he frequently invokes Jesus. During his prayer the fireman is in high spirits, and jokes with his assistant.[9] He drops some water at the eastern end of the firestick.

0.30 a.m. The water bucket passes around clockwise. Before he drinks the road man dips the flute into the water, and then shakes it towards north, east and south and blows four short tones. The cedar man wets the drumskin with a scoop from the water bucket twice.

0.35 a.m. At a sign from the road man the fireman strides around clockwise. The road man picks up the flute and the assistant fireman's feather (which since

---

[9] The streaks of humour in sacred ceremonies among Indians always impress the outsider. The serene spirituality of the occasion is as it were balanced by exhiliration and jocularity.

the beginning of the Midnight rite has been resting at the northern horn of the earth crescent). He leaves the lodge. Meanwhile the music and singing start again, and more ashes are heaped onto the middle part of the ash crescent. Suddenly the song stops, and the road man, being outside the lodge, is heard praying. He prays towards the east. Then he blows a long tune on the flute, and in so doing moves the flute firstly against the earth (Mother Earth) and then in a bow upwards (to Our Father). There is more singing in the lodge, and then the same procedure is repeated towards the south. After still more singing the roadman addresses the west, and finally also the north. There is approximately one minute's intermission between the flute tunes.[10]

After the midnight rite is finished the road man returns through the door. Coals are laid out, cedar is strewn over it, and the road man uses the eagle feather to catch the incense and make it suffuse his upper body. Everybody else tries to suck up the aroma with their hands.

0.45 a.m. The drum is passing round again. The order is re-established: everyone who needs to go out must first tell the fireman. Tom Wesaw, my neighbour, approaches me and admonishes me to see him in his home next day, for that will be a powerful day, good for information on Peyote. He adds, "Don't you feel there is something powerful here. Yes, Peyote is more powerful than the Sun Dance."

1.10 a.m. The Peyote passes around for the fourth time. Tom Wesaw states that the Holy Spirit is with us now. He relates to his Peyote experiences. The singing continues, and every singer performs four songs and then takes a pause.

1.45 a.m. The drum and leader's paraphernalia pass me again. Tom Wesaw makes a comment upon the cigarette butts placed at the end of the crescent: they indicate close friendship; the first smoke is a kind of "peace smoking".

2.10 a.m. The whole group of Peyotists is now radiating peace of mind and amiability. Everybody smiles in a friendly manner at me when the Peyote drink is handed over to me. We are all one, partakers of the same oneness.

2.30 a.m. Tom Wesaw urges me to pray to the Peyote button that is the power of God. Ray Wichy rolls a cigarette and prays to the four spiritual beings – Our Father, Peyote, Jesus and Mother Earth. He beseeches them to bless his boy and all of us. The dish with Peyote buttons is now resting in front of the drummer.

2.40 a.m. The singing and rattling is intense as Wichy continues to pray for himself, but quite audible. Now and then somebody leans his head into his hands and prays. The singing is high, tense and quick, the singer George Wesaw twists his whole body in violent fury. Wichy prays incessantly, even during breaks in the singing. On one occasion the road man sucks intensely from the drumskin.

2.55 a.m. The drum passes me by.

---

[10] On this occasion I could not, of course, witness the outdoor rite. Its symbolism was explained to me by Tom Wesaw.

(3.30 a.m. I notice I easily become emotional.)

3.35 a.m. Gilbert Day rolls a cigarette and prays for the sick boy. He then hands the cigarette over to the road man, to induce the latter to pray. The fireman watches very closely that the firestick is put back after use in its right place in front of the ash crescent. While the singing continues Gilbert Day goes on praying, more quiet now, but weeping, more and more weeping. Tom Wesaw criticizes me because he cannot hear me pray: if, he says, I pray quietly the others cannot join me in my prayer.

4 a.m. The drum and the paraphernalia pass me, again.

4.25 a.m. The road man takes a piece of the Peyote stew, lifts it in a circle over the Peyote button of the earth crescent and delivers it to Gilbert Day. All eagerly wait for the dawn.

4.30 a.m. The ashes are modelled into an eagle. There are scores on its wings and its tail, and a square deepening on its back, like this:

4.50 a.m. When Tom Wesaw learns that I have just had a hallucination of a woman, singing from on high he is most interested and says, "it is power".[11] I am now forced to take my third drink of Peyote tea.

---

[11] Cf. above, Ch. I:1 and 3. It is to me completely inconceivable how this experience could take place since at that time I was not familiar with La Barre's statement (1960, p. 50) of the Southern Plains belief that the Peyote woman could be heard singing when a supposed "female" peyote button was eaten, nor were there singing women present in the lodge, and as far as I know none of the present men had similar experiences. In short, the psychological frame of references for such extraordinary experiences was missing.

Here are some other examples of similar auditory sensations in the Peyote lodge which remind of my own experiences. Vecsey was told that in former days you could hear the voice of "the first peyote woman", singing high over the men's songs. However, he says, these were rare occasions (Vecsey 1988, p. 196). In a Lipan Apache Peyote session a supernatural woman, who might have been "a modified Virgin Mary", talked from the top of the Peyote tipi (Opler 1938, p. 279, Stewart 1948, p. 35).

Similar auditive hallucinations may be received by North American Indians during traditional tribal ceremonies. James Howard reports that during Shawnee ceremonies "an extra female voice, that of Our Grandmother, is sometimes heard above the brush arbor joining in the singing of the women" (Howard 1981, pp. 258 f., 282). "Our Grandmother" is the supreme deity of the Shawnee. One wonders whether influences from Peyotism, known to the Shawnee since 1890, have not put their stamp upon the elaboration of Shawmee ceremonialism.

4.55 a.m. Coals are put in the deepening spot of the ash eagle whilst Tom Wesaw is praying. He then lays cedar over the coals. With the aid of the lone eagle feather Gilbert Day, and thereafter Ray Wichy, draw the scent to themselves.

5.10 a.m. Dawn is approaching. The smoke rises from the glue on the back of the ash eagle.

5.15 a.m. The drum with paraphernalia is passing around. The singer usually has his neighbour as the person to drum for him, but some drummers are tired now, and others take their place.

5.40 a.m. The firestick is used to make the sign of a cross just behind the fire. All paraphernalia have now reached the road man, and the singing and drumming stops. (Important disruptions of activities always take place when the regalia have returned to the road man.)

5.45 a.m. The road man calls for "morning water": he makes four long and six short whistles on the flute. After that, the drum chief beats the drum, and the singing starts again.[12] The road man's wife[13] enters with a bucket of water that is placed over the cross sign. The fireman spreads out a blanket for her to sit on just south of the fire place. In the light of dawn the ash eagle shines resplendently white. After a while the road man finishes the song and lays out all his paraphernalia in front of him. The cedar man stands up, prays the morning prayer (the same long prayer which was previously quoted) and strews cedar over the coals. Everybody takes in the aroma with his hands and strokes it over the upper body. Mrs. Wesaw rolls a sacred cigarette, and her little son takes a seat close to the exit. A quiet passivity rules the lodge. The tobacco which is mixed with cornhusk is praised, "smokes better now, sacred now", says the road man.

6 a.m. Sun-up. Mrs Wesaw prays publicly for the sick boy, for those present, for the tribe and for all nations – four prayers in all. She weeps, shaking violently, during the prayer. Having finished it she gives her cigarette to the drum chief who in his turn hands it over to the road man. The road man prays for a long time, repeating all the wishes that have been put forward during the ceremonial session. In the middle of his prayer he breaks in with two English phrases, of which at least the first one has Christian background: "what mistakes we make forgive us," and "may he [the sick boy] become rich, not die." On both occasions he starts weeping. When he has ended his speech he disposes the cigarrette on the top of the ash eagle's head, in the direction of the bird's length.

6.40 a.m. Mrs. Wesaw pours out some sacred water for herself and her boy in cups. Thereafter the water passes clockwise round the lodge. The drum chief pours some water on the drumskin before he fills his own paper cup, and the

---

[12] This is the "morning water song", directed to the woman who carries in water. Miss Stenberg learned that the first song is a prayer to God for taking pity on the worshippers and blessing the woman, the second song concerns the daylight brought in by her, and the third and fourth songs praise God for his gift of water that keeps the world alive: Stenberg 1946, pp. 124 f.

[13] The "morning woman" is always the road man's wife. One particular reason for this may be that the ceremony lodge is raised on his ground.

road man dips his whistle and blows it four times before he pours out water for himself. The last one to fill his cup is the fireman. "No water in the world tastes so good as this," comments the road man, "it is the best there is." The fireman places the bucket at the door. Mrs. Wesaw walks round the lodge, clockwise, takes the bucket and steps out. The cross sign is smudged out.

6.50 a.m. Drumming and singing start again, the sick boy's father introducing the singing. The fireman's assistant blots out the ash eagle in such a manner that a wooden board draws up the tail over the head and the wings towards the earthen crescent; the final result is that the ashes fill out the space between the horns of this crescent. The road man takes up four songs. Everybody looks satisfied and regards me in a very friendly way.

7.10 a.m. The singing has stopped, and Mrs. Wesaw comes in with a water bucket, a bowl with corn, another bowl with fruit, and still another one with meat. They are all arranged in this order between the crescent and the entrance. New ashes are heaped on the old ashes, "cedar leaves" are put on top, and all inhale the aroma. Mrs. Wesaw takes a seat just south of the door (for women are supposed to sit close to the door) while her husband, the road man, sings four songs, accompanied by the drum chief's beating the drum. This is "the closing song".

7.20 a.m. Standing up the road man prays, his hands grasping two eagle fans, each one containing twentyfour feathers and provided with profusely embroidered handles, from which strings of beads hang.

7.30 a.m. After the prayer the road man removes the Peyote from the crescent and stows away his paraphernalia in a wooden case. He says that he Peyote makes you first feel bad, perhaps vomit, but you get better as you pray. The water bucket now circulates among the partakers, clockwise, and everybody fills his cup. Three charcoals are placed on the crescent, one at each point and one in the middle. They represent, Tom Wesaw tells me, "the protection of the road of life. The old Indians said, if you place them on your forehead they will shine into heaven, and you go safely there." After the water bucket the corn bowl circulates, then the fruit, lastly the meat. The corn and fruit is put in the paper cup, but the meat is served in a small bag. Everybody receives a tea spoon to eat with.

8.05 a.m. After the meal the vessels are rearranged close to the entrance, but in reverse order. The cult members disperse. The last words of Tom Wesaw are, assuringly, that he never gets tired from a Peyote meeting.

Later in the day, "a powerful day", as Tom Wesaw said during the Peyote night, I visited him for further discussion on the sacred herb. After having commented favourably on my behaviour during the vigils, apparently a stereotype to please white visitors,[14] he said the following about my audition in the night:

---

[14] Stenberg remarks that the Peyotists stress "the bravery of those who endure large doses and long meetings"; she earned herself the reputation of being "a tough lady" (Stenberg 1946, p. 129 and n. 5). Tom Wesaw said to his son about me, "Our white brother has a strong mind", referring to my taking notes during the whole night.

"It's a voice from the drum, some say, from the feathers in your hand – that is what I was told. That is all Peyote's work." George Wesaw interpreted the hallucination his own way, and with clear reference to the possible success of his mission last night: "If you hear a woman's voice in the Peyote lodge, that means that somebody who is sick will get well again. That woman's voice is the holy spirit. It is very seldom you hear that woman's voice, so say the old-timers."

III. Why Peyote Spread: the Indian Testimony

1. The General Persuasion

It seems legitimate that an investigation of the motives behind the spread of Peyote first of all takes into consideration the Indian point of view – that is, the persuasion of the Peyotists themselves. Now, the dispersion of the Peyote religion is after all a comparatively recent phenomenon, and there is the theoretical possibility that old Indians of the past, and old Indians still living, could contribute to our stock of knowledge. It is usually admitted that memories of historical events in a tribal society may reach back three generations.[1]

Here, however, we must distinguish between events as they happened and motives as they are conceived. As I found among the Shoshoni, the stories of what had taken place were well remembered and could be supplemented and confirmed by written documents. The motives of the acceptance of Peyote were however interpreted in the light of the informants' own idiosyncrasies at the time they were interviewed. Besides, Peyote's blessings were always the same, what my informant felt had also supposedly been felt by his teachers. Peyote is good for you, Peyote makes you feel good, Peyote cures you, Peyote helps you in distress – these were the standard answers. It is of course natural that a believer in Peyote should see it that way. The deeper religious aspects as well as non-religious factors are usually not available in the manifest declarations of believers.

On the other hand, Indian pronouncements give us a clear comprehension of how they look at the motivations of Peyote diffusion. Besides pointing at the general benefits Peyote may conduce they underline the beauty of the ritual and its supernatural provenience. The grandson of the famous Kiowa chief Santanta, or White Bear, described the attraction of the ritual in the following words: "It is our contention that the ritual itself, well-designed, simple, yet uniquely beautiful and moving is one of the principal reasons why the Peyote religion remains so popular with American Indian groups who have received it in the diffusion process."[2] This esthetic evaluation seems however to have sprung forth from an individual already attending to the ritual rather than from a Peyote beginner; the Kiowa Sun Dance (held until 1887) would have been just as attractive. The esthetic factor for diffusion could not have been so decisive.

More importance should be given to the conviction of a divine sanction for the appearance of Peyote. Such a conviction may take two forms. Either it is

---
[1] This is a widely debated subject. See e.g. Euler 1967.
[2] Howard 1967, p. 21.

incapsulated in a statement of religious belief.[3] Or it is brought forth in an origin legend, a tale of a meeting between a human being and a spirit. Now, a normal pattern in North American Indian religion is that a supernatural sanction is mediated through a myth or a legend. In this connection a religious statement is, either, a contraction of the belief contents of an oral tradition, myth or legend, or a reference to a set of (religious) premises which should be known to the listener. It is mainly the latter alternative that applies here. Religious statements refer to the Bible and the teaching on the Bible.

La Barre provides a good example. The Oto Indian Old Man Green counteracted a Protestant minister, unfriendly to Native religion, by quoting Genesis 1:12. Here we are told how, after the creation of green herbs, God contemplated the creation and "saw that it was good". Green's comment was, "Peyote was there then. If you condemn Peyote, you condemn God's work."[4] Admittedly, this is a forced apologetic situation for the Peyote believer, but we may observe that his weighing in of Native and Christian beliefs apparently guided him to this statement of faith.

In the same spirit other Peyotists make reference to Jesus' words of the Comforter, the Holy Ghost (John 14:16).[5] Slotkin has quoted many Bible sentences which, to the Peyotist, vindicate a Christian sanction of the use of the sacred herb.[6]

In the Christianized forms of Peyote worship such sanctions are important. The use of Peyote is presented there as a phase in God's plan for the salvation of mankind, or at least – since the salvation concept seems a bit foreign to Peyotism as religion (see Ch. IV:3) – for the assistance of mankind. Peyote arrived because God ordered it. Indeed, intellectual supporters of the Native American Church like J. S. Slotkin adopted this view which they considered to be equivalent with White Christian fundamentalism.[7]

The original supernatural sanction is however supplied by the origin tales which most probably antedate the Christian influence. In spite of their frequency they are however of less importance.

2. The Origin Legend of Peyote

In a very ambitious study Christopher Vecsey has collected and analyzed practically all extant Native American narratives on the origins of Peyote.[1] He pre-

---

[3] Cf. Hultkrantz 1968 a.
[4] La Barre 1975 b, p. 102.
[5] The same passage is also used – perhaps as a loan from Peyote theology – to justify traditional Native beliefs, see Hultkrantz 1981 a, p. 227.
[6] Slotkin 1956 a, pp. 65 f.
[7] Slotkin 1956 a, p. 66.
[1] Vecsey 1988, pp. 150–205.

sents sixty stories from over twenty tribes and quotes Omer Stewart's pronouncement that every one of the fifty Peyote-using tribes in North America could supply at least two of these origin stories. As Vecsey points out, these stories are accepted despite their mutual incompatibilities; Stewart's assertion that the narratives, or myths as he calls them, mean less to Peyotists than their own personal experiences of the herb seems quite to the point.[2] Moreover, as Vecsey rightly insists, Peyotism has indeed a more diverse history than these origin tales indicate.[3]

Vecsey differentiates between five types of origin tales. In the first type Peyote reveals itself to the Indians, whether it happens to a person in distress or to someone who is searching for power. In the second type an Indian acquires the Peyote ritual from an enemy tribe with whom he and his people thereafter are on friendly terms. There is a third type in which a young man is brutally clubbed down by a stranger and then – according to the young man – is taken in his unconscious state to a distant tipi and is there introduced into the Peyote ritual. The fourth type of origin story tells how a fallen Indian visits the lodge of his enemies, gives them Peyote, and reconciles the two tribes with each other. A fifth type of story relates how a small band of Indians were besieged by their enemies in a cave or went astray and were very close to starvation when one of them, exhausted and delirious, found the juicy, nourishing green peyote herbs growing there. Thus they were saved.

All these accounts give us, as Vecsey points out, a picture of Peyote as a means of salvation in times of need and distress. They show us, as he says, a close adaptation to the patterns of the North American Indians, and particularly Plains Indian, religiousness.[4] With Vecsey we can also stress that these narratives clearly demonstrate that the supernatural is the precondition, and the human the condition, by which Peyote worship is created.[5] Indeed, many Peyote believers think, like those among the Wind River Shoshoni, that religion was introduced in the world through Peyote; before Peyote there was no religion (see Ch. II:1). As the Taos claim, aboriginal religion is in comparison no real religion, no belief in anything supernatural at all.[6]

In this perspective the origin traditions of the Peyote may be conceived to constitute some sort of rational foundations of a new, separate religion. They do not as such proclaim a final, universal religion; – we shall return to this problem in the sequence (Ch. IV:8). However, they seem to designate the occurrence of a "true" religion, value the new (and Christian) label of religion – the Native

---

[2] Stewart in Vecsey 1988, p. 153. Vecsey draws here on Stewart's personal communication with him. See also Vecsey 1988, p. 174.
[3] Vecsey 1988, p. 173. I am however less convinced when Vecsey claims (p. 168) that the stories were not meant as "strict historical guides". To the believers they are documents of historical depth.
[4] Vecsey 1988, p. 169.
[5] Vecsey 1988, pp. 200 f.
[6] Parsons 1936, p. 64; cf. Vecsey 1988, p. 170.

American Church – in contradistinction to other aboriginal American religions. At the same time these traditions are, as was pointed out, scarcely valid doctrinal documents of the Peyote religion. There is reason to ponder on this statement a little more, and in that connection catch a closer view of some of the oral traditions.

In order to disentangle the cognitive values of the origin traditions we have to consider the differential truth they hold for the scholars and the Indians. Like all other oral traditions the Peyote tales may contain information of historical value to scholars, but this is difficult to evaluate and is mostly contained in occasional episodes of narratives which, in the judgement of the Peyotists, have occurred in a not so distant past. It is more interesting to observe the Indian understanding of their epical religious traditions.[7] One of the chief characteristics of these traditions is that they are either focussed on the beginning of times and refer to a mythic, instituting and modelling world, or referred to later times when humans, mysterious animals and spirits appear on the scene. Using the mythology applied since the days of Grimm we may make a distinction between myths and tales, or legends.[8] The myth involves only supernatural beings, usually gods, and takes place in primeval times, whereas the (belief) legend describes a contact between supernaturals and humans in a later, historical time.[9]

The indigenous traditions about the origins of the Peyote religion are overwhelmingly legends, in the sense above.[10] They mostly refer to the Southern Plains tribes in Oklahoma (Caddo, Comanche, Kiowa, Kiowa Apache, Lipan Apache, Tonkawa) and to groups on the Plains periphery in the Southwest (Mescalero Apache, Taos). Mexican tribes such as the Huichol also exhibit origin traditions, but these have another, mythical stamp: they portray Peyote's creation by the gods, not its communication with man.[11] When Northern Plains tribes speak about the origins of the Peyote religion they usually connect the story with some Southern Plains tribe. Whereas as a rule they combine the Sun Dance origins with their own tribal group because the ritual is so old that its true history has been forgotten, the mythic imagination surrounding the Peyote religion has a restricted sway since this religion is so very recent.

The Plains and Southwestern origin traditions are legends because they reflect, as La Barre has observed, a period of the beginning inter-tribal contacts,

---

[7] See e.g. Hultkrantz 1981 a, pp. 10 f.
[8] Although some Indian tribes make a similar formal distinction, most do not, and the position taken here is "etic" rather than "emic", to quote Kenneth Pike.
[9] I see no reason why this classification should be abandoned when it comes to North American Indians, which several Americanists demand. As admitted it is altogether etic and a valuable instrument in comparative research.
[10] It seems that institutional myths recede for legends in North America, cf. the origin legend of the Plains Indian Sun Dance. The visions have here created a continuum between the other world and this world.
[11] Concerning Huichol origin traditions, see Lumholtz 1900, pp. 17 ff.

after the disappearance of mutual tribal warfare.[12] Some authors, like David McAllester, assume that some of these traditions are truly historical. There is, for example, a Comanche tale describing how a Comanche war leader, having lost all his warriors and being scalped and stripped by Carrizo Apache, sought up the Carrizo camp where a Peyote meeting was held, and asked his enemies to hand over Peyote to his tribesmen; this they promised to do, and they kept their word.[13] However, a variant of this story has it that the war leader and his followers were unhurt, that the hostile tribe was White Mountain Apache, and that these taught the Comanche war leader the Peyote ritual.[14] Whatever historical reality might have lain behind this tale, it is certainly a legend – a historical legend – as it is told. The supernatural element is scarcely perceivable.

It is possible to arrange the origin legends into two groups, one presupposing a secular, the other a supernatural origin. However, the supernatural element is present also in the first category. Thus, the Comanche or Kiowa account of the warrior chief who visited the enemy camp[15] points out that the Peyote leader knows in advance the coming of the visitor: this shows how the Peyote gives the power of divination. In an Arapaho tradition of the achievement of Peyote by the Caddo it is related that the Caddo warriors on the war path lost their way and scattered. One of them was so weak that he lay down to die. He saw a green herb close by, and hungry as he was he ate it. It made him feel restored, so he ate more, and fell asleep. In his sleep Peyote talked to him, told him that the heavenly god had put Peyote on earth for the Indian, and gave him instructions.[16] The legend may very well have some basis in reality, including the supernatural dream; but if so it is scarcely the origin of the Caddo Peyotism it refers to.

The Caddo legend seems more likely to be part of a common Peyote origin tale, the self-revelation of Peyote. Typical for this version is the following Kiowa narrative, recorded early on by Mooney. Two young men went on the war path, but did not return home as expected. Their sister withdrew to the hills to bewail their death. In the night, when she was asleep, the Peyote spirit came to her. Peyote told her that her brothers were alive, and that in the morning she would find something close to her head that would bring them back. When she woke up she found Peyote cactus close by which she brought home. She told the people her story and the instructions she had received, and a regular Peyote meeting was held. In their visions the participants saw the two young men walking in a desolate place. A rescue expedition was sent off and they were found. The girl who founded the Peyote rite has since been venerated as the Peyote woman.[17]

---

[12] La Barre 1975 b, pp. 60 f.
[13] McAllester 1949, pp. 14 ff.
[14] Wallace and Hoebel 1952, p. 334.
[15] This story is common on the southern Plains, cf. La Barre 1975 b, p. 90.
[16] Stenberg 1946, p. 139.
[17] Mooney 1897, p. 330.

This is a widely diffused origin legend,[18] and occurs in many variants. The Kiowa Apache, for example, tell about a Lipan Apache woman and her boy who discovered Peyote.[19] Their tribe had been defeated in combat and scattered, and the woman and her son were left alone without food or water. As the boy was walking around while his mother slept he heard a voice from above that admonished him to eat "something green" ahead of him. He picked a green plant – the Peyote cactus – and ate it. Soon his hunger was gone. He told his mother about his experience, and she also had some Peyote and felt satisfied. She prayed to the power that had given them the wonderful herb, asking for water and for the way back to her people. Both requests were granted: it thundered, and rain fell; and in a nightly dream she was told by "someone" to ascend a certain mountain, which she did, and there she found her people. After their reunion the boy put up the first Peyote lodge.[20]

In a Taos variant the deserted warrior hears a singing and rattling near him and discovers the Peyote.[21]

It is not my intention here to list versions and variants and their distribution. The important thing is that these origin traditions refer the spread of Peyote to supernatural intervention. Occasionally, as in Mexico, they give evidence of how Peyote was created in primordial times – hence they may be called myths. More generally, in any case north of the Rio Grande, these traditions describe how people achieved Peyote – these are the legends. The historical times they reflect seem to be fairly recent, and the nucleus of the stories may contain a grain of truth, at least in some cases. At the same time there is a striking likeness between these stories and narratives of visionary meetings with supernatural animals in situations of stress.[22] This then would mean, at least on the Plains, that man received Peyote because the powers felt pity on him. Peyote was resorted to because it could save man when nothing else could help him. It cured him, it relieved him of hunger and thirst, and it revealed to him his way.

This is, to the Indian, the real reason why Peyote spread.

---

[18] Cf. La Barre 1975 b, pp. 28 f., Petrullo 1934, pp. 34 ff. The tale has been internalized in supernatural experiences of a Southern Paiute collecting Peyote at the Rio Grande in 1968, see Stewart 1987, p. 292.

[19] A Lipan Apache tale describes however a visit to the mythical Peyote people who are "eating each other", see Opler 1940, pp. 56 ff. Could the neighbouring Tonkawa people – known for their endocannibalism – have stimulated this thought on cannibalism?

[20] Brant 1963. See also Brant 1950, pp. 213 ff.

[21] La Barre 1975 b, pp. 13 f.

[22] La Barre 1975 b, p. 29.

IV. Why Peyote Spread: the Research Opinion

1. Trends of the Discussion

James Mooney who gave the first extensive account of a North American Peyote ceremony ascribed its popularity to the stimulant properties of the herb – "a source of inspiration, and the key which opens to them /= the Indians/ all the glories of another world" – and to its use as a panacea in medicine.[1] This was the first appreciation of the causes of Peyote attraction. We notice the cautious dual motivations, the chemical properties of Peyote, and the practical use of Peyote.

Mooney was careful in his evaluation of Peyote's toxicological qualities, but to many medical students and to the political authorities, as well as the missionaries, these qualities were decisive. Thus, this view of Peyote, although adapted to the particular problem of cultural conflict, is echoed in a paper written about fifty years after Mooney's article. The authors, W. Bromberg and C. L. Tranter, there define Peyote as "an anodyne to ease the pain of conflict which the clash of cultures engenders".[2] Here Peyote is presented as little less than a tranquilizing drug, and one can understand the authors when, from these premises, they consider Peyote consumption a little constructive way of managing a repression of cultural conflicts.

This one-sided representation of Peyote, developed further and having become popular through the writings of Aldous Huxley, has fortunately not left any traces in scientific writings on Peyote today. Nobody dreams of referring the diffusion of Peyote to its chemical properties. On the other hand, they cannot entirely be let out of the picture. Mooney was the first to understand that we need a more complex approach to the problem.

It seems easy to agree with Mooney and to postulate that Peyote had medicinal functions because it had stimulant properties. Several documents from the past inform us that such ideas guided the formation of Peyote practice in the old days. As Stewart says, referring to the old Peyote complex prior to 1900, "Peyote was used primarily as medicine and to induce visions by individuals seeking supernatural revelation."[3] We shall later analyze the import of the connections between medicine and such supernaturalism (Ch. IV:5). What is

---

[1] Mooney 1897, p. 329.
[2] Bromberg and Tranter 1943, p. 527.
[3] Stewart 1970, p. 790.

important to realize is that the Peyotism that spread over the Plains in the 1880s and became thereafter a full-fledged religion must be judged as such. Once we have skipped the one-faceted explanation that Peyote is a "narcotic" cactus and we face the fact that the Peyote movement has all the characteristics of a religion we must consider its acceptance and diffusion in a broader perspective. A similar point of view has been developed by James Howard in an analysis of the Kiowa chief White Bear's Peyote ritual:

> Attempts to explain the continued popularity of the Peyote religion solely in terms of the physiological effects resulting from the ingestion of peyote have, we believe, been overstressed. We would like to see, in future studies of the Peyote religion, more attention given to learning what individual peyotists themselves regard as the most important and satisfying elements in the Peyote complex. The tacit assumption, shared by the general public and many anthropologists, that the *substance* peyote is the major *raison d'être* for peyotism, in our own opinion falls short of the mark.[4]

We may endorse Howard's general plea, but query his contention that individual Peyotist motivations could be satisfactory at all levels of investigation.

First of all, Peyotism has, as for instance David Aberle has underscored, a polyvalent character: for some individuals it is a religion of miraculous curing, for others one of transcending knowledge, and for still others a release from guilt, etc.[5] What Aberle does not say is that these are examples of mostly covert motivations, to be contrasted with overt or conscious motivations of a type we have already discussed: "Peyote is good for you", and so on.

Secondly, our investigation needs an historical perspective. We are not *in et per se* concerned with how Peyote eaters react today unless they are the first generation of Peyotists in a particular tribal group, or their present behaviour may be considered to psychologically illuminate the process of acceptance. We are concerned about the Indians' original reactions to Peyote when it was introduced north of Mexico. What causes lay behind the enormous expansion of Peyote worship in North America? We know that south of the Rio Grande Peyote was part of the cycle of cult festivals of the vegetational year, and thus had a different character than north of the boundary line.[6] In North America the adherence to the Peyote religion was a matter of individual choice.

The differences between today and yesterday may be considerable. For example, the Peyotism of the Delaware (Lenape) Indians was investigated in the field for the first time by Vincenzo Petrullo in 1930. William Newcomb performed a new field investigation in 1952. He found that the ceremony was still

---

[4] Howard 1967, p. 21.
[5] Aberle 1982 b, p. 16.
[6] It should be noted however that according to Spanish sources Peyote was used for divinatory purposes in Central Mexico during the XVIth and XVIIth centuries, see Stewart 1987, pp. 19, 24 f.

the same as twentytwo years earlier. However, he noticed that great changes had occurred in the reasons for the religion's appeal to the people: "The modern attractions of the peyote cult are particularly strong in its aspects as an *Indian* ceremony and as a rallying point for Pan-Indianism, rather than in the solace it offers to 'a subjugated people'."[7] Similarly, George Spindler emphasizes that in the case of Menomini Peyotism "uni-causal explanations are totally inadequate, since Menomini peyotism started with an historical accident, got under way because a few individuals were in a ready state, and finally became firmly established not from any single cause but from a combination of factors."[8] The testimony is unequivocal: the first adherents may have had other motives than those living today.

Thoughtful students who have tried to reveal the decisive factors behind the diffusion of Peyote have thus been confronted with a methodological dilemma.[9] How can we know the deeper motivations for diffusion when, in most cases, the occasion for this process is so distanced in time, and the eyewitness accounts of Indian reactions so few? Or, when there are so many occasions, for different tribes in different situations and at different times? The obvious answer has been, not to dig up possible notes on psychological reactions in the past (since we do not know what they mean), but to contrast the Indian situation at a given moment with the Peyote configuration. Still, some lessons may also be achieved from the psychologists' workshops where contemporary situations are concerned; the works of Louise and George Spindler offer good examples of how group interests and individual conditions may operate in contexts of Peyote diffusion (cf. Ch. IV:4, below).

It holds as a rule that most theorists have anchored their explanations to one tribe, the tribe they are most familiar with. Only some few students, in particular perhaps Robert Bee, Weston La Barre, O. C. Stewart and J. S. Slotkin, have based their conclusions on a wider reading (or experience).[10] On the whole, the one-tribe researchers tend to generalize their findings, or to create general hypotheses.

Most students of Peyote who eschew the narcotic-herb hypothesis seem to be aware of the multitude of factors at work in Peyote dissemination, and some are satisfied with this observation, or stress its importance. Malcolm Arth, for instance, holds that among the Omaha, "the several factors are not isolated within the culture. Each acts to reinforce the other, and it is this solidly reinforcing combination of functions that insures the position of peyotism and maintains it."[11] Of course, just as there are always manifold causes of any cul-

---

[7] Newcomb 1956, p. 211.
[8] G. Spindler in La Barre 1960, p. 57.
[9] Unfortunately, several scholars are not aware of the dilemma!
[10] Bee 1965, pp. 24 ff., La Barre 1975 b, passim, Stewart 1987, passim, Slotkin 1956 a, pp. 8 ff., 17 ff.
[11] Arth 1956, p. 28.

tural origins, so are there several causes behind a revivalistic movement such as Peyote.[12]

In most cases the scholars nevertheless single out some few specific traits, or even one dominant trait, which they consider to be more important than others. The former method is represented by, for instance, Mirosława Posern-Zielińska who defines three basic factors in the "process of sacralisation" of Peyote: its hallucinatory properties, its fame as a healing plant, and the long tradition of using it in magic contexts.[13] The tendency to select one particular trait among several others was much *en vogue* during the first decades of Peyote studies. For instance, whereas Ruth Shonle did not deny the role of other factors, like the segregation of Indians on reservations and their cultural disorganization, she emphasized the preforming visionary pattern as the decisive factor.[14] On the other hand, Richard Schultes considered that the principal appeal of Peyote has been its supposed therapeutic qualities.[15] By the time he was writing La Barre published his classic study of the Peyote cult in which the perspective was broadened. With all its undeniable merits Schultes' paper represents a last echo of what I have called above the "one-faceted explanations".

The multi-faceted approach with preferences for some more important aspects seems to give more justice to the complex situation. Sometimes however even a broad causative scheme may miss important clues. In an ambitious effort to count for the range of causes and effects Peter Gerber distinguishes five main causative categories: the historical background, the destruction of traditional social units, the conflict between white and Indian value systems, the social identity and the Peyote meeting as a reference group, and the personal identity and the anomy of Native people.[16] Gerber's main emphasis seems to fall on the safety of belonging to a unified group, whereas the purely religious factors are played down. Edward F. Anderson's judgment makes a rather plain impression: "The Peyote Ceremony has considerable influence on the Indian's life, it offers him prayer for his soul, food for his stomach, health for his body, prestige and self expression. It allows for the venting of certain aggressive feelings and, to a degree, soothes the ever-pressed sense of cultural loss."[17]

Omer Stewart, again, questions most of the theories that have been proposed on the spread of Peyote, being of the opinion that they can be confuted by ethnohistorical documents.[18] His arguments will be examined in the following. Stew-

---

[12] Cf. La Barre 1971, p. 26.
[13] Posern-Zielińska 1972, pp. 246 f.
[14] Shonle 1925, pp. 58 f. She does however also indicate Peyote's curative properties as one decisive factor, cf. p. 53.
[15] Schultes 1938, pp. 703 f.
[16] Gerber 1982, p. 302.
[17] Anderson 1980, p. 48.
[18] Stewart in Lynch 1984, p. 180.

art's own preference, the import of Peyote missionaries, is somewhat along the one-faceted line of approach.

An interesting angle of incidence is represented by Couch and Marino who, in their article on Chippewa-Cree Peyotism, comprise the arguments for the diffusion of Peyote into two categories: the cultural compatibility theory, which correlates the success of a new belief system with its positive degree of integration with inherited culture, and the cultural disintegration theory, which considers the disintegration of old values as a prerequisite for the acceptance of a new belief system.[19] La Barre is connected with the former and Shonle and Opler with the latter theory. The opposition between the two theories is however just elusory since cultural relics and values are not necessarily compatible with each other.

In their evaluation of the causes behind the spread of Peyotism in North America the majority of investigators have been united on two points: that there is no compelling, habit-forming effect from the use of Peyote, and that the psychic pressure in the acculturative reservation situation accounts for the quick positive response that Peyote has met with in so many tribes. Some weight has been laid upon the pre-existence of a visionary pattern among the Plains Indians, conditioning individuals for a positive response to Peyote visionary experiences. Attention has been paid to particular psychological and sociological features like anxiety, aggression and status situation. Pan-Indianism has been stressed as a major cause of the growth of Peyotism. The existence of a possibly earlier "mescal" ritual on the Plains that could have offered a ready mould for Peyotism has been observed. Christian influences may finally have contributed to the formation and role of the Peyote religion.

In the following we shall see how these different possible factors have been analyzed by the scholars and how they may have formed the growth of Peyotism.

2. The Peyote Religion as a Crisis Religion

The history of the Peyote religion as presented in the foregoing has clearly shown that there are three major roots of this religion as it is displayed today north of the Rio Grande: Mexican pre-Columbian Peyote rituals, intertribal and local Indian Peyote patterns, and the white man's religion and ideological assumptions.[1] The intermingling of these three components was apparently a

---

[19] Couch and Marino 1979, p. 7.
[1] La Barre terms the first two constituents "an authentic pre-Columbian native core" and "an intertribal 'ecumenical' syncretism of residual Indianisms": La Barre 1970 a, p. 281. Cf. also La Barre 1971, p. 22.

slow process in the beginning but had a quicker pace after 1880 – indeed, it almost looks as if an explosion of spiritual power had fired Peyotism at this time. The term "crisis cults" has been used for religions which arise from conditions of cultural stress and shock. It would seem that the Peyote religion belongs to this category, although I would prefer to call it a "crisis religion".[2]

There is an almost general agreement among students that the growth and spread of the Peyote religion about 1880 must be seen in connection with the tremendous change that Indian society, particularly on the Plains, underwent in those days. We know the general features of this process: extermination of the wild, and therewith the basis of Plains Indian sustenance and of the conditions for the continuation of the old way of living; military defeat, followed by the removal to reservations and the forced abolishment of tribal political autonomy; an increased accommodation to white society, causing the breakdown of tribal customs and values, with conflicting value attitudes and ideological compromises as a consequence; and the emergence of new trends of thought, belief and action. Peyotism enters as a link in this process. However, opinion differs among scholars as how to interpret its place and import in the scheme of development.

Here follow some examples of this discussion.

The importance of external influences for the diffusion of the Peyote ritual was discussed by Ruth Shonle in her famous paper. Although she focussed on the vision (quest), particularly as concerns the Plains Indians, she also paid attention to the import of the reservation system and the improved communications. The segregation of Indians on reservations, she decreed, "was perhaps the most important factor fostering diffusion". Reservation life meant that the barriers between the tribes broke down, that tribal unity was dissolved, and that mutual tribal hostility disappeared together with the buffalo, the free hunting grounds and the old social organization. The Ghost Dance religion filled the religious vacuum for a time, its most lasting effect being the friendly intertribal contacts it inspired. "The dissemination of the peyote cult flowed easily along the newly opened channels of friendship." The new means of easy communication, postal service and railway travel, favoured a quick dissemination of the Peyote religion.[3]

It is easy to concur with Shonle's main thesis that a new intertribal ethos and improved facilities of communication paved the way for Peyote. If we concentrate here on the communications factor – the intertribalism will be discussed in a later context (Ch. IV:8) – its importance has again been stressed by Aberle and Stewart in an analysis of the diffusion of Peyote to the Ute and Navajo reservations. In their most conscientious work the authors point out the differential availability, as well as differential appeal, of the Peyote religion; the pattern of

---
[2] Cf. La Barre 1971, p. 11. On the concept "cult", see above, the Introduction.
[3] Shonle 1925, pp. 56 f.

contacts and the network of communications of Peyote users are studied.[4] Such an investigation furnishes us with geographic and socioecologic aspects of the diffusion process.

Slotkin has summed up the changes introduced by the whites on Indian land. He mentions the removal of Indians to reservations; the destruction of the buffalo, the chief source of existence for the Plains Indians; the invasion of Indian grounds; the introduction of new diseases resulting in devastating epidemics, and of alcoholic beverages against which the Indians had little resistance; unlimited control of Indian society by whites; ban on warfare and thereby destruction of the tribal status system; disintegration of the Native social and political organization; end of nomadism and confinement to reservations; introduction of agriculture; Christian mission, and ban on old ceremonies (such as the Plains Indian Sun Dance).[5] Of these items, the impact of Christian mission stands out as the most crucial factor for Peyote proselytization, since it serves as a model (cf. Ch. IV:10). No particular investigation has been performed of the influence on Peyotism of the other external factors mentioned by Slotkin. However, it is easy to see that they all had their bearing on the acceptance of Peyote.

The expansion of Peyotism was thus related to the conflicts between Native and white cultures, in the broadest sense. Anthropologists have created a conceptual framework for the processes taking place when cultures (and religions) clash, *acculturation*. The concept has here been discussed in an earlier connection (see under Introduction). Acculturation analyses reproduce a cultural (religious) situation in which one culture is open to varying impacts from another, or in which two cultures mutually influence each other. The end product of this process may be cultural pluralism, syncretism or complete assimilation. Where acculturation is vigorously objected to the outcome may be persistence of traditional culture, or even revitalization of this culture. It may also happen, however, that the rejection of a foreign value system, such as religion, gives rise to new movements which combine Native and foreign values, on a conscious or unconscious level.[6] The Peyote religion is obviously such a new movement. It operates as a crisis religion within the acculturation brackets.

Since the concept of acculturation was not used in anthropological debate until the 1930s we do not find any culture contact analyses of the Peyote religion before this time.[7] (That the Peyote religion manifested a form of culture contact was clearly conceived before this date, but the methodological devices and strategies were not at hand.) Melville Herskovits who, together with Robert Redfield and Ralph Linton, issued a Memorandum on acculturation in

---

[4] Aberle and Stewart 1957. Stewart (1987, pp. 63 ff.) mentions the spread of English as a promoting factor.

[5] Slotkin 1956 a, pp. 12 ff.

[6] This survey is based on the analysis of the acculturation concept that I have presented in Hultkrantz 1973 b, pp. 214 ff., and Hultkrantz 1960, pp. 17–23.

[7] Cf. Hultkrantz 1960, ibidem.

1936,[8] defined in 1948 the Peyote religion as "acculturation, cultural transmission in process".[9] This emphasis on process in the study of acculturation has since been linked to the personality studies in some important American anthropological investigations of Peyote.

The acculturation model has been used to explain the rise and expansion of the Peyote religion north of the Mexican border. It has been applied in particular to studies of psychological reactions. As we shall see, the meeting of cultures provides for a cultural shock which however may be resolved within the confines of the Peyote religion. The adjustment of the individual to his changing milieu within a Peyote context has been studied by several noted anthropologists.

There are though also other types of studies using an acculturation approach, such as diachronic investigations of the development of the culture-contact situation in Peyotism. The detailed research by Aberle and Stewart on Ute and Navajo Peyotism just referred to furnishes us with excellent examples. There are also interesting analyses of structural relationships between Peyotism and traditional religions. Such studies give us a glimpse of the abilities of the Peyote religion to take over traditional tribal religious values.

This latter approach may be illustrated with Roland Wagner's discussion of Navajo Peyotism.[10] In his lucid paper on the subject Wagner tries to demonstrate the different structural character of the ritual units in Navajo tribal religion and in their Peyotism. He claims that, conceptually, the two religions have been merged in the Navajo mind, but that etically they remain two different complexes. Their fusion is merely a matter of ritual additions (addition of the Peyote button to a Navajo ritual chant, of the Navajo singer's sacred pouch to the Peyote ritual equipment). However, in a few places there has been a real combination of ritual units to form a new level of syncretism: the old ceremony Evil Way, used for exorcism of witchcraft, has partly been joined to the Peyote ritual, taking the place of the Midnight water ceremony; and the dry painting ritual of the Navajo ceremonies has been inserted in place of the Morning water ceremony.[11] The author points out that the organizational flexibility of Navajo religion (which manifests Evon Vogt's "incorporative" pattern of integrating new materials) and the potentiality for innovation in Peyotism have both supplied a matrix for the mutual acculturation.[12]

It would seem that the Peyote movement would fit in excellently in acculturation analyses. Still, a well-experienced anthropologist and sharp-eyed Peyote

---

[8] Redfield, Linton and Herskovits 1936.
[9] Herskovits 1948, p. 540.
[10] Wagner 1975.
[11] Cf. also the reporting on a fusion between Peyotism and traditional disease diagnostics in Cooper 1984, pp. 105, 111 n. 92, and the information of an association between traditional ceremonials and Peyotism in Gill 1979, p. 21.
[12] Wagner 1975. Vogt 1961, pp. 328 f.

observer like David Aberle has refuted this kind of analysis as rather pointless in the first edition of his now classic book on Navajo Peyotism. He found that the Navajo, when they accepted the Peyote religion in the 1930s, were the least acculturated tribe in the United States.[13] Right from the beginning, he says, Peyotism met bitter opposition, and this opposition has since continued.[14] It was said that it was foreign, non-Navajo, since it cannot be traced from the mythic era when the supernatural beings operated within the country of the sacred peaks.[15] It was also said to be harmful, like the *Datura,* deranging the mind and even causing death.[16] In spite of these supposed shortcomings Peyote was accepted – but, Aberle interposes, not as a part of an acculturative process, rather as a means for overcoming an economic crisis.

This sounds very materialistic, but is not meant that way, as Aberle clearly demonstrates in the introduction to the second edition of his book.[17] What he refers to is the consequence of the reduction of sheep herds in the 1930s. The over-grazing of the sheep had caused erosion of the soil, so that the Navajo were compelled to cut down the numbers of their sheep to such an extent that their natural and social order was disrupted. To the Navajo this was however against the will of the supernaturals. In their interpretation, the supernaturals punished them with drought and erosion because they had reduced the number of their sheep.[18]

Aberle emphasizes that because of these events and their apprehension of them the Navajo suffered from deprivations of possessions, status, behaviour and worth.[19] (In his second edition, Aberle adds deprivation of power, both social and religious.) Deprivation, not acculturation, is to Aberle the decisive clue to Peyotism. The Peyote religion has, according to Aberle, an ideology well suited to the deprivations encountered by the Navajo and other American Indians as well. At the same time he discards acculturation as a valid operative concept in this connection.

Aberle had started his work on the premiss that Peyotism is a religion of transition, a religion which could facilitate the adjustment of Indians who had become uprooted from tribal tradition but failed to become assimilated into the larger society.[20] He quotes Slotkin who assigns the Peyote religion preferentially to those people who are intermediate in acculturation, and George Spindler who, as we shall see, refers the Peyotists to the second of five levels of acculturation among the Menomini (below, Ch. IV:4). Aberle compares these con-

---

[13] Aberle 1982 b (1966), p. 3.
[14] Aberle 1982 b, p. 18.
[15] Aberle 1982 b, p. 209.
[16] Aberle 1982 b, pp. 207, 210 ff.
[17] Aberle 1982 b, pp. xxiii ff.
[18] Aberle 1982 b, pp. 199 f.
[19] Aberle 1982 b, pp. 336 f.
[20] Aberle 1982 b, p. 244.

clusions with his own data from the Navajo, and the outcome is negative.[21] He finds that the level of acculturation is non-essential to the degree of Navajo acceptance of Peyotism, indeed, he even regards acculturation as an inhibitory force in the spread of Peyotism among the Navajo.[22] "In sum", concludes Aberle, "as respects acculturation, peyotists and non-peyotists do not differ significantly from each other in self-image, church membership, adherence to traditional tabus, education, material possessions, children's education, plans for children's education, or attitudes towards children's subsequent occupation."[23] Perhaps most astonishing is Aberle's information that he could find no differences between the two groups with regard to knowledge of Navajo religion, transmission of Navajo religion or participation in Navajo religious practice (as singers or diviners).[24]

It seems to me that Aberle has modified his view of the import of acculturation in the second edition of his book on Navajo Peyote Religion. Discussing my own and Fred Voget's criticism of his avoidance of an acculturation theory he ends by saying that "there is more agreement among the three of us than might appear. We all see deprivation as resulting from the particular kinds of acculturation experiences and domination known to Native Americans, and we all connect that deprivation with the acceptance of Peyotism."[25] Aberle's words here agree rather well with my own position that Peyotism may be associated with deprivation on account of cultural loss in acculturation.[26]

In contradistinction to Aberle I maintain that the Navajo are one of the most acculturated tribes in the U.S.A. – acculturated in the sense that they offer a picture of adaptation (syncretism) of Native and foreign cultural traditions. They achieved horses and sheep in the seventeenth century, and learned to shear, spin and weave the wool from their Pueblo Indian neighbours. They also obtained silver from the Spaniards and gradually developed their own silverwork. It was particularly after the resettling on the reservation lands in 1869 that silverwork and sheep industry took on imposing dimensions.[27] In other words, Navajo Indians have long been in a state of "transition". The significant fact is that they managed to remain that way, in contradistinction to their Apache congeners east of the Rocky Mountains.[28] This established balance explains why they kept out

---

[21] Aberle 1982 b, pp. 306 ff.

[22] Aberle 1982 b, pp. 243, 279, 308 ff. It is a bit strange however that Aberle assesses acculturation over time by using only one criterion, the level of education (pp. 308 f.).

[23] Aberle 1982 b, p. 250.

[24] Aberle 1982 b, ibidem.

[25] Aberle 1982 b, pp. xxvii f.

[26] Hultkrantz 1975, p. 75. Cf. also Wilson 1973, p. 430. It is more difficult to follow Wilson's thesis that Peyotism took over because of its small expenses (op. cit., p. 428).

[27] For a perusal of the evidence, see Underhill 1956, in particular pp. 33 ff., 41 ff., 155 ff., 177 ff., 186 ff.

[28] Cf. in this connection Roland M. Wagner's discussion of transition and acculturation, quoted in Aberle 1982 b, pp. xxix f.

of Peyote for so long, but also why there are no palpable differences between Peyote eaters and others in cultural possessions, life orientation and values. Aberle is undoubtedly right in assuming that deprivation of many sorts – to the Navajo, first and foremost deprivation of supernatural aid[29] – paved the way for Peyotism. We are satisfied here to state that the Navajo acculturative situation offered opportunities for the adoption of Peyote, although traditionalism in religion had to be overcome.

I think we may assume that, at least initially, the Peyote religion has operated in an acculturative situation. It is less certain that the latter should be considered as the ultimate cause of the acceptance of Peyote. It may facilitate this process, but – isn't it superficial to ascribe the introduction of a new religion only to a general cultural process?

3. Peyote and the Situation of Cultural Shock

Several authors have emphasized the negative psychological consequences of the acculturation situation, the "cultural shock" and its aftermath. It stands to reason that it is difficult to reconstruct, from our scanty source materials, the nature of the shock that opened the gates for the Peyote religion. The authors apostrophied in the following mostly refer to the general human condition: there is a psychological rule that governs everybody. This may be so. Still, the particular reactions of Indians undergoing cultural loss are difficult to grasp even if you are contemporaneous with them and are a close neighbour.

It is the consensus of the aforesaid authors that the disturbances resulting from the cultural shock were resolved within the frame of the Peyote religion. The sharing of values in the group, the togetherness in a solid unit of likeminded fellows, and the peace and harmony that is felt in the circle of meditating Peyotists during a Peyote meeting is seen as a contrast to the anxiety and mental deprivation following the loss of traditional tribal values.

The cultural shock at the breakdown of Indian political and cultural autonomy had many dimensions, correlated with the particular changes that were brought about. They implied the painful clash with a foreign, white culture, its technological superiority, its exclusive value pattern, its different religious ideology and monopoly in religious matters. They also implied the Indian defeat in the military struggle against the vast white population that swept over the country, and the subordination of the Indians under a new political and economic system authorized from a foreign source. Furthermore they meant the loss of traditional culture, its value system and religious convictions, at least to a certain extent. They meant frustration, hopeless resignation, and deprivation.

---
[29] Aberle 1982 b, p. 200.

This was a new saddening experience for the Indians. Certainly, they had suffered before. American Indian history is rich in examples of white exploitation of the indigenous tribes – witness, for example, the gruesome persecutions of Indians in the Eastern Woodlands, and the reckless extermination of Indian tribes in California.[1] Indians had themselves annihilated Indian tribal groups on the Plains in the eighteenth century, Iroquois had swept away Iroquoian and Algonkian peoples in the seventeenth century, and so on. All this was familiar experience to North American Indians.

There was also, and above all, the sufferings of everyday life. The hardships in areas where habitations were fragile – tents, wickiups, brush shelters – in a harsh climate, the starvation, the ailments, the many deaths, all these trials were part of existence since days of old, and people were used dealing with them.

Then there were the rituals in which suffering was a meaningful part. The hardships of daily life were magnified in order to gain the compassion of the powers. Thus, both in the vision quest and the Sun Dance of the Plains pain was an essential ingredient, an instance of the dramatic action. Abstinence from food and drink, exposure to cold, and self-mutilation belonged to these rituals.[2] This was the way to achieve supernatural aid. Only by sacrificing oneself could the petitioner attain the blissful relationship with the supernatural world.[3]

All these forms of suffering were, however, usually interpreted from a positive point of view. They constituted just a passing phase in existence, and were supposed to serve defined goals, seen from a higher, religious and universal perspective: you died for your people, you underwent suffering in a difficult situation but hoped to get through it and reach a happier state. Or you suffered voluntarily (ritually) in order to achieve supernatural gratification: blessings, supernatural power, harmony. Concentration was on the good life, the "beauty way", as the Navajo say, the harmony between man and cosmos. Even nature was, among the hunters, something good, something that was imbued with good medicine, revealing God and the spirits.[4] Shortcomings in this life depended on a lack of harmony with the supernatural world.

The cultural crisis at the end of the last century entailed however another kind of suffering, a suffering which seemed to be without end, without any hope for

---

[1] Cf. for instance Heizer and Kroeber 1979.
[2] Cf. Hultkrantz 1983 b, p. 101.
[3] Clifford Geertz thinks that suffering is one of the gateways to religion. He also considers that, as a religious problem, the problem of suffering is not how to avoid suffering but how to suffer, how to make the physical or psychic pain bearable, "sufferable", see Geertz 1966, p. 19. Plains Indian rituals offer many examples of how religious petitioners have tried to augment their physical pain until they have fainted. Cf. for instance Catlin's description from the Mandan *Okeepa* ceremony, Catlin 1967, pp. 65 ff.
[4] Cf. Hultkrantz 1981 a, pp. 117 ff.

the future. The very foundations of Indian existence – economic, social, traditional, religious – seemed to have been crushed. Here is not the place for quotations from the many lamentations made by American Indians on this matter; suffice it to say that the bitter, resigned comments are legion. Some investigators have tried to pinpoint the underlying fears of the Indians at this moment in their history. Thus, Underhill refers to the general feeling among the Plains tribes that they had been deserted by their spirit helpers.[5] This is an interesting point of view since it emphasizes a religious cause of the depressing situation. Indeed, not only guardian spirits, but also the spirits of the game were thought to have disappeared; the buffalo, for example, were said to have gone underground, to a place from whence they had once ascended.[6] The spirits were evidently understood as part of a life and culture that was threatened with extinction. The relation between old spiritual beliefs and the new cultural situation was somewhat incongruous.

Underhill's view is perceptive and deserves attention. Other authors have proposed explanations which have been more in line with conventional psychological and sociological theories of the day, and less in tune with Indian ideas. Richard Schultes, for instance, indirectly underscores the problem of individual and collective human survival when he refers to the life-sustaining properties and medicinal virtues supposed to pertain to Peyote.[7] In the first edition of his book on Peyote David Aberle prefers to see deprivation in possessions, status, behaviour and self-esteem among the Navajo as decisive factors behind the situation that made Peyotism possible.[8] In the second edition of the same book however he adds a fifth and, as he says, crucial kind of deprivation, through loss of power.[9] Peter Gerber seems to explain Peyotism almost entirely in sociological, sociopsychological and economic terms.[10] While such theories always contain a part of the truth their main failure is their disregard of religious factors and a religious frame of reference.

If some Marxistically inclined authors have overrated the significance of economic causes it is worth noting nevertheless that economic deprivation has meant a good deal in the chaos that preceded the adoption of Peyote. This was particularly so among the Navajo, as Aberle has shown so convincingly (cf. above, Ch. IV:2). The Navajo reduction of sheep in the 1930s has its counterpart in the loss of buffaloes on the Plains in the 1860s and 1870s: both processes meant impoverishment and hardship for the Indian herders and hunters.

---

[5] Underhill 1952, p. 143. The Shoshoni in Wyoming informed me that the spirits nowadays have retired from areas inundated by electric cables and power stations.
[6] Mooney 1896, p. 906. For the retirement of game spirits in the Woodlands area, see Martin 1978, pp. 148 f.
[7] Schultes 1938, p. 706.
[8] Aberle 1982 b (1966), pp. 326 ff.
[9] Aberle 1982 b, p. xxiv.
[10] Gerber 1975, pp. 171 ff.

However, as Aberle has realized, the economic deprivation is only part of the picture. Another important factor is social deprivation. As Gary Witherspoon emphasizes, the social life of the Navajo is primarily organized around the sheep herd.[11] Within a resident group like the one at Rough Rock, the status of people corresponds closely with the number of sheep in the herd.[12] Mary Shepardson and Blodwen Hammond conclude that traditional social interaction patterns, rules of residence and forms of marriage are adjusted to sheep holding. Indeed, "the whole value system is integrated about the sheep herds".[13] On the Plains, the keeping of horses formerly induced a similar ranking.

All these factors are of considerable importance, but they must be seen in their mutual connections and, as Aberle correctly states, they must be coordinated with the crucial factor, the loss of power. Now, Aberle here refers to secular powerlessness, but he thinks it has connection with supernatural power. Just as the old social power system was reciprocal and non-hierarchical in Navajo matrilinear groups, supernatural power was immanent and bound up with nature and livestock in the old days. And just as reciprocal secular power was supplanted by the white man's hierarchical power, the immanent spirits were supplanted by Peyote's transcendent power.[14] So far Aberle.

This may sound plausible, but is not convincing: as Aberle remarks himself, traditional Navajo religion has not lost its grip, and Peyote brought no qualitatively different power, but additional power. The superficial parallels between secular and supernatural power, actualized by authors like Swanson, Burridge and Jorgensen – all approvingly cited by Aberle – are misleading.[15] There may be formal and linguistic conformity, but the two kinds of power are basically not comparable. Nevertheless, Aberle's introduction of the religious dimension in a discussion that has been conspicuously void of the role of religious values is most welcome.

The need to observe the religious factor as such in a discourse on Peyote will be dealt with in the sequence (see Ch. V). Here we can note the following. In a social group where there is a strong religious sentiment among the average individuals, and the formalized religion is traditional (as it was among North American Indians at the time of the Peyote expansion, or just before this expansion), the cultural shock is also a religious shock that will be resolved within the religious framework. Stewart, quoting Kroeber, speaks in Peyote connections about "the cultural disintegration theory", according to which "peoples experiencing cultural disintegration and degradation will readily accept new religions,

---

[11] Witherspoon 1973, p. 1444.
[12] Witherspoon 1973, p. 1443.
[13] Shepardson and Hammond 1970, p. 242.
[14] Aberle 1982 b, pp. xxiv f., 202.
[15] Swanson 1960, Burridge 1969, Jorgensen 1972.

especially those which promise the miraculous restoration of former conditions of life."[16]

There is, of course, the question of the quality of such a religion. What does it stand for – militant aggression, as was obviously the case in the Ghost Dance, or, as Roland Wagner expresses it, "passive acceptance of a situation of enduring deprivation"?[17] The latter answer was given by Bernard Barber when he claimed that Peyotism "crystallized around passive acceptance and resignation in the face of the existing deprivation. It is an alternative response which seems to be better adapted to the existing phase of acculturation." Better than the Ghost Dance, Barber thinks.[18] Wagner has rightly recognized the same interpretation in the writings of a sociologist like H. D. Lasswell and an anthropologist like Clyde Kluckhohn. The latter's view of Navajo Peyotism in its initial phase about 1940 is particularly interesting since Kluckhohn had a well-established field contact with these people. In Kluckhohn's appreciation the Navajo response to crisis was a substitute for aggression, called by psychologists "leaving the field", and manifested in social withdrawal and flight from reality through the use of narcotics. The Navajo tried both ways, Kluckhohn informs us, but without great success (at that time). Peyote, he says, met with opposition from the Indian Service (as being a supposed narcotic drug), and he adds: "The use of alcohol is much more widespread."[19] Peyote and alcohol as alternative drugs!

Wagner vigorously attacks the thesis that Peyote religion is another worldly escape from a painful reality. He emphasizes its pragmatic character, its power to bring about significant changes for the better in everyday life. It restores people's health, helps them to live more satisfactory lives, extends non-kin ties to other people. "Peyotism is not an attempt to flee from reality, but rather an attempt to deal with it in another form."[20] Wagner agrees with Aberle that Peyotists are not defeatist, but persevere in their opposition against civil and religious authorities, and that Peyote is tough medicine.[21]

It is easy to accept Wagner's points of view so far. There is indeed nothing escapist in the Peyotist attitude, but rather the reverse in their fight against law courts and prohibitionists. Peyotists are not noticed for their passive equanimity, they are activists at the same time as they are introverted religiously – as American Indians have always been. Wagner goes too far, however, when he denies that Peyotists "cling to another-worldly religious creed".[22] All religions

---

[16] Stewart 1944, p. 90. Cf. Kroeber 1925, pp. 868 f., and 1948, p. 568. Kroeber does not systemize the concept in the way Stewart does. Also La Barre refers to Kroeber as the originator of the concept, see La Barre 1960, p. 52. (The quotation in La Barre is however from Stewart, not Kroeber as La Barre insists.)
[17] Wagner 1975, p. 197.
[18] Barber 1941 a, p. 669.
[19] Kluckhohn 1967 (1944), pp. 90 f.
[20] Wagner 1975, p. 204.
[21] Cf. Aberle 1982 b, pp. 109 ff.
[22] Wagner 1975, p. 201.

are *par définition* other-worldly, although they do not necessarily tend to world denial which is something else. Wagner's position in these matters will be further discussed in Ch. V:1.

In most parts of the world cultural shocks due to western impact have engendered new religions in which ideas of salvation have been of paramount importance.[23] The believers are promised deliverance from their sufferings in a new order of existence in this world, or in another world. The well-known "prophetic movements" in Africa and Melanesia offer good examples.[24] In North America, the Ghost Dance religion was a prophetic movement which was highly salvation-conscious.[25] However, the Peyote religion stands apart from this general pattern. It certainly implies a conversion in a psychological sense, an acceptance of a set of spiritual values,[26] but it does not presume an outspoken salvation consciousness.

A study of the Peyote doctrine as presented by Slotkin, for instance, corroborates this statement. The Peyote Road elaborates an ethic characterized by Christian virtues, brotherly love, care of family, self-reliance and avoidance of alcohol (not always Christian). In particular, Peyote teaches each man and woman what to do and what not to do. Whoever follows the Peyote Road will have comfort and happiness in this world and be blessed in the next world.[27]

Like Christians, Peyotists speak of the good road that leads to God and the bad road that leads to hell. However, this is a late interpretation, pertaining to the time when Peyotism turned to Christianity. The stress is generally on the common blessings provided by Peyote, and not on the salvation from this world or its present condition.[28]

Why, then, did not this idea of salvation become attached to the Peyote movement? The answer is simple enough: there was no sudden change of the world expected, there was no immediate eschatological perspective. In contrast to the Ghost Dance Peyotism grew imperceptibly stronger, without a revolutionary program. No upheaval of social, political or religious institutions was foreseen, just a quiet evolution of Red Indian spiritual life. No dramatic salvation was implied.

---

[23] Salvation could here be defined according to the suggestion in the Encyclopedia Britannica as "the deliverance or redemption of man from such fundamentally negative or disabling conditions as suffering, evil, finitade, and death", see Wheeler 1974.

[24] For quick references to the main literature, see La Barre 1971, pp. 4–6.

[25] Reference is here made to such items as the purification from white influence, and the alienation from white persons: a this-world salvation.

[26] I am aware that psychologists of religion would question the unqualified use of the concept of conversion and, particularly, would distinguish between personal decision and conversion. However, there is little opportunity here to make such distinctions; only Radin's account of a Winnebago Indian's transition to Peyotism may be used (Radin 1920).

[27] Slotkin 1956 a, p. 71.

[28] Slotkin observes (p. 113) that there are some exceptions to this rule, people who believe that when all tribes have eaten Peyote the world will come to an end. The reference is here to Winnebago beliefs probably inspired by Christian thoughts. Cf. Radin 1923, p. 418.

In this respect Peyotism was close to traditional American Indian spirituality which knows no sharp eschatological break with past conditions in a future prospect. Eschatology, in the strict sense of the word – not so generally used among students of North American Indians – means the doctrine of judgment day and ending times, the events when the world comes to an end. Such a doctrine did not exist in aboriginal North America. It is usually combined with the idea of an ethical dualism between two major divinities, and the demand on man to cooperate with the good divinity. This ethical action facilitates salvation, whether it is enacted on a national (Israel) or universal (Parsism, Christianity, Islam) level.

A dualism between a good and a bad divinity has existed over wide areas of North America. However, it was restricted to the myth, and had little to do with the ethical behaviour of man.[29] Furthermore, the American Indian time perspective was horizontal, not vertical. Year followed year in an unbroken chain, like undulations (Arne Runeberg). There was a beginning far away, which was reinvoked by man when he performed his great ceremonies; but there was no end, unless (as in California) an earth-quake broke the quiet trot. Such a calamity could happen, but so far the world seemed to remain fairly intact. There was, in other words, no true eschatology.

In the absence of eschatology and real dualism, a word like "salvation" is devoid of meaning. It has, nevertheless, been used by a scholar of religion in a paper on salvation among North American Indians. The author is a Belgian, Anne Dorsinfang-Smets. It is apparent that she uses the word salvation in a very wide, indeed, loose sense. Her main example from North America, the Grand Medicine Ceremony *(midewiwin)* of the Ojibway and their neighbours around the western Great Lakes, certainly does not convey any idea of salvation. It is life, a prolonged life and health that the initiates hope to gain; they are not granted salvation in the moral and other-worldly senses that we use the word in.[30] It is true that the the Winnebago Medicine Ceremony promises a safe reincarnation.[31] However, it is scarcely meaningful to call the chance to metempsychosis a salvation.

If the Peyote religion does not bring salvation it has however in a way a cleansing function like salvation. I am here referring to the practice of confessing sins sometimes occurring during Peyote rituals. There was no Christian prototype for this custom. Peyotism here associated to extant American Indian ritual observations.

As indicated by several scholars, the custom of public confession is very ancient in America.[32] La Barre lists it among a great many tribes from Aurohuaca in Colombia to the Eskimo.[33] He states its appearance among the Itelmen

---

[29] Hultkrantz 1979 b, pp. 32 ff., and 1984.
[30] Dorsinfang-Smets 1962, pp. 119 ff.; cf. Hoffman 1891.
[31] Radin 1945.
[32] See the references in Hultkrantz 1979 b, p. 88, 1992 p. 158.
[33] La Barre 1947, pp. 302 ff.

of Kamchatka as a proof of its high age – a proof which perhaps is not so convincing since the Itelmen like other Palaeosiberian tribes had a close cultural connection with the Indians of the Northwest Coast.[34] There is scarcely any doubt however that in America this custom was pre-Columbian.[35]

La Barre is undoubtedly right when he observes the re-emergence and spread of the confession complex "in the modern religion of the Plains, the peyote cult".[36] Its connection with Peyote seems to date from the old Mexican Peyotism. Thus, among the Huichol of Mexico the pilgrims who seek to obtain the sacred cactus confess their sins, the women to Grandfather Fire, the men to the winds.[37] North of the Rio Grande individual confessions are part of the nightly ritual among the Iowa, Omaha, Oto and Winnebago.[38] "Some time before dawn," writes La Barre, "when the effect of the morphine-like alkaloids of peyote is at its height, many members rise, on the exhortation of the Road Chief, and accuse themselves publicly of misdemeanors or offences, asking pardon of any persons who might have been injured by them."[39] From all appearances this must be considered a local elaboration of the Peyote ritual.

The presence of this psychotherapy in the Peyote religion obviously represents a last off-shoot of the custom, as La Barre reminds us.[40] It is possible that confessions, like another cathartic measure, vomiting, were part and parcel of the Peyote movement from its start. In this connection it is interesting to note that the Creek, when taking their emetic *Ilex cassine* (cf. Ch. I:2), also resort to purgatory confessions.[41]

However, it is important to observe that whereas sin, in the old tribal religions, was interpreted as a break of a ritual taboo, it takes on a new meaning in the Peyote religion. It stands here for wrong deeds committed against a fellow-human of one's acquaintance or of the ritual group. There is scarcely any doubt that this change in meaning must be retraced to Christian missionary impulses. We have reasons to presume that the change occurred in the Peyote ritual some time during the past two hundred years. The change facilitated that the confession became in part what Barber calls "a mechanism for the dissolution of individual anxieties".[42] In other words, it relieved the Indians of the psychic disturbances caused by the cultural shock.[43]

---

[34] Cf. for instance Bogoras 1902, Czaplicka 1928, pp. 492 f., Gurvich 1988.
[35] La Barre 1947, ibidem.
[36] La Barre 1947, p. 307.
[37] La Barre 1975 b, p. 30, quoted from Lumholtz 1902 II, pp. 129 ff. In pre-Columbian Mexico Mother Earth – who is sometimes identified with the Peyote woman of the later Peyote religion – received confessions of sin, cf. Pettazzoni 1931, pp. 191 ff.
[38] La Barre 1975 b, pp. 52 n. 115, 99, Stewart 1987, pp. 163 f.
[39] La Barre 1947, p. 301. We are reminded of the sensitivity training fashion of the 1970s!
[40] La Barre 1947, p. 307.
[41] La Barre 1947, ibidem.
[42] Barber 1941 b, pp. 674 f. Cf. also Stewart 1987, p. 182.
[43] See also Ch. V:3.

4. Peyote as a Means of Personal Adjustment

Modern investigations of the ways in which contemporary Peyotists evince accommodations to present-day cultural situations may seem unwarranted for the problem posed in this book, the causes of the adoption of Peyote in Indian communities. However, overtly or covertly such investigations have been used for the solution of this problem. Something can also be said in favour of this argument. Although admittedly relating to a time when the Peyote religion was mostly well established in its area of diffusion these studies may possibly illuminate some of the forces at work in the personal motivations, manifest or latent, for the acceptance of Peyote. In single cases, such as the Navajo, such studies may reveal the interactions between personalities and an expanding Peyotism.

Much has been said in American personality-and-culture research about the ways in which Peyote restores the emotional and social security of individuals suffering from cultural loss. Allen Dittmann and Harvey Moore made an investigation of Navajo dreams in order to find out the ratio of psychic disturbances among Peyote adherents in comparison to other individuals. They studied the dreams of fiftynine Navajo among whom were twelve Peyotists. The two researchers reached the conclusion that the Peyotists were more disturbed than the rest of the examined Navajo. This could mean that those who are emotionally disturbed join the Peyote movement where they find "a reintegrated outlook and restructured goals and group memberships".[1] However, it could also mean that the disturbances owe their origin to the marginal and "outlaw" position of the Peyote believers among the Navajo at the time of the investigation (1957). Admittedly, the last alternative seems less likely.[2]

The most penetrating of the psychologically slanted studies dealing with Peyotism in acculturation have been written by Louise and George Spindler, and concern Menomini Peyotism.[3] Like most other acculturation studies these papers refer to the time after World War II, which means that the conditions at the time of the Menomini acquisition of the Peyote religion are not accounted for.

In the eyes of these authors the Menomini Peyotism offers "a unique variation of culture conflict resolution within the transitional position".[4] By "transitional" is here meant a level of acculturation halfway between the least acculturated Menomini, the Dream Dance group, and the most acculturated, bridge-playing and tea-drinking group. Using projective tests (Rorschach) the authors found the members of the Peyotist transitional group expressing anxiety and loss of control, at the same time as they exhibited a high degree of "introspective fan-

---

[1] Dittmann and Moore 1957, p. 643.
[2] Cf. also the comments in Aberle 1982 b, pp. 269 ff.
[3] See especially G. Spindler 1955, and Spindler and Spindler 1971.
[4] Spindler and Spindler 1958, p. 219.

tasy" that in the opinion of the authors seemed to be "a direct function of identification with cult ideology and experience in cult ritual".[5] This is a curious assessment of the fact that Menomini Peyotists are religious (of course). In another paper which George Spindler has written together with Walter Goldschmidt there is a keener awareness of the importance of the religious factors in an analysis of acculturation. Here, of all social criteria the authors have selected religious affiliation and orientation as the "crucial indicator".[6]

It should be mentioned that also among the Navajo Peyotists seem to hold a transitional, intermediate level of acculturation, if we may believe Roland Wagner.[7]

A closer view of the process of psychic change in Menomini acculturation is offered in an interesting article by Louise Spindler. She finds that there is, among the Peyotists, an emotional crisis as a consequence of the conflict between old Menomini and white cultures. This clash in values is too much for them, and they face a breakdown of emotional control, accompanied by manifestations of diffuse anxiety. However, although the shock is traumatic these Menomini do not give in to the demands of white society. They find means for a harmonious adjustment and a resolution of their value conflict in the Peyote religion.[8]

It is noteworthy that the observation of the Spindlers of a differential anxiety in Menomini groups facing acculturation is at variance with Irving Hallowell's analysis of corresponding reactions among the neighbouring Ojibway Indians. At one reservation (Flambeau, Wisconsin) Hallowell found anxiety and a low degree of psychological adjustment as a characteristic of individuals on all levels of acculturation.[9] The loss of the old religious value system is pointed out as the root of the evil.[10] To my understanding this explanation may hold good also for other Indian populations. It is apparently in particular sensitive and *religiously* motivated persons who suffer from anxiety in the culture-contact situation. This is what my own experiences from an Indian reservation have convinced me about. There are certainly also more mundane aspects of the acculturative situation that may have destructive results, such as the fight for survival, among the Plains Indians in particular,[11] the deprivation of social order and familiar social groups, and so on. However, a closer investigation will perhaps show that even in these instances the loss of religious value patterns and religious beliefs, the ideological foundations of existence, have been decisive for most religious people – and what Plains Indians were not religious at the time when their culture collapsed.

---

[5] Spindler and Spindler 1958, p. 220, G. Spindler 1955, p. 207.
[6] Spindler and Goldschmidt 1952, p. 73.
[7] Wagner 1974; cf. the report of this work in Aberle 1982 b, pp. xxix f.
[8] L. Spindler 1952, p. 595.
[9] Hallowell 1967, pp. 351, 356.
[10] Hallowell 1967, p. 357.
[11] La Barre 1947.

This digression from our subject – so important for the theme of this book – should not conceal the importance of the discovery that Peyotists belong to an intermediate acculturative group. They have more or less left their old traditional religion, or combined the latter with their new creed. They have not yet reached the level of assimilation where Christianity, agnosticism or atheism offer alternatives. They are the people in between.

To return to our main issue, anxiety, then, is the reaction of the religious individual in a conflict situation where his established religious values are at stake. The Peyote religion offers a new retreat, but, if we may trust the Menomini data, a retreat which does not always give full emotional security. Perhaps the fact that the new religion is not shared by all members of the community upsets the mental balance of many believers. The resolution of the value conflict is apparent, not real, as long as the individual has not attained complete control of his situation. Religious and social motivations join forces to create a new harmony.

The Navajo as described by Aberle and others present an interesting case where individualism and anxiety reduction occur side by side. Guy Cooper has aptly comprehended the situation.[12] He points out how the changes in the Navajo society and economy of the 1930s made traditional religion inadequate to cope with the new conditions (stock reduction, wage-labour, adaptation to white technology, education and health). Traditional sanctions which were inherent in the application of traditional religion "were replaced in peyotism by self-responsibility and a system of morality which provided an anchor in a period of confusing upheaval." Peyotism encouraged a sense of individual and family responsibility which helped to overcome the difficulties, thus facilitating a more individualistic stance, adjusted to white society. It also alleviated the traditional Navajo fear of the dead and witchcraft.

5. Peyote as a Medicine

The argument for the quick adoption of Peyote which has perhaps received the most positive response is Richard E. Schultes's. To this eminent down-to-earth botanist it is obvious that the therapeutic and stimulating properties of the Peyote plant have been responsible for the establishment, spread and, partly, maintenance of the Peyote religion.[1] There are indeed many facts that speak in favour of his theory.

---

[12] Cooper 1984, pp. 103 f.
[1] Schultes 1938, pp. 703 f. It should be mentioned that Radin (1914, p. 12) was among the first to express the view that the curative function was the primary factor in causing the appeal of Peyotism. La Barre underlines that doctoring at Peyote meetings is of primary importance and is in a majority of cases the purpose of calling a meeting (La Barre 1975 b, pp. 85 ff.).

First of all, as Schultes demonstrates, the Peyote bulb is used in Mexico and the United States as a medicament for a variety of varied diseases. It is often taken without any ritual by single individuals. For instance, Kiowa Indians pack Peyote buttons around an aching tooth, and Shawnee use Peyote tea as an antiseptic for open wounds.[2] Furthermore, Schultes shows convincingly that the first tribal Peyote leaders were converted when they had tried Peyote and found that it cured them from some disease they had. It was, says Schultes, this healing property of Peyote that swept aside conservative opposition. Finally, Schultes adduces examples of how modern Peyote rites are arranged in order to cure sick persons. Schultes's own experience of such a rite is worth quoting in detail:

> The Kiowa leader who conducted the curing rite which I witnessed treated a young man suffering from tuberculosis. Leaving his place shortly after the ritual of the Midnight Water, the leader walked to the patient, lying at the side of the tipi. The fire-man handed the leader a cup of water, and the leader offered several prayers in which the words Jesus Christ were frequently used. He handed the patient fourteen mescal buttons which he himself had partly masticated before the treatment. While the patient was swallowing them, the leader waved the cup of water in cedar incense produced by throwing dried juniper needles (*Juniperus virginiana* L.) into the altar fire. He also wafted this incense to the patient's bared chest with an eagle feather fan. Following this, he chewed several more buttons, expectorated them into his cupped hands, and anointed the patient's head with the saliva while praying. Then he picked up a glowing ember from the altar fire and, placing it almost in his mouth, blew its heat over the patient's chest. The ritual ended with a long prayer.[3]

This description of a Peyote curing rite is in no way unique, on the contrary, but it illuminates the way in which a Peyote leader has usurped the functions of the medicine man in traditional Native religion. The methods used by the Kiowa leader remind us of the practices of the medicine man, or shaman.[4] The sweeping of the patient's body with a feather fan, the use of incense and the smearing of the patient with saliva are all methods used by the Plains medicine man when curing.

---

[2] Schultes 1938, p. 706. Cf. also Robert Bee's report on a Prairie Potawatomi woman who kept a small bottle of Peyote in her handbag which she used "just like aspirin": Bee 1965, p. 26. See also Stewart 1987, p. 330.

[3] Schultes 1938, pp. 709 f. "Mescal button" here of course stands for Peyote button. Setkopte, one of the first Kiowa Peyote leaders, was cured from consumption by eating Peyote, see Stewart 1987, pp. 81 f. On prayers for the sick in the Peyote ceremony, cf. Stewart 1987, p. 38 (after Mooney).

[4] The distinction between shaman and medicine man is difficult in medical connections. As I see it all doctors who cure with supernatural sanctions are medicine men, but only those who make use of ecstasy in their operations could be called shamans. It is important to note that this terminology is the scholar's etic evaluation, but not the Native classification. See Hultkrantz 1985, and compare Hultkrantz 1973 a, 1993.

The closeness of the Peyote ritual to the ritual of medicine men is also obvious from the Peyotism of the Mescalero Apache. It seems that here Peyotism occurred in the service of shamanism.[5] According to Morris Opler not only did the arrangers of a Peyote ceremony need the permission of the medicine man, the ceremony itself took the form of "a gathering of shamans under the control and guidance of the peyote chief".[6] The situation is certainly partly explanatory against the background of the ancient position of the medicine man among the Mescalero (cf. Ch. I:2), but it also gives evidence of the recognition of Peyote as a medicine to be handled by medicine men.

In this connection it should also be remembered that two dominant Peyote leaders among the Wyoming Shoshoni, father and son Wesaw (see Ch. II:3), both claimed to be medicine men and were honoured as such in their own faction of Shoshoni society. Among the Kiowa Apache shamanism is now practically dead, and about 1950 there were only two practising medicine men, both ardent Peyotists and carrying out their curative functions during or immediately after Peyote meetings.[7]

Stewart has distinguished the roadman originally as a medicine man: "Generally, the person who wished to become a roadman was already distinguished as a medicine man."[7] Interestingly, Stewart stresses that at the ritual Peyote meeting among Nevada Indians "Peyote helps cure all diseases and reveals many things: the location of lost objects or persons, future events, and proper behavior, among others."[8] In other words, Peyote has taken over all the shamanic tasks! The difference is however that in Peyotism the source of healing is less pronounced the doctor, it is the Peyote. Now it could be objected that like the shaman depends on his guardian spirit, the roadman depends on Peyote. However, Peyote is not just the roadman's adviser, Peyote illuminates the minds of all members of the cult group. Furthermore, the guardian spirit directs the shaman or medicine man who is the claimed doctor, whereas in Peyotism Peyote itself is said to be the doctor. Or put in another way, Peyote cures without the intercession of a human doctor.[9]

This is the regular procedure, but there are exceptional cases where shamanic doctoring has occurred in the Peyote lodge. If as I think such events were more common in older days – when traditional practitioners appeared as roadmen – the medical import of the Peyote ritual might have been stronger than it is today. Anyhow, our records show that in more recent times the curing performed by medicine men in the Peyote lodge is mostly incidental and not part of the Peyote ritual as such. Furthermore, except for the sacred Peyote atmosphere there is no-

---

[5] See also Bee 1965, pp. 20 f.
[6] Opler 1936, p. 151.
[7] Stewart 1987, p. 68.
[8] Stewart 1982, p. 202.
[9] Hultkrantz 1992, p. 90.

thing that directly connects the doctor's actions with Peyote and its ritual in such cases. The medicine man simply makes use of techniques that are familiar to his respective tribe.

Some examples. Among the Lipan Apache the medicine man sucks the disease away during the Peyote meeting.[10] Among the Kiowa Apache shamanism is now practically dead, but around 1950 there were two practising medicine men, both ardent Peyotists carrying out their curative functions during or immediately after the Peyote meetings.[11] Aberle and Stewart report that the Ute shamans in some places are Peyotists.[12] They tell us that "shamanistic sucking can be added to the peyote meeting, or slipped in during a lull in the regular peyote ritual."[13] A remarkable curing in a Gosiute Peyote circle has been reported by Stewart. A little girl was treated here by the Qglala Sam Lone Bear. The medicine man but hot coals in his mouth. "Flames came out of his mouth. He blew the flames on the child's chest and back. He prayed to have God cure her. She is still alive."[14] Lone Bear was a devious and scandalous person, but he was as much a curing shaman as Peyote proselytizer.[15] Stewart watched among the Arapaho how at one séance the roadman served as "sucking shaman" during the midnight break.[16] In this connection it should also be remembered that two dominant Peyote leaders among the Wyoming Shoshoni, father and son Wesaw (see Ch. II:3), both claimed to be medicine men and were honoured as such in their own faction of Shoshoni society.

These examples show that occasionally the medicine man works like an old-time doctor curing people from the intrusion of pain, the most common healing method among North American Indians.[17] However, as a roadman in the Peyote tipi he mostly abstains from playing an active role in curing.[18] At most he ritually handles the fan, anoints the patient's forehead, and blows on him, as was the case in the Kiowa Peyote healing observed by Schultes. These are vague gestures derived from the old shamanism. For, as noted above, it is Peyote that heals the patient. By eating Peyote, drinking the sacred Peyote "tea", praying to Peyote – together with the other cult members – the sick person becomes convinced that he will regain his health. Peyote is the doctor. In this perspective the

---

[10] Opler 1938, p. 284.
[11] Brant 1950, p. 220.
[12] Aberle and Stewart 1957, pp. 34 ff.
[13] Aberle and Stewart 1957, p. 36. In another connection Stewart mentions however that such cures have not been observed during the Peyote ritual (Stewart 1987, p. 375). Whatever the truth, Stewart notes that there are several common features between old Ute shamanism and Peyotism (Stewart 1986, pp. 676 f.). We hear of Ute Peyotists who later became sucking doctors (Aberle and Stewart 1957, pp. 35 ff.).
[14] Stewart 1987, p. 266.
[15] Stewart 1987, p. 267; cf. op. cit., pp. 178 ff. and passim.
[16] Stewart 1987, p. 375. Cf. also Kroeber 1902–07, p. 405.
[17] Hultkrantz 1989, pp. 341 f., 343 ff., 1992, pp. 159 f.
[18] La Barre 1975 b, pp. 81 ff.

roadman becomes more a priest supervising the ritual than a charismatic medicine man.[19]

The medicine man's role in the growth and development of the Peyote religion is not easy to explain. He certainly was a guiding figure in Mexico and among the Mescalero. But the shift from a cultic ceremony in an ethnic religion to a divergent sect, or an independent religion in its own right, has apparently made his position more ambiguous. In some tribes, as among the Washo, there arose a deadly rivalry between medicine men and Peyotists. It seems that such fights ensued from the fact that the medicine men in such places had a fairly prominent social standing, whereas in other places where the difference between medicine man and common man was slighter, as on the Plains, little rivalry developed.[20]

Peyote's connection with shamanism as illustrated in the foregoing material introduces us to a holistic interpretation of Peyote medicine. In other words, this evidence signifies that Peyote should be regarded as a medicine in the traditional Indian sense – not as a pseudo-rational "pill", as Schultes thinks, but as an ingredient of a supernatural cure.

It is apparent however that Schultes has consciously avoided this interpretation. His article which we have referred to here is directed against Ruth Shonle's effort to prove that Peyote spread as a means of causing visions (cf. Ch. IV:7). As a natural scientist and experienced Peyote investigator Schultes found it imperative to point out the practical, medical implications of the use of Peyote. Although Schultes cautiously talks about "the supposed therapeutic properties of the plant" in the introduction to his article[21] he ends it by stating that Peyote "has been shown to possess actual therapeutic possibilities", whatever that means.[22] In pointing out the supposed medical value of Peyote Schultes is right, to a certain extent. His main fault is that he does not recognize the importance of the general setting in which Peyote is used as a medicine.

At first sight Schultes's thesis is well founded. If we go through the accounts on Peyote we have from former days and more recent times we easily find that most of them relate how people turned to Peyotism either from pure curiosity, or from the desire to be cured from a disease that no other treatment supposedly could heal satisfactorily. It seems indeed that other motives cropped up only secondarily, in retrospect or as later incitaments.[23] Stewart for instance asserts that, since Washo and Paiute Peyotism was first presented and advertised as a curing ritual, "the greatest number of arguments in its favor have to do with its

---

[19] Hultkrantz 1992, p. 140.
[20] See further Ch. IV:10.
[21] Schultes 1938, p. 699.
[22] Schultes 1938, p. 712.
[23] Cf. for instance Aberle 1982 b, pp. 186 f., Stenberg 1946, p. 133, and Stewart 1944, p. 72. Among the Oglala, however, Peyote has lost its power to heal in the present time (Steinmetz 1980, pp. 107 f.). One Oglala sees the purpose of Peyotism in clearing the mind (op. cit., p. 90).

therapeutic value."[24] It is also true that ever so many meetings today are held to cure sick people, or to ensure that the hospital treatment of a sick person will succeed, as I have found to be the case among the Wind River Shoshoni.[25] Verne Dusenberry's main Peyote informant among the Cree of Montana, Tom Gardipee, reported that his people might hold Peyote meetings to ask for the recovery of a sick person, or as the result of a vow if a certain sick person had recovered from an illness. All the night through the attendants of the meeting smoke for him or pray to the Peyote to heal him. According to Gardipee such meetings are just as powerful as the Sun Dance.[26] We may add that the vow to hold a Peyote meeting in case a sick person's health improves is most certainly patterned on the well-known Plains Indian custom of vowing to set up a Sun Dance if a relative or friend recovers from an illness (cf. above, Ch. III:1).

As the Cree example suggests, the emphasis on curing is facilitated if the Peyote procedures can be integrated with extant curative patterns. In spite of the distance and initial enmity between Peyotism and tribal religions the Peyote ritualism slowly and imperceptibly adjusts itself to the old curative patterns, or even absorbs the latter. Schultes has demonstrated this applies to the Kiowa Indians, as we have seen. The Plains Cree are another example. Two more illustrative examples will be adduced, one from the Washo on the Nevada-California border, the other from the Navajo of the Southwest.

Among the Washo the roadman in the Peyote rite has indeed taken over the medicine man's therapeutic functions. He can look into a person and see what is wrong with the latter, he fans the afflicted part of a sick person with eagle feathers, and he removes the disease with prayers. In some respects the patient performs acts which in traditional religion are handled by the medicine man: in traditional religion the medicine man sucks out the disease object and spits it out in the form of, for instance, a snake. In the Peyote ritual it is the patient who vomits up the disease object which appears as a snake, an insect or an inanimate thing.[27]

The Navajo feel that the Peyote religion is a greater threat to their tribal religion than Christianity because in contradistinction to the latter it is a curing religion.[28] As we know the whole traditional Navajo religion revolves around disease and curing. Many long and detailed Navajo ceremonies further therapeutic aims. Here Peyotism enters the same market, so to speak, although in a more charismatic, less ceremonial way. As Aberle says, the Navajo move from one healing religion to another.[29] Only recently the Navajo have tried to

---

[24] Stewart 1944, p. 84.
[25] See also Stewart 1944, pp. 73 ff., 84, Aberle 1982 b, p. 125, and Smith 1974, p. 167.
[26] Dusenberry 1952, p. 177.
[27] Merriam and d'Azevedo 1957, p. 618.
[28] Aberle 1982 b, p. 223.
[29] Aberle 1982 c.

adjust Peyotism to the old indigenous rituals, creating old form rituals around Peyote.[30]

It is obvious that during modern reservation conditions health has come more into focus in ceremonial life than was probably the case in earlier times. Arth attributes the important role of curing in Omaha Peyotism to the high rate of tuberculosis on the Reservation.[31] It is possible that the epidemic diseases introduced by the whites have contributed to the greater emphasis on curing in Indian ritualism during the last hundred years or so. At the same time the earlier Indian occupation with war, hunting, fishing and gathering has more or less fallen into oblivion, and therewith also the rites concentrated on such pursuits. Peyotism with its strong medicinal effects has filled an important function in this development. It has stepped in on the Indian scene at the right moment.

All these facts, not observed by Schultes, speak in favour of his theory of the health concern as the primary appeal of Peyote. And yet, his approach is too narrow; it is the approach of a naturalist rather than that of a student of Indian culture and religion. La Barre was the first to see this deficiency in Schultes's approach. He has repeatedly stressed that the curative functions of Peyote must be seen within the frame of the old vision quest and its religious and culture-ideological premises.[32] As we have stated, Schultes wanted to substitute his "medical" theory for Shonle's "vision" theory. In order to implement this change of causation he was forced to make an artificial, non-genuine distinction between the vision-giving power and the curative functions of Peyote. It was the latter, and not the former, which according to Schultes had facilitated the spread of Peyotism.[33] La Barre points out that it is here that Schultes goes wrong. La Barre, himself a decided protagonist for Shonle, makes clear that the medical properties of Peyote are part of a larger complex, the vision quest. As La Barre accurately says, "Plains 'medicine power' is supernatural in origin (the vision), not pharmaceutical."[34] If Peyote has medicine power it is not because it is a pharmaceutical medicine, a drug, but because it transmits supernatural power (cf. Ch. V:2).[35]

With reference to the opposition in scholarly circles against the alleged role of visions, to which we shall return later (Ch. IV:7), and with due respect to the decisive element in the visionary experience, it is better to underline "super-

---

[30] Gill 1979, p. 21.
[31] Arth 1956, p. 25. Mooney considered that all Indian youngsters coming back from schools in the humid east suffered from weakened lungs, see Stewart 1987, p. 219.
[32] La Barre 1939, 1946, 1960 pp. 45, 52, 54.
[33] Schultes 1938, p. 712.
[34] La Barre 1960, p. 52.
[35] Bee refutes La Barre's interpretation, arguing that hallucinogenic and therapeutic qualities are distinct considerations (Bee 1965, p. 27). He has here unfortunately – and to no small extent because of La Barre's emphasis of vision instead of supernatural power – construed a distinction where there is none. Cf. the following.

natural" rather than "vision". If Peyote had been a medicine among medicines, the user of Peyote could just as well have turned to other medicaments available in a pharmacy. However, he does not do that. He surrounds the use of Peyote with a religious ritual, he even prays to Peyote. It is here a question of a religion, not just the taking of a medicine. In this respect Peyotism is on a par with shamanism for which the medical effect is an application of the religio-magical apparatus.[36]

The ritualistic value of the Peyote and its relationship to an occasional, certainly secondary non-ritual use of the cactus has been correctly appreciated by Aberle who writes, "Peyote is sacred and not to be used for curiosity or amusement, nor casually by people who are not members of the church. It is to be taken ritually, in the right place, at the right time, in the right manner, and for a purpose. It is a sacrament. A member may take peyote outside of meetings for curative purposes."[37] Non-ritual use of Peyote for medical reasons is thus reserved for Peyotists.[38] Perhaps Schultes would have hesitated in his prompt interpretation of Peyote as just a medicine if he had meditated the all-embracing medical use of Peyote. In all groups it is said to be good for everything and anything. For example, Sol Tax indicates that among the Fox the main reason for a person's association with the Peyote religion is the herb's curative efficiency for everything.[39] Such a marvellous medicine is not profane, it is surely supernatural.

In western and southern North America there is a widespread belief among Indians that there are certain plants which radiate powers of an unusual kind. They are often thought of as human beings of different sexes.[40] It is not enough to say, as Radin does, that man's attitude to such plants is the same as ours to medicinal plants.[41] The relationship is far more magico-religious.

The Wind River Shoshoni, for instance, respect and venerate a plant of this dignity which they call *toyaratuwara* ("mountain rose"). Its botanical identification is uncertain: it may be *Primula Parryi,* a primrose growing on the foothills and mountains, possibly a kind of shootingstar *(Dodecatheon).* This plant is supposed to have supernatural power and is consequently very dangerous. It has to be picked after due preparation, including cleansing and meditation. The devotee prays to the plant to aid him and not harm him because he has picked it. It has to be dug up in a prescribed way, and turned with its root upwards. The man who unearths the plant will use the root as a supernatural power which can grant him all kinds of help that he requests, such as healing power against all

---

[36] Cf. my analysis of shamanism and medicine in Hultkrantz 1985.
[37] Aberle 1982 b, p. 180.
[38] Driver and Massey have observed that the non-ritual use of Peyote is most varied and may have many aims, such as divination, reducing thirst, hunger and fatigue, and curing of different types of ailments. See Driver and Massey 1957, p. 270.
[39] Tax 1937, p. 268.
[40] Cf. La Barre 1975 b, pp. 12 note 14, 13.
[41] Radin 1923, p. 419.

kinds of diseases.[42] We have seen (Ch. II:3) how other Plains tribes also pray to magic plants. The same attitude to powerful plants may be noted in many other cases, for instance, at the gathering of *Datura* among the Zuni.[43] And it holds good for Peyote to which a person prays and smokes before cutting.[44]

It has been speculated that such beliefs about plants belong to a specific, partly plant-gathering culture, represented in North America by the so-called Desert Culture which once comprised parts of Northern Mexico, the Southwest and the Great Basin, but in historical times mainly survived in the Basin area.[45] The Desert Culture may be a good operational concept for archaeology, but we know very little about its connection with a specific plant-ideology.[46] The veneration of particular plants as supernatural is most certainly a part of that attitude to psychedelic plants which La Barre has found widespread in aboriginal America (see also Ch. V:2).

Peyote belongs naturally within this context. It has supernatural qualities, and therefore also medical effects.

It is quite another matter that Peyote sometimes may have a clinically observable effect on persons committed to alcoholism.[47] However, this should not be interpreted as proof that Peyote qua medicine cures alcohol addiction. Indeed, La Barres studied an Osage Peyotist who was suffering from alcoholism,[48] and Stewart observed that on the Ute reservations with the highest percentage of Peyotists there is also the largest proportion of problem drinkers.[49] Some medical observers report that former alcohol abusers in Saskatchewan attributed their non-drinking habits to participation in the Peyote religion.[50] Curtis gives a vivid picture of how a Cheyenne Indian was freed from heavy alcoholism through Peyote.[51] Peyote's contribution to health is that as a religion it will demand a personal decision from its practitioners to abstain from competing drugs. The Winnebago John Rave, who introduced Peyote among his tribesmen, gave up drinking in connection with his conversion to Peyotism (Ch. V:1). Radin attributes the abandonment of drinking among Winnebago Peyotists to Rave's influence, and not to the effects of Peyote: when Rave's influence declined the number of Peyotists committed to drinking increased.[52] However, the general attitude is that Peyote demands abstinence from alcohol (cf. Ch. I:3). The Ute and Navajo, for instance, insist that Peyote ethics keep a man from

---

[42] From Hultkrantz, Wind River Shoshoni Field Notes.
[43] Driver and Massey 1957, p. 273.
[44] Stewart 1987, p. 186.
[45] Jennings 1964.
[46] See however Schuster 1964.
[47] Cf. Pascarosa and Futterman 1976. See also Morgan 1983, p. 94.
[48] La Barre 1941, p. 42.
[49] Stewart 1979/80, p. 293.
[50] Roy, Choudhuri and Irvine 1970.
[51] Gifford 1976, p. 47.
[52] Radin 1920, p. 431 n. 126.

drinking,[53] and the Lakota do not want to accept as Peyotists persons conducive to drinking habits.[54] Thus, Peyote may deliver a person from alcoholism, but not as a consequence of its medical properties. Normative requirements for Peyotist followship constitute the basis of Peyote's power at this juncture.

Disregarding this particular issue we are able to state that when Peyote becomes attractive as a medicine it is due to its general supernatural properties. Its supernaturalism is primarily revealed in its marvellous effects on the mind – in particular, the visions – and in its supposed effects on bodily health. Even when doses of Peyote are privately taken as a medicine, it is not a matter of pharmacological assumptions but of religious conviction. The medicinal functions of Peyote cannot be divorced from its general supernatural qualities.

6. Peyote as an Expression of Religious and Ritual Continuity: Peyote and the "Mescal Bean Cult"

The Peyote religion has found its greatest following among the Plains Indians, be it their reservations are still situated in their old hunting grounds or congested in Oklahoma. Peyote scholars have long been aware of this particular adaptation of the Peyote religion to the Plains Indians. There is, of course, the ponderous fact that southern Plains groups were the first to overtake and elaborate the Mexican Indian ritual. We also know that these groups created the outlines of the forms of ritual that are now in use, and that the whole Peyote ritual in many respects evinces the colourful Plains patterning.[1]

Scholars have however gone further than this and tried to prove that Peyote took over religious rituals that had, for a long time, owned much attraction on the Plains. Two rituals have been particularly mentioned, the Red Bean "cult" and the vision quest. Both of them are apparently ancient and vanish in the mists of the prehistoric past.

The Red Bean, or Mescal Bean ritual has been studied by Weston La Barre, James H. Howard, Rudolph Troike, William Merrill and Omer Stewart. They all disagree considerably on the origins of the "cult". To La Barre, this is a ritual that originated from Mexico, spread via the Apache and possibly preceded the Peyote religion in Texas and on the Plains.[2] To Howard, it is the matter of a "cult" that crystallized on the Great Plains. He surmises that it paved the way for the Peyote religion – which he identified as Plains Indian in origin – and

---

[53] Aberle 1982 b, pp. 180, 212, Smith 1974, p. 174. Cf. also Stewart 1987, p. 91.
[54] See for instance Steltenkamp 1982, pp. 64 f.
[1] La Barre 1975 b, pp. 54 ff., 57 ff.
[2] La Barre 1960, p. 48, 1975 b, p. 121. Cf. Ripinsky-Naxon 1993, p. 168.

even provided the ritual model for this religion.[3] As Troike has convincingly argued, the "mescalism", as it has been called, was no real cult, since as far as we know the mescal bean was never an object of worship.[4] Merrill and Stewart go even further, they deny that mescalism in any manner cleared the way for Peyote diffusion.[5]

At this juncture it is appropriate to briefly present the so-called "Red Bean Cult". It surrounds the consumption of a psychotropic plant, *Sophora secundiflora* Ortega, which grows in northern Mexico and the southern parts of Texas and New Mexico. Its range is vaguely similar, but in the north somewhat more extended, to the natural range of the Peyote cactus.[6] It may be described as an evergreen shrub with violet flowers and fruits that hold one to four bright red beans. These contain the highly toxic substance sophorine which, if consumed, may produce nausea, convulsions and even death.[7] The Red Bean, or Mescal Bean "cult" was spread over the Central and Southern Plains. It was upheld by a particular society which had nightly vigils. The members sang while shaking gourd rattles or drumming, and from midnight until dawn they kept drinking a brew of pounded mescal beans. Vomiting was frequent as a result of this drinking. Finally, there was a feast of vegetables in the morning. Common Plains paraphernalia and ritual orientations enveloped the meeting.[8] It is apparent that there is a general likeness to the Peyote ritual.

However William L. Merrill has questioned the assumption that the Mescal Bean could be considered a precursor to Peyote. One of his arguments is that the beans were mostly used as beads, not for consumption.[9] Stewart, referring to Merrill's findings, pays particular attention to the fact that there are no sources for a Mescal Bean ritual in northern Mexico, that few "mescalists" lived within the natural range of *Sophora,* and that most mescalists are to be found north of Oklahoma.[10] He endorses Merrill's conclusion that there is no evidence for an impact of Mescal Bean ceremonialism on the Peyote religion.[11]

It is however difficult to accept this conclusion. The source material is too fragmentary and sparse to allow long-range results. We cannot tell for sure whether an original Mescal Bean ceremonialism occurred in Mexico or not. In any case, it is not important to the problem of whether or not it was a Plains

---

[3] Howard 1957.

[4] Troike 1962, p. 947. The Pawnee kept their red beans in a sacred bundle which was not allowed to touch the ground and was used as good medicine on the war path. However, it was scarcely the object of a cult.

[5] Merrill 1977, Stewart 1979/80, 1980, 1987, p. 8.

[6] Stewart 1980 a, p. 299, fig. 2, 1987, p. 6, map 1.

[7] La Barre 1975 b, pp. 126 f., 218 f.

[8] Reference is here to the Iowa as described in Skinner 1915, pp. 718 f., and to the Pawnee as described by M. R. Harrington in Skinner 1926, pp. 245–247.

[9] Merrill 1977.

[10] Stewart 1979/80, pp. 281 f., 1980 a, p. 306.

[11] Merrill 1977, p. 60.

Mescal Bean ritual that had an impact on Peyote ritualism. If mescal beans were used as beads this does not diminish the value of the historical information that there were mescal bean societies with a ritual around the consumption of the bean. The crux of the matter is, if mescalism preceded Peyotism on the Plains. We have no certain empirical proof that this was the case (although Harrington asserts that it happened among the Pawnee),[12] but the decline of mescalism and quick spread of Peyotism may suggest it. The fact that in historical times few tribes using the mescal bean lived in the natural area of the plant does not prove the contrary. Did not most Peyote tribes reside outside the regions where Peyote grows? When Stewart points out that among the original Peyote groups only the Kiowa Apache have been known to eat mescal beans we may counter with the question of whether or not the impact of mescalism on Peyote ritual could have taken place in other Plains groups.

Perhaps a firmer grip of the matter could be gained by a closer study of the mescalism complex. Howard recognizes two ritual forms, one practised by some tribes who incorporated the "shooting" ritual of the Central Algonkian Midewiwin ceremony, and the other reminding us of the Peyote ritual.[13] Troike suggests a finer classification into four complexes, the Peyote – Mescal Bean ceremony (where the mescal bean is a substitute or supplement), the shooting ceremony which is not an integral part of mescalism, the Mescal Bean medicine society (often with deer ceremonialism), and the deer dance which is an element in some of these medicine societies.

La Barre has accepted Troike's classifications and deductions, and it seems indeed that his presentation throws the right light over the mescalism complex. The important representatives of mescalism are the members of the Mescal Bean medicine society, by Troike defined as "a bundle society of medicine men in which the mescal bean is used for a variety of ritualistic purposes, including intoxication and purification, and in which a deer or elk dance, sometimes associated with hunting and first-fruit ritualism, forms the principal ceremony."[14] Howard's suggestion that the Wichita and Pawnee were probably responsible for the origins of this society tallies with Troike's conclusion from a diffusion analysis.[15] Single elements may have a more southern origin, for instance, the combination of mescal and deer symbolism sounds Mexican Indian (compare Peyote origins!), and the use of the mescal as an emetic was possibly, as both La Barre and Troike suggest, a substitution for the "black drink" of the Southeast.[16] The black drink was associated with first fruit ceremonies,[17] and also with medical cure, just as the mescal bean was in the Mescal Bean medicine

---

[12] Skinner 1926, pp. 245 f. Cf. also La Barre 1979 a, p. 36.
[13] Howard 1957, p. 85.
[14] Troike 1962, p 955.
[15] Howard 1957, p. 84, Troike 1962, p. 956.
[16] La Barre 1975 b, p. 26 n. 17, Troike 1962, p. 956.
[17] See above, Ch. I:2 n. 13.

society. As to bundle societies in general they were as we know a typical Plains Indian phenomenon.[18]

Evidently the integration between mescalism and the shooting ritual of the Medicine Society of the Ojibway and surrounding Algonkian and Siouan tribes seems to be a fairly recent phenomenon. However, the case is more complicated than the above-mentioned anthropologists seem to be aware of. The shooting ritual does not only occur in the Midewiwin,[19] it is also found in the Sun Dance of the Plains Indians, in particular among the Kutenai and Kiowa.[20] Here, a feather containing supernatural power "kills" the dancers, just as the candidates of the Midewiwin are "killed" by the *migis* shells. The killing symbolizes the transference of supernatural power, a transference which is so revolutionary that it demands a symbolical death and renewal-of-life rite. In the Shoshoni Sun Dance, a man who faints from exhaustion while dancing is supposed to be knocked out by the supernatural power inherent in the Dance.[21] The Blackfeet wear a little pouch of leather hanging around their neck, containing a stone. A Piegan Blackfoot informant told me that this is a medicine which a man might achieve by being shut up, together with one of the elders, in a dark tent. There is suddenly wind and voices: the spirits have arrived, they are flying around, and they throw something at the Sun Dance candidate. When the spirits have left he discovers a stone on the floor: that is what afflicted him. My informant added that this was not originally a Blackfoot rite but a new practice that had spread among the Blackfeet and other tribes in the area.[22]

These data underline, I think, the difficulty of arriving at certain conclusions because of the paucity of information. During the last decades field ethnographers have only been slightly interested in the religious complexes of North American Indians,[23] and much material pertaining to the Woodlands-Plains religious continuum has never been written down. If we dare to make an effort at interpreting the sparse and uncertain data that exists we may reach the following hypothetical results. It seems that an ideology of transmission of power through a death and resuscitation ritual has been spread in the Plateau-Plains-Woodlands areas since bygone times, and has been realized in two main ceremonies, the Sun Dance of the north[24] and the Mide-

---

[18] Cf. for instance Wissler 1941, pp. 113 ff.
[19] Hoffman 1891, pp. 215 ff.
[20] Shimkin 1953, p. 406.
[21] Shimkin 1953, p. 425.
[22] Interview in Alberta, 1977. The ritual frame of the shooting rite is here obviously the Spirit or Conjuring Lodge (Cf. Hultkrantz 1981 a, pp. 61 ff.). However, the Blackfeet, like other tribes, lack the shooting rite in their regular Spirit Lodge (Schaeffer 1969, p. 16). Nor does it occur in the traditional Sun Dance, cf. Wissler 1918.
[23] Hultkrantz 1983 b, pp. 59 ff.
[24] The Kiowa are here included among the Northern Plains tribes, since they resided there before the eighteenth century and probably received the shooting feature in their Sun Dance during that time.

wiwin.[25] Indeed, these two great ceremonies may originally, as has been suggested, have been connected with each other.[26] In recent days the death and resurrection ritual has regained new power as a pan-Indian complex. It has, however, its roots in very ancient cultural strata, for it occurs in different parts of North and South America.[27]

If these conclusions hold – and I think they do – the association between mescalism and the shooting ritual could be much older than has generally been supposed. Howard has been interpreted as having traced the mescalist influence on Peyotism from the north, but this was apparently not his intent.[28] It is of course impossible to derive mescalism from the north, but we cannot exclude that a mescal bean society including the shooting ritual has existed for centuries before Peyote appeared on the Plains. Troike's objection that Howard only records two mescal bean groups with shooting ritual, the Omaha and Delaware,[29] is no longer tenable since now also the Kiowa and Prairie Potawatomi can be adduced.[30] Among the Omaha we can possibly study how the connections between mescalism and shooting medicine society took place. Here, the shooting incident is a feature in both the Shell society and the Wichita dance society, the latter of which used the mescal beans.[31] Shall we dare the conjecture that the Wichita dance society took over the shooting ritual from the Shell society? This society is a counterpart to the Midewiwin.

On the other hand, nobody would probably deny that ultimately the use of the mescal bean is of southern extraction. T. N. Campbell informs us that mescal beans, found together with objects which suggest their ritual use, belong to archaeological complexes from the Pecos River (Focus) and the Edwards Plateau (Aspect), dating from between 7500 B.C. to A.D. 1000.[32] Later dates have pinpointed the beginnings of the use of mescal beans to 8440–8120 B.C.[33] Of course, this is no proof of the presence of mescalin at this early date – but it cannot be excluded. Campbell associates the early use of the mescal bean with hunting rock drawings, and La Barre is sympathetic to this idea.[34] However,

---

[25] In an earlier connection I have expressed my skepticism concerning Harold Hickerson's post-contact dating of the Ojibway Medicine Lodge (Hultkrantz 1979, p. 122 n. 12), a dating which now however seems to be taken for granted (Stone and Chaput 1978, pp. 605 f.). My doubts remain. The close connection between the Sun Dance and the Medicine Lodge as evidenced by the shooting act indicates in my view a considerable age of the Medicine Lodge. Two present-day German scholars, Werner Müller (1954, pp. 8 ff.) and Wolfgang Lindig (1970, pp. 76 f.), also emphasize the pre-contact age of the Ojibway Medicine Lodge.

[26] Müller 1954, pp. 135 ff.

[27] Hultkrantz 1979 b, p. 123.

[28] Cf. La Barre 1957, p. 711, 1960, p. 48, Howard 1960.

[29] Troike 1962, p. 947.

[30] Howard 1962, pp. 125, 128 f.

[31] Dorsey 1884, pp. 349 f., Fletcher and La Flesche 1911, pp. 509 ff., cf. Fortune 1932, pp. 110 ff.

[32] Campbell 1958.

[33] La Barre 1975 b, p. 258.

[34] Campbell 1958, p. 158.

interpretations of rock drawings are always a hazardous enterprise, and their connections with ritual practices are extremely difficult to establish.

The following picture seems to emerge. The mescalism appeared north of the Rio Grande before Peyote and was elaborated on the Plains into a ritual on the Plains Indian pattern. In the northern and central parts of the Plains mescalism amalgamated with the shooting rite.[35] The forceful effects of mescal consumption reminded the initiates of a transition to a new state, and the "killing" by shooting expressed the same general idea. The integration between the two complexes indicates, in my opinion, a considerable age for the mescalism on the Plains. In any case, it is probable that the Mescal Bean medicine society paved the way for Peyote in this area.[36] Troike is certainly right when he dismisses Howard's theory of a direct cultural impact from mescalism, except in some smaller details, and instead suggests a previous conditioning of Plains people to the use of the mescal bean, a conditioning which facilitated the diffusion of Peyote.[37] The ritual frame was partly the same for Peyotism and mescalism, set by the common Plains pattern.

What caused Peyote to get the upper hand over mescalism? There were probably two reasons for this. Firstly, the mescal bean belonged to a closed society, its consumption was not open to everybody. Secondly, it has been described as five times stronger than Peyote. A person who drinks the mescal tea sees the world intensely red, loses his sensibility and falls in a coma that may last for hours.[38] This was obviously not a means for bringing man in touch with the supernatural world in an easy way.

7. Peyote as an Expression of Religious and Ritual Continuity: Peyote and the Vision Quest

It was Ruth Shonle who, in an article seventy years ago, was the first to emphasize Peyote's connection with the past Plains culture through its bestowing of visions. Shonle noted that the Peyote religion spread mainly among the Plains tribes, and she found a solution to this mystery in two decisive factors, the impediments of a diffusion further west in the guise of competing new religions

---

[35] Of course we do not know when this happened, but most probably in pre-contact times.
[36] This is also La Barre's opinion, cf. La Barre 1957, p. 710. In this article La Barre even embraced Howard's idea that the red bean ritual shaped the form of the Peyote ritual, a position he abandoned after the publication of Troike's article.
[37] Troike 1962, pp. 958 ff. Among minor cultural influences from mescalism on Peyotism may be mentioned the use of mescal beans for necklaces and belt ornaments, the occurrence in Peyotism of the flicker as spiritual messenger, and the combined or alternating use of the mescal bean in Peyotism among Apache, Tonkawa and Ponca.
[38] Cf. for instance Howard 1962, p. 131.

(like Shakerism in Washington and Oregon) or fixed ceremonial routine (the seasonal division of ceremonies among the Pueblo Indians of the Southwest), and in the vision-giving power of Peyote.[1] As Shonle remarks, visions at puberty occurred in many other areas, but on the Plains also mature men sought visions.[2] The visions produced by the Peyote fitted in with the vision quest of the Plains.

We are reminded here of the fact that the vision quest was a dominating religious custom in large parts of North America. It was the main channel for the individual to attain communication with spiritual powers, to acquire their help and assistance. The most well-known visionary experience was associated with the quest for guardian spirits.[3] The guardian spirit, revealed usually in a sought vision, promised the visionary its own particular powers provided that its instructions and rules were followed. There is no doubt that the guardian-spirit complex had its roots in the oldest American cultural stratum, the hunting culture. It has affinities with the North Eurasian hunting ideology,[4] it is mainly spread among hunting tribes in North America, and it is almost non-existent among profiled agricultural groups, such as the Pueblo Indians. The guardian spirit responded to the needs of the lone hunter.

On the Plains where as we noticed also mature men acquired guardian spirits in visions, often one spirit after another, the vision quest was of primary importance.[5] Whoever glances through Robert Lowie's well-known account of the Crow religion, for instance, cannot escape the impression that this religion was saturated with the guardian-spirit quest and its ideology.[6]

These were the facts to which Ruth Shonle could associate. In her opinion the Peyote religion gained an easy footing on the Plains (in particular) because it produced visions which were equal in importance to the ones received in a regular vision quest. She offered some examples of Peyote visions, but not too many, since she had not waded through the material.[7] Earlier Paul Radin had suggested a collection of accounts of Peyote visions,[8] but nothing of the sort has been done. Nor will it be done here – that would be a Herculean task. However, a reading of Peyote documents from the Plains area gives ample evidence of the occurrence of visions at Peyote séances. Most of them record Peyote visions from bygone days, but there are also accounts of visions from our own time.

For example, there are several instances of Peyote visions among the Oglala

---

[1] Shonle 1925, p. 58.
[2] Shonle 1925, p. 59. Cf. Hultkrantz 1986 a.
[3] Benedict 1923.
[4] Cf. Hultkrantz 1981 b, p. 18.
[5] Benedict 1922.
[6] Lowie 1922.
[7] Shonle 1925, pp. 70 ff.
[8] Radin 1914, p. 20.

Lakota in Steinmetz' presentation of their modern religious scene.[9] Lakota visions may be very powerful. The medicine man Leonard Crow Dog reports that people "get out of themselves, far away, high up in the air, seeing their bodies way down there on the floor."[10] However, there is no reference any more to guardian spirits, as in the old visions. The Minneconjou Lakota Lame Deer, "a medicine man in the old Sioux way", speaking of Peyote, remarked, "I want my visions to come out of my own juices, by my own effort – the hard, ancient way. I mistrust visions come by in the easy way – by swallowing something."[11] He did not dispute, however, that Peyote gave visions.

Several students have accepted Shonle's argument as being the most persuasive and forceful proposition as regards the spread of Peyote. La Barre is entirely convinced. He states laconically that the appeal of Peyote depends on the visions it induces (and which confer medicine and curative power).[12] La Barre's insistence on the importance of visions for the spread of the Peyote religion is however only partially based on Shonle's argument. It is primarily a consequence of his conviction that in America any visionary state, be it a dream or a waking vision, is in itself "a manifest experience of the supernatural".[13] Hence, he goes on, narcotic and other drugs are intimately connected in American Indian religion with "dream-visions and supernatural power".[14] As we shall see, the relations between drugs and religious experiences can be debated (Ch. V:2).

However, La Barre is mistaken in presuming that *any* visionary state involves a supernatural experience. Not every dream or vision communicates a religious revelation. This was pointed out long ago by Lowie,[15] and an unpublished investigation of mine on the subject confirms his conclusions.[16] To adduce one example, the Wind River Shoshoni make a difference between the common dream and the "power-dream" *(puhanavuzieip)*, in which a supernatural being appears and grants powers.[17] The visions of the vision quest are certainly power dreams, and Shonle's discussion concerns this type of visions.

Peyote consumption is not just expected to give dreams, it is expected to give *sacred* dreams, because the perspective is religious. Narcotics like tobacco may be enjoyed without sacred objectives, but Peyote is usually taken in a religious

---

[9] Steinmetz 1980, pp. 94, 95, 97–106. Cf. also the rich material in Steinmetz' unpublished field notes.
[10] Lame Deer 1972, pp. 221 f. Cf. Morgan 1983, pp. 95, 97. Cf. also the similar Omaha vision reported by M. R. Gilmore and quoted by Shonle 1925, p. 71.
[11] Lame Deer 1972, p. 217.
[12] La Barre 1960, p. 45.
[13] La Barre 1970 a, p. 143.
[14] Ibidem. Cf. also Stenberg 1946, p. 130.
[15] Lowie 1915, p. 221.
[16] Hultkrantz, Basic Sources for Eschatological Beliefs among North American Indians (Ms.).
[17] From the author's Wind River Shoshoni Field Notes.

setting. It may, as some individuals put it, "feel good".[18] But it gives religious comfort and visions.

Other students have received Shonle's proposition less favourably. One of the first objections came from Vincenzo Petrullo, the writer of the first book on Peyote. According to him, there could be no comparison between the fasting and self-torture of the Plains vision quest and Peyote visions; furthermore, he found no information available that Peyotists seek individual power.[19] As to the first of these arguments Petrullo misses the central point, namely, that it was just the easy way of acquiring visions that made some Indians so eager to try Peyote. Even so, achieving a vision at a Peyote session has sometimes been considered an ordeal.[20] Petrullo's second argument is a bit doubtful, for the Peyote bulb itself is a source of power to everybody, as the origin myth reveals.[21] "I am the power of Our Father", says Peyote in one origin myth.[22] Among the Reese River (Yomba) Shoshoni of Nevada it is reported that by taking Peyote a person could acquire the power of the rattlesnake.[23] Moreover, a Winnebago serving on a destroyer in the Pacific during World War II carried a bundle of Peyote around his neck. It enabled him to see better than others in a blackout.[24] Similar reports are coming from the Potawatomi, emanating from before the days of their cultic Peyotism: Potawatomi medicine men carried peyote in their medicine bags.[25]

However, Petrullo is right if he means that, as a rule, no Peyote man has a qualitatively different spiritual support than his fellow-believer. Still, it seems less realistic to deny that Indians have sought power in the Peyote ceremony. Religion has always been a matter of power, supernatural power, to the American Indian. And power may come through visions.

Another critic of Shonle's thesis was Bernard Barber. He did not doubt that visions were important in Plains Indian culture as well as in Peyotism, but this in itself could not, he opined, explain the wide diffusion of Peyote.[26] However, there is information that Peyote was taken just in order to produce visions. According to Ruth Landes, Prairie Potawatomi braves consumed Peyote to induce prophetic visions in connection with war parties. This was decades before the elaborated Peyote religion turned up. Often the war leader and his assistant fasted, smoked, and ate the Peyote in pulverized form – because "they were

---

[18] Cf. also La Barre 1975 b, pp. 23 ff.
[19] Petrullo 1934, p. 22.
[20] See for example Stenberg 1946, pp. 129 f. Cf. Vecsey 1988, p. 176.
[21] See Ch. III:2. Cf. also Underhill 1952, p. 143.
[22] McAllester 1949, pp. 14 ff., 17.
[23] Stewart 1987, p. 272.
[24] Stewart 1987, pp. 330 f.
[25] Bee 1966, p. 195.
[26] Barber 1941 b, p. 675.

grown men and often had no teeth" – and thereafter they received visions revealing the numbers and the location of the enemy.[27]

The talented biologist, Richard Evans Schultes, has also opposed Shonle's theory. In his judgment, the Peyote vision is incidental and the medicinal reputation of Peyote fundamental "in the establishment, spread, and, to some extent, in the maintenance" of Peyotism in the United States.[28] In particular he adduces the following five objections to Shonle's argument – objections which however have little bearing power as far as I can find:

(a) Peyote visions are relatively rare. Since Peyote is a hallucinogenic drug this sounds unlikely, particularly when large amounts of Peyote are consumed.[29] Some modern field-workers tell us that no particular attention is paid to visions, and this may be true for the present time, particularly in Peyote communities outside of the Plains area. If the expectancy of visions is suppressed it may happen that none turn up. The present author has received visions (illusions) after having eaten a few Peyote morsels.

(b) Peyote visions are avoided as being wrong. They are indeed, in some non-Plains cultures, and therefore do not appear there.

(c) Proselytes do not mention visions as an appeal. This is in the main correct, but there are exceptions. Through Peyote the Winnebago S.B. was happy to receive the visions he could not have at his puberty fasting.[30] The paucity of information on the subject is due to the fact, underlined by La Barre, that the vision is part of the complex "medicine power", and its function is presupposed in the taking of medicine.[31]

(d) Very early writers do not emphasize Peyote visions. The early source writers, like Sahagún, do occasionally mention visions, but they were probably more observers than participants and thus failed to notice the subjective reactions of the Indians.

(e) Peyote has spread to areas where the vision was of little importance in adult life. This is true; but it is the point of my presentation that the visions primarily facilitated the diffusion of Peyote on the Plains, the center of adult visions.

Even such a good field observer as James Howard tries to play down the importance of visions in Peyotism. He thinks that auditory and visual hallucinations are rare (surprisingly he bases his presumptions here on his own experiences of eating Peyote),[32] and considers that many visions in Peyote séances are not due

---

[27] Landes 1970, p. 192. Similar prophetic visions have occurred among adherents of the Peyote religion, see La Barre 1960, p. 49 (quoting Spindler).
[28] Schultes 1938, p. 704. Cf. above, Ch. IV:5.
[29] Cf. Slotkin 1956 a, p. 41: "...visions are both common and vivid."
[30] Radin 1920.
[31] La Barre 1939. See also Ch. IV:5, 10.
[32] In this work visions have not been distinguished from auditory hallucinations since the auditory element is strong in all Peyote visions, perhaps – as Vecsey thinks – prevailing over the visual element (Vecsey 1988, p. 177). Cf. Ch. II:3 n. 11.

to the hallucinogenic properties of the plant but are due to lack of sleep, hypnotic drumbeating and staring into the fire.[33] Produced by Peyote consumption or through other means, the visions referred to by Howard are actually true visions.

A most cautious attitude to the problem of the influence of the vision quest is taken by Malcolm Arth. He states that visions are not important to later-day Omaha, at least not in the Peyote rituals he has attended. However, he adds the supposition that possibly the element of vision-seeking was more important at the time of the adoption of the Peyote religion than it is today.[34] This seems most probable. Arth introduces here a dynamic perspective on Peyote development which should not be overlooked in the reconstruction of Peyote adoption.

Not unexpectedly students affiliated with the Native American Church disclaim the "vision theory". The Native American Church represents a reorientation of the Peyotism into a "full" religion, an all-encompassing, institutionalized and still spiritual organization. Any reminder that it owes its beginnings to the vision quest is not likely to be approved by all its adherents. On the other hand, the visions of the Peyote religion may be apprehended as a bridge to traditional Indian religion.

This is how J. S. Slotkin evaluated the vision. He considered that the prime reason for the rapid diffusion of the Peyote religion was its program of accommodation between the old and the new, and among the elements of religious adjustment he mentions the visions which, to him, grant the individual socialized help and moral strength. Within the Peyote religion there were two influences that fostered change of the old vision quest: the need for social reorganization, and the adoption of the white man's concept of supernatural aid. The Peyote promised everybody who tried it a vision, one could not fail.[35] All this comes close to the position taken by Shonle.

On the other hand, Omer Stewart completely dismisses the importance of visions to the Peyote ritual. This is strange in view of what his own field data from the Washo and Northern Paiute told him: "Peyote visions of dead relatives in a happy state, of God and Jesus welcoming the Indians in a beautiful land ... are proof that peyotism is the true Indian religion"; "... in most hallucinations the Indians find divine instruction."[36] However, Stewart maintains that only three or four Peyotists share this opinion; most informants think visions are incidental, and seven report seeing nothing. From these statistics Stewart draws the conclusion that "visions are merely part of the religious aspect of the cult", and he takes exception to Shonle's and La Barre's opinions on the importance of visions.[37]

---

[33] Howard 1967.
[34] Arth 1956, p. 26. See also, for the Oglala, Steinmetz 1980, p. 89.
[35] Slotkin 1956 a, pp. 35 f.
[36] Stewart 1944, p. 86.
[37] Ibidem. Cf. Stewart 1987, pp. 91 f. Stewart refers i.a. to the Caddo John Wilson who saw visions as signs of disease (op. cit., p. 92). However, this evaluation may be due to his Christian background.

Now, Stewart's standpoint is certainly influenced by the fact that his field work belongs to the Great Basin area, not to the Plains. He has himself found the vision quest largely failing in traditional Basin religion: with some Northern Paiute exceptions, power was received in unsought dreams, and mostly by becoming medicine men *in spe*.[38] If the waking vision had no particular background in the area it is natural that its importance in the Peyote ritual could be insignificant, and its role as a pathway to Peyotism inconsiderable. Here is the basis of Stewart's generalization that the vision quest has had a slight impact on the spread of Peyote.

David Aberle's discussion of the meaning of visions in the Navajo Peyote religion is very careful. He refuses to comment on the controversy regarding the influence of the vision quest on Plains Peyotism,[39] a problem which he considers requires a closer analysis. He restricts himself to the Navajo Peyotism where, he thinks, visions are not the critical issue. They are, he says, rare, or absent in very many cases, devalued by some Peyote believers, but welcomed by others.[40] Visionary experience is never rejected, points out Aberle.[41] On the contrary, Peyote people complain when they have no visions. The vision is not desired as such, but for its meaning, and particularly as communication with a deity.[42]

That visions should be less highly rated among the Navajo seems to tally with their overall idea that dreams and visions are dangerous and forebode death.[43] Indeed, it is remarkable that the Navajo tolerate, and even wish for visions during the Peyote sessions. Perhaps the accepted use of *Datura* for divination has paved the way.[44] According to Robert Bergman, M.D., Navajo Peyotists seldom experience visions, but when they do, they see beautiful colours in the fire. In times of stress, such visions are more common. Thus, a man praying for his wounded eye saw the water bucket, as it passed around the circle of Peyote eaters, walking towards him as a little woman.[45] Roland Wagner informs us that the Navajo do not as a rule receive visions in Peyote séances because they do hot eat enough Peyote. Their restricted consumption produces "a noticeable alteration of mood, to heighten the senses, but certainly not enough to stimulate full-blown visions".[46] This moderation may be related to the above-mentioned fear of visions.

Aberle's emphasis that it is not the vision as such, but its meaning that mat-

---

[38] Stewart 1941 a, pp. 413, 443. Cf. also Park 1938, pp. 22 ff., and 1934, pp. 99 ff.
[39] Aberle 1982 b, p. 340.
[40] Aberle 1982 b, p. 6.
[41] Aberle 1982 b, p. 219.
[42] Aberle 1982 b, pp. 8 f.
[43] Haile 1940, p. 359.
[44] Aberle 1942 b, p. 219.
[45] Bergman 1971, p. 696.
[46] Wagner 1975 b, p. 200.

ters, seems correct. This meaning can be expressed as God or power.[47] Guy Cooper associates the break-through of Peyotism with the reactions of many Navajo against the exclusive access to power by the specialists of the traditional ceremonies. A more personal access to power is offered in the Peyote religion. Cooper thinks that the Peyote practices are similar to an earlier Athapascan shamanic tradition suppressed by the later (agricultural) Southwestern Emergence Mythology.[48]

If the Navajo possibly revived an older visionary tradition with the Peyotism their neighbours the Pueblo Indians had certainly no such ties with the past. The Pueblo Indians, well-known for their ceremonialism and lack of marked individualism, had little visionary activity, and practically no Peyote rituals (cf. Ch. I:2).[49] La Barre sees in this circumstance a confirmation of Shonle's theory that Peyotism spread where visionary patterns prevailed.[50] He concludes that "the contemporary Indian use to produce hallucinations conforms precisely with the aboriginal vision quest".[51] Peyote, in other words, has supplanted the old vision quest.

At this juncture a closer look at the Peyote situation in the Pueblo Southwest could be instructive. The Pueblo Indians lack the vision quest, except the Indians of the Cochiti pueblo,[52] and even spontaneous visions are not too frequent.[53] The evidence for the pueblo of Taos is conflicting. According to Elsie Clews Parsons, it is the pueblo where the individualism of the close neighbours, the Plains Indians, had its strongest impact.[54] As we know, the Taos Indians were in the past periodically buffalo hunters on the Plains. Parsons did not find any vision pattern among the Taos Indians, but another researcher, Harold Lasswell, did. He states, "Typical visions show the individual as a successful hunter, farmer, trader, orator, lover."[55] In any case, it was in this partly individualistic, partly collectivistic context that Peyotism found inroads. As previously said (Ch. 1:2) Taos is the only pueblo where the Peyote religion has secured a firm footing. The Pueblo situation, and the exceptional case of the Taos will be dealt with in more detail in Ch. VI:4.

With some reservations, then, it is possible to say that a pre-existent vision pattern has contributed positively to the spread of Peyotism. This is far from the claims of a recent symposium on Peyote that there is a general rejection of the

---

[47] Aberle 1982 b, pp. 11, 193. See also below, Ch. V:1.
[48] Cooper 1984, pp. 104, 115.
[49] Benedict 1923, pp. 36 ff.
[50] La Barre 1939. Of course, La Barre also mentions other causes for the Pueblo resistance, such as their repugnance to alcoholic drinks and other psychotropic substances (La Barre 1972, p. 277).
[51] La Barre 1970 a, p. 149.
[52] Cf. Benedict 1923, p. 39.
[53] Cf. Underhill 1948, p. 1. Underhill deviates from Benedict on this point.
[54] Parsons 1936.
[55] Lasswell 1935, p. 237.

view that the core of the appeal of Peyote has been the vision experience.[56] It seems possible to evaluate the influence of the vision pattern of Peyote as follows:[57]

(1) All assessment of the place and meaning of Peyote in Amerindian religion must proceed from the recognition that Peyote is a hallucinogen with the power to create visions, auditions and other extraordinary effects. It would be too hasty to say that it propels religion (see below, Ch. V); but, as Michael Harner has turned it, as a powerful hallucinogen it brings the individual face to face with visions and other overwhelming experiences tending strongly to reinforce his faith in the supernatural world.[58] It is therefore natural that Peyote has easily spread where patterns of visions have been elaborated; indeed, most Peyote accessions have probably developed on the vision patterns.[59] Roland Wagner considers the vision experience to be the only validation necessary for innovations in the Peyote ritual.[60] We may with La Barre say that tribes with such visionary patterns have been "pre-adapted" to Peyotism.[61]

At the same time we must accept, with Aberle, that the vision stands for supernatural power. In the old days it was power from the guardian spirits, in the Peyote context it is power from God, or from Peyote.[62] The Wind River Shoshoni, for instance, had no longer any use of guardian spirits for the common man when the reservation existence took over from the earlier hunting and warring life: the individual protecting spirit was succeeded by the Peyote that promised health and happiness in this new type of existence. Only medicine men continued to find recourse to the old spirits.[63] The vision as such was particularly well qualified in the American Indian milieu to serve as a vehicle of the supernatural message. E. A. Hoebel makes the point that God, as preached about by the Christian missionaries, has always appeared to the Indians as a remote, abstract being. However, he has taken form through the traditional Indian vision experience. "When God speaks through peyote he is an understandable God

---

[56] Lynch 1984, p. 181.
[57] To the following, cf. my points of view in La Barre 1960, p. 57.
[58] Harner 1973, p. xi; cf. also op. cit., p. 51.
[59] Underhill 1957, p. 132. It is symptomatic that the last Oto Indian to receive a puberty vision, Charles Whitehorn, became a leader of Peyote due to this vision (Whitman 1937, p. 82 note, cf. Stewart 1987, p. 120).
[60] Wagner 1975 b, p. 174.
[61] La Barre 1972, p. 277. It should be mentioned that many Peyote songs appeared as parts of visionary states, just as in ancient times a guardian spirit could present his client with a song (McAllester 1949, pp. 36, 47).
[62] Still, Underhill says that Indians in Peyote visions have seen guardian spirits as in the old days; some saw angels, or God (Underhill 1965, p. 267). The Winnebago S.B.:s visions of an eagle and a mountain lion during a Peyote rite (Radin 1920, p. 440) remind us of the experiences during a vision quest, but we do not learn that these beings conferred power on S.B. Most visions have however a Christian reference. For instance, a Pawnee man frequently had visions of Christ during Peyote sessions (Murie 1914, pp. 636 f.). Cf. further below.
[63] Hultkrantz 1981 a, p. 223, 1986 b, p. 45.

who tunes man's emotions to set their spirits soaring."[64] In traditional Indian religion the Supreme Being spoke through the spirit world, in visions.

Aberle creates an unnecessary opposition between vision quest and power search. He insists that repeated recourse to healing religions among former Navajo Peyotists suggests that the search for supernatural power, but not for visions, should constitute the central appeal of Peyotism.[65] As it stands this statement is contradictory, for power may be discharged through the vision channel; the vision mediates the form of power. This stricture does not of course disqualify Aberle's observation that the Navajo have not sought visions as a primary goal in their Peyotism.

(2) Whereas the old vision quest could supply the forms of communication between man and the supernatural in the Peyote religion, in particular on the Plains (where the model for Peyote visions was set), the forms and meanings of the vision changed drastically in Peyotism. This process was accompanied by a proceeding weakening of the importance of visions as the Peyote spread outside the first nuclear diffusion area and the institutionalization of the Peyote movement took form. It is here a question of the old battle between spirit and organization in religious development.

First of all, the vision was reduced to one part of a circumstantial ritual with many other components. The evaluation of its importance changed with time and place, but it was and is mostly a sign of the connection with the religious world. Occasional pronouncements that visions are bad and should be avoided are untypical and usually derive from areas outside the old vision-quest territory.

Secondly, instead of hard-to-get and capricious visions as in the old days, Peyote visions are easily caught – anybody can attain them – and they are not as frightening as the old visions often were. Even the Navajo find that the Peyote vision almost always conveys an assurance of bliss.[66] Moreover, Peyote visions are often stronger and more compelling to the skepticist than are Plains sought visions, and they may reach a truly hallucinatory (not just pseudo-hallucinatory) level.[67]

Thirdly, there is a qualitative difference in content between the visions of the vision quest and Peyote visions. The most general observation is not that the guardian spirit of yore, but current aspects of the supernatural world – God, Peyote, Mother Earth, and so on – are revealed in the Peyote vision. For instance, a Ute Peyotist confessed that "Jesus, as a little man, had descended through the smoke hole of the tipi, had walked on the peyote road marked on the moon, and had assured him that this was the one true Indian religion."[68] Besides, there are other psychic phenomena not usually experienced in the

---

[64] Hoebel 1949, p. 126.
[65] See Aberle's abstract of lecture in Lynch 1984, p. 180.
[66] Cf. Bergman 1971, p. 696.
[67] Hultkrantz in La Barre 1960, p. 57.
[68] Stewart 1948, p. 18.

vision quest that appear, illusions, feelings of unity and sympathy with one's fellow-beings, etc. With reference to the Washo Stewart asserts that the Peyote vision gives no personal power, man considering himself protected by God's power. The vision may expose earlier personal actions, for instance, misdeeds, rather than guardian spirits.[69] This may indeed be true in many cases. We have to reckon with visions changing over time, and with the fact that in areas where the vision quest was uncommon in earlier days visions may evince some deviating features.[70]

8. Peyotism and Pan-Indianism

To many students of acculturation the major value of the Peyote religion lies in the fact that it facilitates the ideological adaptation of Indian groups to a transitional cultural situation – a station on the road between Native Indian and modern Western culture. Characteristically such a religion would preserve many elements of the past which are not only able to survive because they fit in with the new situation, but also may develop into fundamental bricks of the emerging religious structure. However this does not imply that these elements would necessarily be part of the traditional tribal religious system. The main thing is that they express their "Indianness".[1] Underhill for instance heard the Indians say, "to us peyote came, and not to the whites". She adds, "Peyote, it is obvious, gives a wide range of belief, and its real unifying factor is that it is Indian, something for the Red Man alone and which the white can share only with his permission."[2] And Stewart working among the Washo and Paiute assures us that to many of them the Peyote religion "represents the return to a real native faith, containing the teachings of all religions in an understandable Indian form".[3]

Several other researchers have regarded the progress of Peyotism as being

---

[69] Stewart 1944, pp. 82, 85.

[70] Conversely, on the Plains it could happen that vision seekers turned to Peyote séances. Fred Voget mentions how the Crow William Big Day who had accepted Peyotism in a traditional Plains Indian form – the "Tipi Way" with eagle-feather fan for curing and smoking of tobacco in prayer – tried this out. He took a small tipi to the mountains, held a Peyote meeting together with a good friend for three nights and days, and finally had a vision of a spirit in the form of a bird. This was thus a somewhat irregular guardian-spirit quest. See Voget 1984, pp. 131 f.

[1] For the new Indian generations, the "Indianness" of an object, a social fact, a belief is not restricted to tribal heritage, it encompasses all things and states attributed to American Indians in general. The differences between tribes are played down in modern Indian consciousness. Cf. below.

[2] Underhill 1952, pp. 143 f., 147 f.

[3] Stewart 1944, p. 83.

dependent on the fact that it is an Indian religion. Peyotism could achieve a quick acceptance because it is Indian – in contradistinction to the alien Christianity.

We do not need to presuppose that this Indian insight of Peyote's native character resulted from a sudden awareness of a common Indian religious identity. The case was much simpler than that. It was easy to find that the values in Peyotism are Indian: they correspond vaguely to earlier beliefs, but are at the same time somewhat different. The more they reminded Indians of their old tribal beliefs, the quicker the acceptance of Peyotism.[4] But even a vague likeness with other known Indian religious manifestations, Indian-like but not traditionally tribal, could pave the way for the transition to Peyotism.

There is to my knowledge only one case in which a Peyote devotee could have mistaken the Peyote religion for his own traditional faith. If Paul Radin is right in his descriptive account from the Winnebago we face here the most surprising fact that a leading Peyotist could interpret the Peyote religion as just another offshoot of his tribal religion.

This Peyote leader was the famous John Rave who introduced the Peyote ritual among his tribe, the Winnebago of Nebraska. According to Radin Rave's belief in the Peyote was in the beginning coloured by his conviction that it was a version of Winnebago religion. "It seems to have been similar to the average Winnebago attitude toward a medicinal plant obtained either as a gift or through purchase. There is only one new note – stimulation by a narcotic [sic]. ... His attitude throughout, both from his own testimony and from that of others, seems to have been practically the attitude of the Winnebago shaman. He even offered tobacco to the peyote."[5] Radin discerns here an extension of the Winnebago cultural background, "there was hardly anything new at all". Consequently, John Rave did not, at the beginning of his Peyote practice, develop any antagonism against his old culture.

However, his attitude changed. When Radin first met him in about 1910[6] Rave showed a violent hatred toward the old Winnebago customs. He discarded "all the ceremonies that they [the Winnebago] were accustomed to perform before".[7] This new attitude was probably not brought about by influences from the Christian religion on Peyotism, for Albert Hensley and his Christianized version of Peyotism had not yet appeared on the scene. It probably rather reflected the increasing hostility of the tribe towards Peyote, and the opposition against John Rave's assuming the role of a tribal leader and reviver.[8]

In this case, then, the Peyote leader "discovered" that his religion deviated

---

[4] The anthropological rules for the spread of innovations (as laid down by Sapir, Linton, Barnett and others) are well-known and will not be commented upon here. Cf. also modern communications theory.
[5] Radin 1923, pp. 419 f.
[6] In 1910 according to Radin 1950, pp. 253, 290.
[7] Radin 1923, p. 393.
[8] Radin 1923, p. 420.

from the religious heritage of his tribe, and therefore turned against his own traditions. In all other cases known to me Peyote converts have been well aware of the differences from the outset. The gap has been obvious. Only the lapse of time has made Peyote compatible – but not identical – with autochthonic tribal religion.

If the label Indianness has been confusing to an Indian Peyote leader it has certainly not always been clear to those who investigate Peyotism. The foreign derivation of the Peyote religion among societies north of the Rio Grande is of course registered by these writers, but somehow some of them have taken it for granted without regard to its implications. From their point of view the exogenous origin of Peyotism is of little consequence. They satisfy themselves with stating that through its Indian origins Peyotism suits the specific conditions in an Indian acculturative situation. It happened to be there at the right moment, and served as a convenient expression for Indian religious and ethnic tendencies just then. Even such a competent field researcher as James Mooney describes Kiowa religion about 1890 as a unit, mixing old tribal beliefs with Peyote notions.[9]

This disregard for the analytical importance of the otherness of the Peyote religion is remarkable. However, it is even more disturbing when an investigator, and a field researcher at that, is unable to see the difference between Peyote and tribal religion.

Molly Stenberg, writing about Peyotism among the Shoshoni and Arapaho Indians of Wyoming (cf. above, Ch. II:1), thinks of it in terms of an asset strengthening the old traditional religions. She assures us that the Peyote religion is "the last remaining pattern of an old culture, which the Indians have grasped as an anchor against the engulfing tide of the imposed white culture."[10] She notes that it is flourishing among the fullbloods "who are most interested in maintaining a vestige of their heritage",[11] and she unveils prophetically, like many others, that the need for the religion will disappear in the modern world. In the progressive dissolution of Indian culture "the Peyote Cult is manifestly a transitional link".[12]

It is possible to observe that here Stenberg has confused two different aspects of Indianness, tribalism and pan-Indianism. By "tribalism" in this context I mean here the guard of inherited tribal values, and by "pan-Indianism" the embracement of shared common values of (supposedly) all Indian tribes.[13] We shall soon return to the concept of pan-Indianism. What matters here is that under no circumstances may the Peyote religion be interpreted as a manifestation of tribalism.

---

[9] Mooney 1898, pp. 237–239.
[10] Stenberg 1946, p. 136. The reader should observe Stenberg's expression in the title of her paper: the Peyote culture.
[11] Stenberg 1946, p. 137.
[12] Stenberg 1946, p. 136.
[13] On the definition of pan-Indianism, see further below.

The account of Shoshoni Peyotism in a preceding context (Ch. II) should have demonstrated the untenability of Stenberg's thesis. We remember how Shoshoni Peyotists, while formally keeping up the old tribal religion, turn against its foremost representatives whom they dismiss as "unworthy" or "no good", how they depreciate the traditional Sun Dance when compared with the Peyote ritual, and how they deny the existence of a real Shoshoni religion before the arrival of Peyotism. It is difficult to see how Miss Stenberg could have reached her conclusions in this particular setting.

A comparison with the Navajo religious situation is rewarding. Aberle writes that "peyotism, with a transcendent God approached by his dependent worshippers and taking an active interest in their moral behavior, stands point for point contrasted with Navaho religion, with immanent spirit approached in reciprocity and punishing only for the transgression of tabus. Peyote prayers are spontaneous, Navaho prayers are compulsive spells. Peyotist dead have spirits which go heaven; Navaho spirits stay around and make trouble or go to a drab and little-described afterlife."[14] No wonder therefore that one and the same individual who tries to keep up both faiths – a situation that also occurs among the Shoshoni (cf. Ch. IV:12) – makes a clear distinction between them. There is indeed no syncretism on this level.[15]

We shall have reasons to return to the important question of the relations, in Indian consciousness, between traditional religion and Peyotism.

The distinction between the Peyote religion and tribal traditional religion actualizes a terminological problem most conspicuous in a discourse on acculturation: may we characterize the strong upholding of a religion that is not part of the tribal heritage, but taken over from outside, as "nativistic" in Linton's sense?[16] Several students have done so, perhaps a bit too hastily, for Linton's concept has to be remodeled in order to justify a phenomenon like Peyotism. As I have noted before (see Introduction), Peyotism does not represent a conscious revival of selected aspects of traditional culture: it is not except in marginal cases the result of deliberate actions, and it is in no sense a perpetuation of tribal culture. In an earlier connection I have accepted an extended version of Linton's concept as suggested by Voget who talks of "reformative nativism", that is, a subordinated group's effort to create a new integration based on a combination of traditional and alien cultural components.[17] In this sense the Peyote religion may be characterized as "nativistic".[18]

---

[14] Aberle 1982 b, p. 198; cf. also op. cit., pp. 202, 353.

[15] Aberle 1982 b, pp. 198 f.

[16] Linton 1943, p. 230. Cf. the discussion in the Introduction, above.

[17] Voget 1956, p. 250.

[18] It is apparent here that attention has moved away from the religion as such to the general values it is thought to express, within the frame of culture, in a specific situation characterized by national subordination. Slotkin's concept of "nativistic nationalism" covers this condition even better, cf. Slotkin 1956 a, p. 6.

It is perhaps even better to abstain from clichés altogether, to simply define the Peyote religion as a movement bringing together tribal and alien values in a new functioning unity. Malcolm Arth has made an effort to elucidate the social meaning and typological classification of Peyotism. He contends that it constitutes "a reaffirmation of in-group feelings" at the same time as it represents an attempt to recapture or maintain the old way of life.[19] The basic quality of the Peyote religion is thus its "Indianness".[20] There is, however, no clear understanding of the import of the alien extraction of this religion.

The presumption that the Peyote religion preserves the old way of life is not indisputable. Referring to the Navajo Aberle rules out this possibility. "For the first-generation peyotist", he writes, "peyotism is not an effort to retain traditional culture. It involves a sharp break with this culture, often with belittling of traditional religio-magical figures and practices." Aberle – who operates with the concept Native culture, and regards Native religion as an aspect of such a culture – therefore criticizes the tendency to consider Peyotism more in terms of cultural retention than in terms of cultural innovation.[21]

However, conditions are more complicated than Aberle seems to think. Firstly, as we have seen in the foregoing, there is a differential attitude to tribal religion among Peyotists, depending on their tribal integration, the character of the old religion, and the cultural ethos. Secondly, Aberle has overlooked the fact that *cultural identity* need not automatically be bound up with *traditional tribal religion*. Dysfunctional religion may indeed be a burden to ethnic coherence. The abolition of the old Hawaiian religion in 1819 is a case in point.[22] In North America, Coastal Algonkians have thrown off most of their tribal religious heritage without giving up their ethnicity. If in a situation of social change it is felt that traditional religion fails to meet new demands it will be either transformed, or substituted by new religious ideas which, however, usually have some general relation to old religious patterns. Peyotists generally want to strengthen their cultural heritage, in a selective way, but tend to disregard much of their religious past that is not suitable for reinterpretation in Peyote terms.

It is against this background that we must evaluate Miss Stenberg's conclusions. When introduced in Wyoming the Peyote religion expressed "nativistic" tendencies, but these were of a wider scope than just a rejuvenated tribalism; indeed, they pointed to a new, all-Indian cultural perspective.

The vacillation between tribalism and Peyotism is not restricted to the Shosh-

---

[19] Arth 1956, p. 26.
[20] As Vecsey (1988, p. 190) puts it, "peyotism has given hundreds of thousands of Indians an opportunity to express not only their religiousness but also their Indianness".
[21] Aberle 1982 b, p. 340. It should be noted that here Aberle discusses Peyotism in general, not just Navajo Peyotism.
[22] See for example Davenport 1969.

oni and Arapaho but has parallels elsewhere. The fullbloods of the Northern Ute back up old cultural ways at the same time as they are Peyotists.[23] The same connection between Peyotism and cultural revivalism characterizes the Southern Ute.[24] The Oglala Lakota have many individuals who "move back and forth between traditional Lakota ceremonies and Peyote meetings according to what best fulfills their needs at the time".[25] And the Cree of Montana consider that, since we are all the Great Spirit's children, a man can be at the same time a Catholic, a Sun Dance leader and a leader of the Peyote congregation.[26]

The Peyote religion is not ethnic, it is intertribal, and was so from the beginning. As even Stenberg observes, in Wyoming the Peyote religion was for long "the only Indian-initiated activity that cuts across tribal lines".[27] A direct expression in institutional forms of this intertribalism is the Native American Church which, like its Christian prototype, has a gospel transcending ethnic boundaries. The Church organization (which is, certainly, of a loose federative kind) has its prerequisites not only in the Christian model but also in the widespread sentiment of common Indianness that has pervaded the Native American world after the end of the Indian wars.[28]

The concept corresponding to this new sentiment is "pan-Indianism".[29] It has been used on several occasions in the past but was definitely introduced as a scientific concept by the late James H. Howard in an article on tribal exchange in Oklahoma (1955).[30] Howard defined pan-Indianism as one of the final stages in "progressive acculturation" in North America, a stage preceding complete cultural acculturation. Its characteristic is that a "super tribal culture" has become established after the loss of tribal identity. The "powwow" has been mentioned as the main social expression of pan-Indianism,[31] and Peyotism as its particular religion.[32] Robert K. Thomas – who somewhat rashly interprets pan-Indianism as an attempt to create a new ethnic group, the American Indian[33] – regards it as a Plains Indian movement. He thinks that the great spatial mobility of these Indians was an important factor in the rise of pan-Indianism.[34] At

---

[23] Jones 1955, pp. 229, 232.
[24] Marvin K. Opler in La Barre 1960, p. 57.
[25] Steinmetz 1980, p. 165; cf. also Lame Deer and Erdoes 1972, pp. 63, 216 f. The latter reference concerns the Minneconjou Lakota.
[26] Dusenberry 1962, pp. 178 f.
[27] Stenberg 1946, p. 93.
[28] Actually, the same feelings had already fired Pontiac and his men, cf. Josephy 1962, pp. 110 f.
[29] The question whether pan-Indianism is, as Washburn says, just a "stopping place" in American Indian development will not be discussed here. Cf. Washburn 1975, p. 251.
[30] Howard 1955.
[31] Cf. Powers 1980, p. 223, and Sanford 1971, p. 222.
[32] Hertzberg 1971, p. 284.
[33] Thomas 1968, p. 77.
[34] Thomas 1968, p. 79.

the same time, Plains culture traits were generalized as expressing this Indianness. The urbanization of the Indians has promoted this development. Thomas concludes, among other things, that pan-Indianism has formed a healing bridge between factions.[35]

As will be shown in the sequence, modern Peyotism may be considered a Plains cultural phenomenon (cf. also Ch. IV:6, VI:3). In so far as pan-Indianism is Plains Indian it is also closely allied with Peyotism. Indeed, one could say that the history of the Peyote religion and pan-Indianism are to a great extent identical. Howard thinks that pan-Indianism as a conscious movement started about 1920 in Oklahoma, and Powers seems to imply that it culminated about 1955.[36] This is to my understanding also the time when Peyotism reached its apex in North America. What has since followed has the contours of a more irregular pattern, involving trends which are both pan-Indian and revivalistic in a tribal context.[37] In religion, this situation corresponds to the coexistence of Peyotism and a renewed tribal religion on a pan-Indian basis.

The pan-Indian qualities of Peyotism are apparent, but there is some uncertainty about what they exactly mean to the devotees. Stewart tells us that to many Washo and Northern Paiute the Peyote religion represents "the return to a real native faith, containing the teachings of all religions in an understandable Indian form."[38] As far as I know this standpoint is exceptional. The rule is simply that, as Aberle puts it, "both in terms of practice and ideology, peyotism is pan-Indian."[39] And Grant, writing on the Kiowa Apache, testifies that Peyote is the religious symbol of pan-Indianism.[40] In other words, the Indian religious heritage has its adequate expression in Peyotism. This conviction contrasts with that of the anti-Peyotists who see Peyotists as dissenters, breaking Indian unity.[41]

Pan-Indianism manifests itself emotionally in Peyotist behaviour. Anyone who has attended a Peyote meeting can observe how sympathy and radiant friendliness set their stamps on the relationships between Peyote participants

---

[35] Thomas 1968, p. 83.
[36] Powers 1980, p. 224.
[37] Cf. Lurie 1968, p. 201.
[38] Stewart 1944, p. 83.
[39] Aberle 1982 b, p. 335; also p. 18. As Aberle points out, sophisticated Navajo Peyotists have chosen an Indian, not a Navajo, identity (p. 351). Cooper thinks he can see a factionalism here between young Peyotists interested in pan-Indianism and traditionalists guarding their Navajo identity: Cooper 1984, pp. 108, 111 n. 107, 116.
[40] Brant 1950, p. 222.
[41] Washo traditionalists detest Peyotists because they dissolve old social loyalties (Merriam and d'Azevedo 1957, p. 616) – a natural reaction in a group whose aboriginal religion is on the verge of vanishing (Downs 1966, pp. 103 f.). Western Shoshoni traditionalists who trace Peyote power from the rattlesnake and the coyote consider Peyotists to be witches (Lieber 1972). Aberle states that in the Navajo community Peyotism has become a centre for factionalism (Aberle 1982 b, p. 221).

from different ethnic groups. Newcomb testifies that Cherokee-Delaware Peyotists in Oklahoma feel closer and more friendly to Peyotists from other tribes than to their own tribesmen who are not Peyotists.[42] My Peyote-taking Shoshoni informants admitted openly that they made similar preferences. Information from other tribes is no different. In some tribes, such as the Delaware, whites were initially not permitted to take part in Peyote meetings.[43] However, where whites are welcome they are treated just as well as other guests, according to my own experience. This is logically seen as modification of the pan-Indian basis of Peyotism. It seems that the love of mankind fostered in the Peyote circle has overruled Indianism.

Of all Peyote-taking tribes only the Navajo, as far as I know, show little practical interest in pan-Indianism.[44] One reason for this could be that they are the most numerous tribe of the United States, and are very much taken up with their own troubles. Another cause could be that pan-Indianism as was said above has its strongest support on the Plains. Another ethnic group, the Oglala Lakota, have two confessional Peyote denominations with different responses to pan-Indianism. In the circles of the Half Moon Fireplace which retains many traditional Lakota symbols there is a strong sense of pan-Indian identity, whereas in the Cross Fire congregation, which emphasizes a Christian interpretation, the identity is Lakota rather than pan-Indian.[45]

From all the evidence we have it seems that pan-Indianism and Peyotism have belonged together from the very moment that the Peyote movement emerged as a brotherhood over the tribal boundaries, that is, with the organization of the Native American Church. It is probably no coincidence that this Church was formed at about the same time as in Howard's opinion pan-Indianism became a reality.

In her pioneering study on the Peyote religion Ruth Shonle has tried to illuminate the rise of pan-Indianism in Peyotism (cf. Ch. IV:2). She points out that the Ghost Dance, the messianic revivalism that followed the defeat of the Plains Indians in the Indian wars,[46] provided vivid intertribal contacts. These friendly relationships represented something new on the Plains where earlier tribal wars had been part of the pattern of life. The reservation life, and the common opposition to white supremacy, paved the way for this new pan-Indianism. However, the Ghost Dance took on a militant and destructive, anti-white direction, culminating in the so-called Sioux uprising in 1890, and was crushed in the massacre at Wounded Knee. In the vacuum that followed the Peyote Way

---

[42] Newcomb 1955, p. 1042. Newcomb assesses Peyotism as one of the strongest elements furthering Cherokee-Delaware pan-Indianism (p. 1044). He also reports that Peyote meetings are always held together with Indians of other tribes.
[43] Petrullo 1934, pp. v f.
[44] Cf. Aberle 1982, b, pp. 222 f.
[45] Steinmetz 1980, pp. 164, 166.
[46] See Mooney 1896.

stood for a compromise with the whites and a continued pan-Indianism that could be deepened and intensified.[47] From this point of view the Peyote religion and its organized backbone, the Native American Church, could for a long time be seen as the major means to communicate pan-Indianism.

There is certainly much that could speak in favour of this kind of interpretation. It has been accepted by such an authority as La Barre.[48] There is however not much evidence that pan-Indianism is a consequence of the Ghost Dance: rather the other way round. Furthermore, Peyotism antedated the Ghost Dance (see Ch. IV:13). It is true that Peyotism could become integrated in the Plains war complex, but it also could have expressed an amicable side. There is, as I see it, great probability that the Peyote religion spread from the eighteenth century and onwards because of the peaceful, intertribal relations that it promoted through its uniform organization and freedom from tribal bonds. After the Indian settlement on reservations these peaceful relations turned into strong feelings of friendship over the tribal boundaries. There is no doubt that Peyotism profited from these sentiments in its further distribution over North America. Pan-Indianism was the natural outcome of the process.

Certainly, in some cases even the Ghost Dance contributed to pan-Indianism, for instance by stimulating relations between Plains and Basin-California Indians. Moreover, its message was that of a close concord between Indian tribes, with the exclusion of the white society – a concord that could mean peace in its western but war in its eastern areas of influence. Slotkin concludes that the Ghost Dance failed because it had a program of opposition, whereas the Peyote religion succeeded thanks to its program of accommodation.[49] We may also say that it was the *friendly* side of the growing pan-Indianism that gained the upper hand in the long run.

It seems that better than anybody else Slotkin has expressed the close relationship there is and has been between Peyotism and pan-Indianism. He defines the Peyote religion as a pan-Indian defense mechanism against white domination – in a mild, accommodating spirit – and singles out intertribal solidarity, intertribal peace ethics and intertribal visiting as the great achievements of pan-Indianism. He thinks that pan-Indianism was furthered by the similarity of cultural conditions on the Plains, both before and after reservations had been established, and by the breakdown of social control and, thus, of traditional tribal customs. The Peyote religion was and is one of the most efficient instruments in this process.[50]

It is indeed difficult to disentangle Peyotism from pan-Indianism. They go together, and instead of pondering over which one was the cause and which one

---

[47] Shonle 1925, p. 57.
[48] La Barre 1975 b, p. 113.
[49] Slotkin 1956 a, p. 21. Cf. our analysis below of the historical relationship between the Ghost Dance and the Peyote religion (Ch. IV:13).
[50] Slotkin 1956 a, pp. 18 f. Slotkin sees it as a fellowship in spirit intersocialization.

the result we should look for the common factors that produced both of them. Slotkin has pointed out some of these factors. Pan-Indianism is not the object of investigation in this work, but it should certainly be possible to find several common denominators of Peyotism and pan-Indianism in this study.

9. The Facility of Peyote Religion

When the Peyote religion spread at the expense of traditional tribal religions it was not only because of its better accommodation to a new situation or the real or supposed qualities of a new drug. The Peyote religion had a structure that made it easily accessible in a time of crisis.

This observation should not lead us to underestimate the tenacious and surviving capacities of the old tribal religions. The breaking up of the traditional tribal life, particularly on the Plains, and the move to sometimes new hunting grounds after the Indian wars certainly weakened these religions which were firmly anchored in the socio-political system and environment of their old hunting grounds. It is indeed remarkable that these religions have been able to survive at all, considering the destruction of tribal life, the prohibitions of white authorities to conduct old-time ceremonials (such as the Sun Dance), and the transformation of values in the modern Indian world. We have even seen these religions becoming revived in the 1960s and 1970s, certainly devoid of many old rituals and belief traditions that have fallen into oblivion, but focused on some major ritual traditions which have been elaborated and reinterpreted with new symbolism.

However, at the beginning of this century Peyotism looked more active, more vigorous, more promising. In comparison to tribal religions it undeniably offered many advantages: besides being well adapted to a changed cultural situation it could be shared by Indians of many tribes, and it presented a unified religious complex, whereas tribal religions are often dissolved in diverse configurations of belief.[1] In particular, the Peyote religion is generally simpler than the traditional religions, and consequently easier to learn.

This facility of the Peyote religion has repeatedly been expressed by investigators of Navajo religion. Thus, Aberle points out that among the Navajo Peyotism with its simple ritual and lack of dependence on elaborate learning and training in a complicated mythology has a great appeal to untrained worshippers.[2] As we know, Navajo ritual and mythology is indeed very complicated, many ceremonies being performed during nine nights' singing of sacred

---

[1] Cf. Hultkrantz 1981 a, pp. 28 ff.
[2] Aberle 1982 b, p. 204.

chants which are parts of myths. Roland Wagner similarly clarifies that the very brevity of the Peyote ritual among the Navajo, and its simplicity, makes it easy to be adopted as a unit, and promotes the retaining of its ritual integrity.[3] Also Guy Cooper reasons along the same lines, emphasizing that in a faster and more mobile world the Navajo experience the Peyote ritual as being "shorter, simpler, less expensive and more spontaneous than traditional ceremonialism".[4]

The Navajo are of course an extreme case, but similar observations have been made among other tribes. Petrullo tells us that one Delaware Indian complained that his old tribal religion was too "heavy", that is, too demanding, for present-day Delaware, whilst he found Peyotism easy in comparison.[5]

It would not be difficult to demonstrate that the Peyote ritual is very elementary when compared with the elaborate rituals of the tribal religions in most areas under consideration here. The obvious exceptions are the Great Basin religions which, for ecological reasons, have had a most limited ceremonial development.[6] It has been pointed out before that the intricate ceremonialism is a characteristic trait of American Indian religions, particularly in the Southwest and east of the Rocky Mountains.[7] Why this is so will not be discussed here – it is obviously a case of a special patterning. The simpler structure of Peyote ritualism is expressed in its short duration (one night), its lack of standardized song contents, its few ritual gestures and opportunities for individual digressions. James Howard rightly concludes that "the ritual itself, well-designed, simple, yet uniquely beautiful and moving is one of the principal reasons why the Peyote religion remains so popular with American Indian groups."[7a] Perhaps this beauty should be further stressed (cf. Navajo rituals which are said to restore beauty). There is no doubt that the simplicity and beauty of the ritual scheme has been promoted by Peyote's intertribal, pan-Indian scope.

The same simplicity characterizes Peyote belief systems. In an appreciation of the Peyote religion on the Plains the German ethnologist Horst Hartmann calls it "a cult without dogmas". Since there are no generally applied prescripts, he continues, each Peyote group may insert its own traditional beliefs in their Peyote faith.[8] There are truly no dogmas – but nor are there any in the old tribal religions. We must make a distinction here between dogma and ideology. Traditional Indian religion has no dogma in the sense of a fixed, closed doctrinal system, but it has an ideology: a world view, tenets about gods and spirits, and so on. Similarly, a Peyote *dogma* should not be expected among North Ameri-

---

[3] Wagner 1975 b, p. 174.
[4] Cooper 1984, pp. 103 f.
[5] Petrullo 1934, p. 76.
[6] Cf. Hultkrantz 1976, pp. 144 f.
[7] See Lowie 1960, Hultkrantz 1981 a, pp. 51 ff.
[7a] Howard 1967.
[8] Hartman 1973, pp. 246, 247. On the uniformity of Peyote ideology, cf. below.

can Indians, not even in the organized Native American Church. However, a Peyote *ideology* would seem necessary. Otherwise, how could the Peyote ritual have a meaning?[9]

George Spindler nevertheless questions whether there really is a common ideology in the Peyote religion. He notes continuity and persistency in Menomini Peyotism, but is uncertain whether there is a general program.[10] The lack of a chapter on ideology in La Barre's *The Peyote Cult* may have contributed to a certain bewilderment here.[11] Peyotists often decline to instruct the field worker about their beliefs, but ask him to take part in the meetings and eat Peyote, experience it. That is, they insist, the only way to understand Peyote.[12] Apparently, the Indian view is that the experiences themselves feed the correct beliefs. This is a consequent religious evaluation.

Still, there is a unifying ideology, a doctrine. Although the Peyotists themselves may express it carelessly – "we all worship the same God and all eat peyote" (Navajo)[13] – observers with deeper insights into the Peyote religion have tried to formulate certain common elements. Sometimes they proceed from some central concept, as Stewart has done. He maintains that the purpose of this religion is to heal and protect human beings "through the worship of God by means of peyote", and then goes on to discuss the theology and the symbolism of Peyote.[14] Others, like Slotkin, prefer a tabular overview.[15] A detailed analysis of the doctrine has been made in the foregoing and need not be repeated here (Ch. I:3). It emerged that the world of powers according to Peyotists is made up of some constantly recurring supernatural beings, and also, a great many spirits of apparently tribal origins differing from tribe to tribe. The pantheon is thus fairly amalgamative, to use Underhill's term,[16] and thereby evinces a structure deviating from ordinary tribal pantheons. This may call for conflicts.

This is confirmed when we hear about ideological clashes between Peyotists and non-Peyotists. It has been mentioned that the Peyote-taking Wind River Shoshoni tend not to believe in guardian spirits, and we know that differences in opinion between Peyotists and tribalists in the same tribe provoked much trouble in the beginning.[17] The same situation has existed among the Washo on the boundary between Nevada and California: the Peyotists fought the shamans

---

[9] I agree of course with Kurt Rudolph that the ideology of a religion only takes in conceptions, ideas, beliefs. See Rudolf 1978, p. 22.
[10] Spindler in La Barre 1960, p. 57.
[11] On this issue, cf. La Barre's statement in La Barre 1975 b, p. xviii n. 1 (discussing my criticism in La Barre 1960, p. 57).
[12] Cf. for instance Slotkin 1956 a, p. 75. Aberle 1982 b, p. 335, Stenberg 1946, pp. 128, 132. My own Shoshoni informants told me the same thing.
[13] Aberle 1982 b, p. 19.
[14] Stewart 1944 p. 64.
[15] Slotkin 1956 a, pp. 68 ff.
[16] Underhill 1957, p. 135.
[17] Hultkrantz 1981 a, pp. 219 f.

and their religious influence, and the old-style visions were suppressed.[18] In the long run this discord entailed the decline of Peyotism.

In other places where local beliefs did not deviate basically from the Peyote ideology, or where they were thought to fit in with the latter, the gulf between Peyotism and tribal religion could be more easily overbridged. The rule is that traditional ethnic beliefs should not be adopted (or rather, retained) by Peyotists if they deviate from the central core of Peyote ideology. The ideological position of Peyotism is well exemplified on the northern Plains where "each local group follows the general pattern, although variations in minor detail of ritual and belief are characteristic".[19]

It would be wrong however to consider the Peyote ideology as such an obstacle in the dissemination of Peyote religion. To those who were not fixed in their old traditional beliefs it offered a simpler way of experiencing an encounter with the supernatural – simpler than the vision quest which required abstinence and suffering and often involved spirit powers of a tricky or even dangerous disposition. It is important to stress in this connection that the ideology was primarily realized in the ritual setting, in the mysterious experiences of the Peyote rite. This is a general Indian attitude to religion. That is why it may sometimes appear, as it did to George Spindler, that Peyotists have no formalized ideology.

In one respect the Peyote ideology delimits itself sharply from old tribal patterns, in ethics. Slotkin makes "the Peyote road" include such universal values as brotherly love, care of family, self-reliance and avoidance of alcohol.[20] We notice the difference with tribal ethics on two scores. In contents, the stress on love, on strict family relations (no extra-marital associations allowed) and on abstinence from alcohol contrasts Peyote ethics to many traditional ways of living. More important still, in basic structure these ethics are adjusted to the pan-Indian demands on the reservations.[21] Aberle has correctly stated that these ethics express the individualism in societies whose kinship organization and social control system have broken down.[22] It is possible to go one step further and say that in the vacuum of tribal disintegration universalistic Christian values have formed vital parts of the ethical program (regardless of whether they were acknowledged as Christian or not). No doubt these individualistic, ultimately Christian-inspired ethics must have paved the way for the acceptance of Peyotism in the new reservation societies. However, this is of course very difficult to prove.

---

[18] Merriam and d'Azevedo 1957, p. 617. Stewart states that "aboriginal Washo-Paiute beliefs have found very little place in the ideology of peyotism" (Stewart 1944, p. 81, d'Azevedo 1986, p. 496; cf. Stewart 1986, pp. 679, 680, and 1987, pp. 273 ff.; Hultkrantz 1992, pp. 144 ff.).
[19] Hurt 1960, p. 16.
[20] Slotkin 1956 a, p. 71.
[21] Aberle 1982 b, pp. 15, 336.
[22] Aberle 1982 b, pp. 16, 202.

We conclude: the mythological doctrine and the ethics of the Peyote movement are concrete and easy to handle. They differ sometimes profoundly from tribal ideology, and thus may invite religious factionalism. In particular they constitute, together with the simple ritualism, an enticing alternative to the often multistructured tribal religion, especially for those who are not too committed to the old religion.

10. The Role of the Peyote Proselytizer

Some authors have stressed the importance of charismatic personalities in the diffusion of the Peyote religion. In particular we may here mention Omer Stewart, but also C. I. Malouf, M. K. Opler, C. J. Couch and J. D. Marino belong here.[1] This gives us reason to ponder upon the leading roles of the Peyote movement.

It has been said before, and it could be repeated here, that Peyotism is no prophetic movement. There are no personalities in the Peyote religion that in essence or importance could be defined as prophets. A prophet is an inspired person who feels called upon to pronounce the will of God, or the powers.[2] Only in the Peyote origin legends do we, as we have seen, find heroes who remind us, vaguely, of prophets: Peyote tells them in their sleep, or in an extraordinary state of consciousness, of the powers it has and instructs them to conduct the Peyote ceremony.[3]

Instead of being a prophet the Peyote leader is, it seems, primarily a priest, a holder of sacred knowledge, a keeper of sacred paraphernalia, and a master of ceremonies (cf. Ch. IV:5). In this respect he resembles a Christian clergyman or priest, and we may well wonder if there is a relationship here. The original Peyote leaders were medicine men more than priests, whereas modern Peyote leaders, members of the Native American Church, are a sort of priest – that is, inspired priests.[4] Quite reasonably this change of roles could have taken place under the strong influence of Christian ecclesiastical organization.

It is not so self-evident, however. The dichotomy between charismatic medicine man and priest has never been absolute in North America. Margot Liberty has shown that on the Plains, among the "nomadic" bison hunters, both "shamans" (as she terms the medicine men) and priests occurred. The Cheyenne, for instance, had both inspired medicine men who cured illness and priests or ritual functionaries who guarded the knowledge of rites and traditions and were "keepers" of tribal regalia, such as the Sacred Arrows and the Medicine

---
[1] Stewart 1944, Malouf 1942, Opler (M.K.) 1940, Couch and Marino 1979.
[2] Lindblom 1934, p. 29, Hultkrantz 1973 a, p. 34.
[3] Cf. above, Ch. III:2, and Underhill 1957, p. 135.
[4] Of course, Peyote leaders have not been installed as priests and are not called priests.

Hat. It is characteristic that one and the same individual could be both priest and medicine man.[5] Undoubtedly also other Plains tribes who kept similar fetishes could be aligned with the Cheyenne – also the Crow, whom Liberty puts in contradistinction to the Cheyenne.[6] Liberty argues that shamans were more common than priests in the Plains area and that priests only appeared "where social organization had become fairly complex beyond the kinship level".[7] I think this is correct in a larger, evolutionary perspective, but not entirely correct on the micro-level. We must bear in mind that former horticultural tribes, like the Cheyenne, gave up all or most agriculture when they migrated into the Plains area, but at the same time kept much of the ritual apparatus that went with their earlier type of culture. Secondarily, their ceremonial behaviour influenced pure hunting groups on the Plains, like the Shoshoni and the Kiowa Apache. (The Crow were themselves matrilinear inheritors of the Missouri horticulturists.)

If we return to the Peyote religion we can state that the latter had risen in a milieu where shamanism and agricultural ritualism were coupled together. To some extent the same double heritage prevailed when the Peyotism was brought over to the Plains. Perhaps it is therefore no coincidence that the Peyote leader in later times stood out as a carrier of double functions: as a spiritual, charismatic performer, an inheritor of functions derived from a "shamanic" past, and as a ceremonial leader, cultic expert and keeper of paraphernalia, a priest.

This deliberation is analytically meaningful, but, from the standpoint of the believing Indians it matters little whether the Peyote leader is an inspired visionary or a cultic servant (according to our categories). To them, he is the proper man to fit Peyote traditions of leadership. Peyotists would say that it is important that he knows his job, that he has a balanced and strong personality, that he has acquired his wisdom from a reputed Peyote authority, and that he is spoken of with respect.[8] Such qualifications in leadership mean also very much for the perpetuation of the Peyote movement. The combination of strong personalities and a particular understanding of the role of the leader may bring about a specific, dynamic and expansive function in the leadership with consequences for the diffusion of Peyotism.

Of the double roots of the Peyote leadership the connection with shamanism, as suggested in Ch. IV:5, is certainly the most interesting. Very many historical and ethnographic documents indicate that the roadman has his prototype in the shaman (some sources even hint that the fireman plays the shaman's curative role). Furthermore, we are told that the first "missionary" of Peyotism was often a shaman, or a former shaman or medicine man.

Weston La Barre who holds the opinion that psychotropic substances have

---

[5] Liberty 1970.
[6] Cf. for instance the numerous keepers of sacred pipes who have to observe particular rituals, as exemplified among the Crow: Lowie 1935, pp. 269 ff.
[7] Liberty 1970, p. 78.
[8] Cf. La Barre 1975 b, p. 100.

been responsible in shaping shamanism points out that the old Mexican Peyotism revolved around the shaman.[9] He explained the differential diffusion of Peyotism from this fact, correlating the occurrence of vision quest, shamanism and Peyotism.[10] We have earlier noted that among the Mescalero Apache the medicine men formed a guild of Peyote eaters, perhaps a forerunner of the later Peyote ritual group (see Ch. I:2, IV:5). As we have also found, Stewart considered that originally the roadman was a medicine man.[11] An instigator of Kiowa Apache Peyotism was the famous Daveko who had been a practising medicine man long before there was Peyotism in Oklahoma; he continued to shamanize until his death.[12] The great Peyote reformer John Wilson was a medicine man among the Caddo before he took over the role as a Peyote roadman and introduced his christianized form of Peyote ritual, the Big Moon.[13] The Southern Ute medicine man Herbert Stacher was a sucking medicine man who became a ranking Peyote leader.[14] His tribesman and colleague, Walter Lopez, claimed that he was a Peyotist even before he became a traditional medicine man – a strange inversion of the rule.[15] Both men introduced Peyotism among the Navajo.[16]

It is known that there has been a considerable antagonism between medicine men and Peyotists in some places, particularly among the Washo.[17] There is reason to believe that in this case it bas been the question of professional rivalry since both shamanism and Peyotism "constitute a medicoreligious complex".[18] The powerfulness of Washo medicine men, in contradistinction to other Great Basin medicine men, has been much talked about; accusations of sorcery have now and then been directed against them.[19] Similar conflicts have been reported from the Northern Arapaho, although their reality is disputed.[20] Among other Indians, for instance the Ute, there is however full harmony between medicine men and Peyotists. Older medicine men who were not Peyotists are said to have attended Peyote meetings and even to have recommended Peyote as an alternative curing method to their own.[21] It seems that the prerequisites have been different on different reservations.

---

[9] La Barre 1975 b, p. 39.
[10] La Barre 1975 b, p. 40.
[11] Stewart 1987, p. 68. See Ch. IV:5. However, Stewart formulated his statement as a a generalization which indeed does not fit all his data.
[12] Stewart 1987, p. 84.
[13] Stewart 1987, pp. 86 ff.
[14] Aberle and Stewart 1957, p. 41.
[15] Aberle and Stewart 1957, p. 35.
[16] Aberle and Stewart 1957, pp. 6, 34.
[17] See above, Ch. IV:9.
[18] Siskin 1983, p. 137.
[19] The antagonism between shamans and peyotists among the Washo has been dealt with in great detail in Siskin 1983. For a concise discussion, see Hultkrantz 1992, pp. 140 ff.
[20] Elkin 1940, p. 242, questioned by Stewart 1987, p. 191.
[21] Aberle and Stewart 1957, p. 35.

The medicine man as Peyote proselytizer illustrates the role of the personality as cultural carrier. Stewart has particularly indicated this factor as being responsible for the spread of Peyotism: "perhaps it was the personality of the peyote proselytor who brought the cult".[22] Couch and Marino agree with this view and make it more precise by demanding that we recognize a high social status for the cultural carrier.[23] The medicine man who has been accepted by his group is no doubt a man of social prestige, and thus destined to be a leader, a reformer, and an introducer of new ideas. It is however, just as important that the new religious ideology has acceptable qualifications.

The shaman or medicine man is, on the other hand, not the only proselytizer with prestige. There is the influential chief, like the Comanche Quanah Parker, or the high-ranking member of a chief's family, like the Shoshoni Charlie Washakie. And there is also the Christian priest or clergyman. It is rather surprising to find that Indians who from the beginning were Christian missionaries became, in time, Peyote leaders. One of them was Jonathan Koshiway, a Sauk and Fox who was a Mormon missionary, a Presbyterian minister, and a sucking medicine man before he became one of the great Peyote missionaries.[24] Another Christian missionary who turned Peyotist leader was the Kiowa Setkopti, reported on by Mooney.[25] Several others could also be mentioned.[26] This data should be collated with Stewart's opinion that "inevitably, as the church spread Christianity and civilization, it spread knowledge of peyote".[27] He means that indoctrination into Protestant Christianity was positive toward Peyote's diffusion.[28] An early learning of the Christian principles was, according to Stewart, an entry into Peyotism. It seems that Stewart here proceeds from his conviction that the Peyote religion has long been a Christian religion.

It was hinted above that Christian models have changed the Peyotist idea of religious leadership. Certainly, there is no doubt that the "priestly" functions in Peyotism were strengthened and expanded under the impact of Christian missions. An organization like the Native American Church is simply unthinkable without inspiration from the Christian Church (disregarding here the influence of the instigator, James Mooney). The singing of Christian hymns,[29] the baptism ceremony of the Winnebago,[30] the reading from the Bible[31] and many other

---

[22] Stewart 1941 b, p. 308.
[23] Couch and Marino 1979, pp. 10 f.
[24] Stewart 1987, p. 167. See Ch. I:2.
[25] Mooney 1896 b, p. 9.
[26] See also Ch. IV:12. In this connection we should not forget that Omer Stewart, who was a white man, started out as a Mormon missionary and ended up as a propagandist – for the Natives – of Peyotism.
[27] Stewart 1947, p. 26.
[28] Stewart 1947, p. 101.
[29] La Barre 1975 b, pp. 82 ff.
[30] La Barre 1975 b, p. 91.
[31] La Barre 1975 b, pp. 73 f.

sacred actions call on priestly service to an extent unknown to the early nineteenth century Peyotism. More important in this connection, the Peyote leader has taken over the foremost function of the Christian missionary.

Robert Bee has mentioned, among the factors promoting the diffusion of Peyote, "proselytization and profit".[32] If this constellation may seem materialistic in outlook this is due to Bee's dependence on Omer Stewart's analysis of Peyote missions to which we shall soon return. First of all we must however consider whether in fact, as Bee presupposes, the Peyote leader has appeared as a proselytizer, just like the Christian priest and missionary.

Proselytization was no natural activity in traditional American Indian religion. Indian religions were "ethnic" or "tribal", that is, they were the concern of the tribe and for the tribe, and not designed for outsiders. Gladys Reichard has interpreted the Navajo Indian's reaction very well: "Proselytism is not so much offensive as incomprehensible to him. Believing that his way of life is invaluable and right, he thinks it should not be dissipated by 'taking it out of the tribe'. He would not try to convert a neighboring Indian or a white man to his religion; he cannot understand why anyone should try to persuade him to abandon his birthright. Nor can he see why anyone should be willing to give away that which he has gained only by great exertion. His reasonable conclusion is, 'Of course your religion is good for you, ours for us. Why should either of us change?' With this rhetorical question he continues on his way without even curiosity about a strange religion from which he is not allowed to select."[33]

The Peyote religion, on the contrary, was and is no ethnic faith. It is intertribal and pan-Indian, and has developed into a "church". As always when a religion is not restricted to national boundaries but demands a solidarity in heart and spirit on a wider scale the spread of its ideas becomes a necessary means for its perpetuation. We could say that Peyotism by necessity became a missionary religion, and that the prototype for its missionary activity certainly was the Christian Church.[34]

It is in this connection that the impact of strong personalities makes itself known. Peyote history is rich in outstanding individuals who have acted as forceful agents for the spread of the religion.

The Comanche Chief Quanah Parker (dead 1911) offers a good example. This legendary hero from the Indian wars was first opposed to the use of Peyote, but having taken part in a Peyote rite in 1884 which cured a stomach ailment he suffered from, he became an enthusiastic devotee. At that date the Peyote road had been known to the Comanche for some time (cf. Ch. I:2), but Quanah became the most famous leader. He had a great persuasive power. In 1906 he invited an

---

[32] Bee 1965, p. 28.
[33] Reichard 1949, p. 70.
[34] Posern-Zielińska (1972, p. 246) reminds us that Peyotism in its first period of dissemination had the character of an uncontrolled cultural transmission which later changed to an organized missionary action.

old friend, Henry Murdock of the Kickapoo, to come and stay with him. Henry Murdock accepted and was invited to a Peyote meeting where he was taught the ceremony. Presented with cultic paraphernalia he returned to the Kickapoo and managed to introduce the ritual among them although they had earlier been bitterly opposed to Peyote. Quanah Parker composed many Peyote songs that he had received in auditive hallucinations during ritual meetings. They became famous and spread widely.[35]

Another influential messenger of Peyotism was the Winnebago John Rave. According to one tribesman, he was a real "bad man" before he became a Peyotist, he had been married many times, and was a heavy drinker. However about 1890 he converted to the Peyote religion, and then introduced it among his own people. Radin emphasizes that up to 1913, John Rave was the ritual leader whenever he was present at a meeting. His position was unchallenged until Albert Hensley appeared on the scene with his Christianized version of the Peyote religion (1908). However, even thereafter John Rave prevailed as the head of the movement, although Hensley's ideas increasingly gained the upper hand.[36]

John Rave was often away on journeys to other reservations and other Indian tribes among which he spread his message. From his Winnebago home in Nebraska he visited South Dakota, Minnesota and Wisconsin.

A third remarkable proselytizer was John Wilson, of mixed Caddo and Delaware descent, who spread the Peyote gospel among the Caddo. He has been discussed by Mooney, La Barre, Stewart and Melburn Thurman.[37] Wilson, a pro-Catholic man, blended Catholicism, Ghost Dance and Peyotism into a unique complex, and introduced the Christianized Big Moon Peyote rite which through him was spread from the Caddo to the Delaware, Quapaw, Osage and, after his death (1901), to the Seneca.

Having discussed John Rave, John Wilson and some other Peyote missionaries Stewart raises the question, "Have these men and other famous proselyters spread the gospel of peyote solely out of love for their fellow men? No doctrine of the peyote cult commands members to go forth and convert other tribes."[38] Stewart argues, a bit surprisingly in view of his commitments to the Peyote movement, that the main cause for proselytizing has been economic profit, and he adduces several cases where Peyote leaders have received large payments for their spiritual services. For instance, one Washo-Paiute Peyote leader, Ben Lancaster, introduced the new religion when he was unemployed and very poor. He exploited his followers economically and used the money he received for his ritual services to make a good living. At the same time he was, nevertheless, a

---

[35] Cf. La Barre 1975 b, pp. 85, 112 f., 116, and Jackson and Jackson 1963.
[36] Radin 1923, pp. 388 ff.
[37] Mooney 1896 a, pp. 903 ff., La Barre 1975 b, pp. 151–161, Thurman 1973, Stewart 1987, pp. 86 ff. (with notes from Frank G. Speck).
[38] Stewart 1944, p. 96.

sincere believer.[39] Also other famous leaders, like John Wilson, certainly earned a lot. Driver and Massey also underline the importance of economic considerations, but think that the social prestige meant more.[40]

Stewart admits, certainly, that the literature contains few direct statements that suggest that financial gain motivated Peyote diffusion, but he considers that our data is incomplete here.[41]

Personally I have never noticed, from my association with Shoshoni Peyotists, that money has played any decisive role at their ritual meetings. Of course, business deals may have taken place without my knowing it, but I doubt very much that they have been as important as Stewart thinks. Moreover, it has long been customary in traditional Indian society to show one's appreciation of a doctor by giving him blankets, horses or, recently, money. A Shoshoni medicine man to whom I was very close – and who was no Peyotist – took it for granted that he should receive money or other valuables in connection with curing. He was proud of this, and in his narratives of his personal success on different occasions of curing never failed to tell how much he earned. There was no greed behind this attitude. He was a generous man, and shared the little he owned willingly with others. No, the fee he received was a measure of his success, his ability as a medicine man. It was, besides, the customary tribute that a medicine man should have.[42]

There is no reason why the Peyote leader, successor of the medicine man, should be exempted from this rule.

Writing about Peyotism among the Washo and Northern Paiute Stewart concludes, "Knowledge of the religion came when individuals desired aggrandizement, social, political, above all, economic; therefore becoming proselyters and deliberately setting about to convert the Washo-Paiute."[43] This is indeed a very cynic presentation of Native Indian religion, and very unexpected from a man who is so close to the Peyote movement. It is so much more surprising since Stewart assigns to proselytism the main role in the diffusion of Peyote.[44]

Of course, in a larger human perspective all our actions have an egocentric bias, whether we work for ourselves or for others. However, in the Peyote context it would seem that the aspiration for social prestige means more than economic gain. Many authors have noted that the Peyote religion bestows prestige and status upon its leaders. Thus, Robert Newberne and Charles Burke, assessing the general extension of the Peyote religion, find that it is due to active

---

[39] Stewart 1944, p. 94.
[40] Driver and Massey 1957, p. 273.
[41] Stewart 1944, p. 97.
[42] Stewart (1987, p. 69) seems to have partly held a similar view. For another opinion, see Petrullo 1934, pp. 129 f.
[43] Stewart 1944, p. 97. See also Jorgensen (1986, p. 679) who wrongly claims that Stewart did not find economic motives behind the Peyote proselytization.
[44] Cf. the summary of Stewart's lecture in Lynch 1984, p. 180.

missionary efforts by persons who thereby want to achieve personal leadership in Peyotism.[45] Malcolm Arth suggests that the Peyote religion restores the lost meaning of the male Indian role, as seems to be the case among the Omaha.[46] With specific reference to the Navajo Bernard Barber asks, "Do the leaders of the new cult come from among the old elite?"[47] Aberle finds that the question is difficult to answer, since the old Navajo elite was no single unit and, moreover, shifted in its composition with time. Still, Aberle thinks that Barber's assumption is partly correct: those who were most deprived of status and wealth would apparently have been most likely to join the new religion. And yet, this was clearly not the case. Because of the antagonism the new religion provoked, becoming a member could result in a loss of prestige in the larger Navajo community.[48] As for the Plains Indians, La Barre considers that Peyotism offered them prestige that they had lost with the cultural and political débâcle at the end of the last century.[49]

We can conclude that social prestige sometimes followed Peyote leadership, sometimes not, and that even the reverse could occur.

However, our main impression is that Peyote leaders wanted Peyotism to grow because they were deeply convinced of its blessings for their people. Of course, in-group feelings, the propagation for one's own little interest group contributed to this conviction, as several sociologically inclined authors have pointed out. In particular, however, the leaders were themselves persons who had suffered and found a consolation in the new religion – this holds good for the leaders in the past in any way. The accounts of hardships and shaking religious experiences told to Radin by Peyote protagonists among the Winnebago give convincing proof of how the wonderful herb restored these men to a life that gave them meaning and spiritual direction.[50] They could gain prestige and, in some cases, more money through Peyote; but their main gain was a new religious certainty and a viable way of living.

This cannot be better illustrated than through some quotations from one of John Rave's Peyote experiences which he related verbatim to Paul Radin. After having seen God, and his own family at home in the middle of the night he exclaimed, "Indeed, it is good. They are all well – my brother, my sister, my father, my mother. I felt very good indeed. O medicine, grandfather, most assuredly you are holy! All that is connected with you, that I would like to know and that I would like to understand. Help me! I give myself up to you entirely!" In a later context John Rave stated, "Whoever has any bad thoughts, if he will eat this peyote he will abandon all his bad habits. It is a cure for everything

---

[45] Newberne and Burke 1922, p. 12.
[46] Arth 1956, p. 27.
[47] Barber 1941 b, p. 675.
[48] Aberle 1982 b, pp. 406 f., 413.
[49] La Barre 1975 b, p. 201.
[50] Cf. Radin 1923, pp. 389–414. See also Radin 1913, 1920, 1926.

bad." Again, "Only by eating the peyote you will learn what is truly holy. This is what I am trying to learn myself."[51]

Like Isaiah John Rave had an overwhelming experience of God's holiness. This, it seems, was the foundation for his missionary zeal. It was also included in the prayer which he used everytime he initiated a new member to the Peyote religion through a simple baptism, "God, his holiness".[52] It is almost sacrilegious to talk about earning profits as the main stimulus of missionary action in this connection. Certainly, a cultural materialist like Radin would have stressed the economic factors in proselytization if he had found them.[53]

Recently an American anthropologist, Francis Hsu (Lang Kwang), offered a new hypothesis to explain missionary activity. He claims that "proselytization was and is an outstanding characteristic of Western positive ethnocentrism in religion, in contrast to the patterns of religion in the rest of the world".[54] He even asserts that all missionaries and missionary movements have been of Western, and secondarily Arab, origin.[55] There is, he says, an inherent impetus in Western culture to change; he calls it "internal impetus to change", in contrast to change resulting from pressure from without, "external impetus to change". He aligns missionary movements with capitalism and free enterprise as varying expressions of expansionist tendencies in Western societies. He contrasts this situation with prevailing historical conditions in such countries as India, China and Japan where all change took place as a result of pressure from other societies and cultures.[56]

Hsu concludes that once this is understood we can see that it was not monotheism – in an absolute sense – in Judaism, Islam or Christianity that was the cause of internal impetuses to change and of proselytization.

We may certainly, question several of these pronouncements. In spite of Hsu's documentation, there was a missionary tendency in old Hinduism – witness the Hinduization of tribes in India and elsewhere, and the conflict between Hinduism and Buddhism is more or less implied. The missionary idea in such religions as Jainism and Buddhism is more or less implied. It is also clear that monotheism, by its very exclusiveness, calls for a propagating spirit to be upheld. Nevertheless, Hsu has rightly seen that the Western world has had a more dynamic missionary spirit than the East.

The reasons for this are, I think, not just the internal impetus to change, unless this tendency is seen as part of a more significant trend (eschatology), but the following:

(1) Missionary movement usually presupposes a multinational community, a

---

[51] Radin 1923, pp. 391–393. For an analysis of John Rave's experience, see Radin 1933, pp. 185 ff.
[52] Radin 1923, p. 389.
[53] Cf. Radin 1957, pp. 40 ff., and 1953, pp. 137 ff.
[54] Hsu 1979, p. 525.
[55] Hsu 1979, p. 522.
[56] Hsu 1979, p. 524.

consciousness of an *oikoumene* comprising many peoples and realms. The religion transcends national boundaries, it is universalistic. Since it is, ideally seen, not supported by any state organizations it is dependent on as wide a following as possible. (This is the general condition for proselytization, also affecting non-national religions in India.)

(2) Eschatology, that is, the knowledge that the drama between dualistic divine powers, and between good and evil forces in mankind is heading towards a final showdown calls for a salvation of as many people as possible. Since man is part in the struggle he has to assist in the salvation process. (This is the motivation *par préférence* in the religions of the Western world: Zoroastrism, Judaism, Gnosticism, Christianity, Islam.)

(3) The compelling force of prophetism sets a pattern of missionary activity transplanted to subsequent religious teachers. (This applies particularly to Judaism and Christianity.)

We may now return to the missionary activity of the Peyote leaders. It is obvious that the Peyote religion, being universalistic (at least aiming at including all Indians) and dependent on its following, presents a case of missionary movement. To a certain extent this universalism and supratribalism were inspired by Christian models, and so was no doubt the missionary activity. The eschatological implications in the Peyote religion are however very weak and of no consequence: Peyotists reckon with a blissful existence in the next life, but they do not count with an ultimate battle between good and bad forces, or with a Judgement Day – unless they have assimilated Christian values to a degree that they regard themselves as Christian.[57] Finally, although prophetism is absent in the Peyote context the compelling force of missionary strength is revealed in John Rave's Peyote experience as described above. Behind it lurks the pattern of conversion transmitted by Christian missions.

In summation, we may regard the proselytization spirit within Peyotism as an indirect testimony of Christian impact and, of course, as an impetus to Peyote diffusion. Its energy was however primarily aimed at American Natives.

11. Peyote as an Instrument against White Domination

In his book on the Peyote religion J. S. Slotkin introduces, in his first chapter, "a theory of nationalism". He proposes the thesis that a subordinate ethnic group attempts to overthrow the domination-subordination relation socially by means of militant nationalism, and culturally by means of nativistic nationalism. Slotkin tries to show, he says, that the Peyote religion is an Indian defense

---

[57] Cf. Slotkin 1956 a, p. 71.

against White domination and its consequences. He finds, however, that socially it is an example of accommodation rather than militant opposition, and culturally it should be understood as a case of pan-Indian nativism.[1] This conclusion is shared by many students of Peyote, although they hesitate to emphasize the particular aspect of opposition. Others, however, have drawn a different conclusion from Peyote's role as a defense mechanism against White supremacy. It seems that Lanternari oversteps the case when he ascribes a militant quality to the Peyote movement.[2] In view of what we have discussed earlier this is missing the point: Peyotism has spread and survived because, in contradistinction to the Ghost Dance, it has presented a more compromising attitude to foreign rule (cf. below, Ch. IV:13).

It is well known that religion is the field where a subjugated group may best articulate its protests against their conquerors. There are however different modes of such protests. As concerns Peyotism the opposition is there, but it is, as Slotkin has implied, a defensive rather than an offensive attitude, a guarding of the Indian, or pan-Indian, heritage against the White lords.

Ruth Underhill's experiences are valuable here. She entirely avoids an aggressive interpretation of Peyotism when she writes, "To the people whose self-respect was gone, who felt lost and inferior, it was a healing belief that to them had come a message no white man could understand. Over and over I have been told this fact and realized how the marginal groups among the Indians, those not yet adjusted to the new culture, cling to this prop for their racial importance. ... Peyote, it is obvious, gives a wide range of belief, and its real unifying factor is that it is Indian, something for the Red Man alone and which the white can share only with his permission. ... What matters is the sense of racial importance derived from a religion all the Indian's own."[3] Thus what we face here is a confession to the Indianness, to pan-Indianism, to the ethnic religious heritage of the Indians. The whites may be invited to join Peyote sessions, but should realize that this is not their religion.

In this vindication of Indian religion there is of course a tacit aggression towards the whites, although it seems that Underhill scarcely noted it. My own experiences from Peyote meetings is that as an invited guest I was welcome. The consumption of Peyote stimulates feelings of sympathy and brotherhood of great intensity, and I was certainly met by such feelings in abundance. However, they reached me as a participant in the prayer meeting, and not as a white man. The white supremacy is challenged in a mild, but determined way: the white ideas are not part of Indian tradition and religion, they do not belong here.

Sometimes, however, there is a more open opposition, for instance, in the reactions against white man's discontent with the consumption of the drug

---

[1] Slotkin 1956 a, pp. 1 ff., 7.
[2] Lanternari 1960, pp. 100 ff.
[3] Underhill 1952, pp. 143 f., 147 f.

Peyote. The Indians manifest in these reactions fear, anxiety and aggression in a mixed composition. In consideration of all the persecution of Peyote from official authorities – administrators, courts of justice, etc., this attitude is most understandable.[4] However, it may take on a deeper import, become a channel of expression for more deep-lying sentiments. "By clinging to peyote in the face of such opposition", says Arth, "the Omaha are indirectly expressing aggression against its opponents."[5] Arth is thus well aware that white hostility to Peyote may bring about a flash of dormant anti-white feelings. Basically, therefore, it is not just white attitudes to Peyote that create Indian irritation, but white domination in general, whereby Peyote offers a *pièce de résistence*.

Aberle informs us that Peyotism, as an ideology, "assures some Navahos that Indians are at least equal to, and in some ways superior to whites – in knowledge, in wisdom, in spirituality, and in possession of a good religion – and superior to traditional Navahos. It supplies an ideological basis for antagonism to whites."[6] Perhaps it does among the Navajo. We must be cautious here, however, and not generalize such findings; the degrees of anti-white feelings vary between tribes and even persons and often reflect particular historical developments. It is difficult to find that Peyote has ever inspired feelings of open hostility. At the worst whites have been forbidden to attend Peyote meetings.[7]

Slotkin stands for the sober judgment that Peyotism "provided a supernatural means of accommodation to the existing domination-subordination relation".[8] It did so by both counteracting and imitating a foreign ideology.[9]

12. Peyote Religion as an Alternative to Christianity and as a Form of Christianity

The connections between the Peyote religion and Christianity are, as has been demonstrated above (Ch. I:2), most complicated: Peyotism appears sometimes as a religion competing with Christianity, and other times as a representation of

---

[4] Cf. above, Cn. I:1, and consult La Barre 1975 b, pp. 223 ff., 265 f., Slotkin 1956 a, pp. 50 ff., 57 ff., Stewart 1961 b, pp. 7 ff., and 1973.
[5] Arth 1956, p. 27.
[6] Aberle 1982 b, pp. 193 f.
[7] There are reports that Peyote consumption can release aggressive impulses, but anti-white thoughts and actions have not figured in these connections. The Boyer team found that the present-day Mescalero Apache suffer from intra-tribal antagonisms which can be bloody and lead to self-destruction, all in consequence of Peyote eating. These antagonisms are referred to a basic weakness in the personality structure: "The physiopsychological effects of the hallucinogen reduced the efficacy of their repression of the hostilities which had resulted from their socialization experiences": Boyer *et alii* 1973, p. 61.
[8] Slotkin 1956 a, p. 20.
[9] On the import of institutionalization of Peyotism, cf. Ch. VI:3.

Christian faith. Peyote students have debated these shifting constellations, sometimes also the role of Christianity in creating presuppositions for the progress of Peyote. This role is closely tied up with the Peyote religion's varying relationship to Christian religion.

It seems that Peyote's main function as an instrument against white domination is, as Aberle points out, to offer an ideology and a ritual that can compete with the Christian religious system. Other students of Peyote are also inclined to regard Peyotism as a response to Christian teaching. Thus Ruth Underhill opines that Christian missionaries built on the Native idea of supernatural help through revelation, but redirected the power quest from success in war and hunting to righteous living, in a Christian sense; whereas the Indians responded by working out their own combination of vision and ethics.[1]

The opinion of the Peyotists themselves bears out this presumption. The Peyote religion is in the eyes of many Peyotists an Indian alternative to Christianity. Miss Underhill heard a Peyote man saying, "Peyote is the Indians' Christ. You white people needed a man to show you the way, but we Indians have always been friends with the plants and have understood them. So to us peyote came. And not to the whites." As Underhill points out, here is a message that heightens Indian self-respect and pride in a situation of loss and defeat.[2] Similar Indian pronouncements have been made by other Peyotists.[3] For instance, a respected leader like John Wilson thought the Bible to be an adequate source of faith for the white man, and Peyote for the red man.[4] Among the Navajo it is said that the white man has the Bible and his Church, whereas the Indian has direct access to God.[5] The Montana Cree believe that their Peyote religion is superior to Christianity.[6] And Shoshoni Peyotists told me that theirs is a very ancient religion, more ancient than Christianity – it is the Old Testament. Apparently the idea is that the Peyote religion can claim the same age as the Old Testament, thus having priority in age to Christianity.

This idea of a differentiated religious heritage is not however only represented by Peyotists. We find it also among adherents of traditional tribal religions. Thus, defenders of the old Shoshoni religion assured me that the white men have the Bible, the Indians their spirits and their Sun Dance.[7] A Sioux chief, Iron Hawk, is said to have proclaimed that while the Great Spirit gave the whites the power to read and write he gave Indians the power to talk with their

---

[1] Underhill 1957, p. 132.
[2] Underhill 1952, pp. 143 f.
[3] Cf. Slotkin 1956 a, pp. 76, 112.
[4] La Barre 1975 b, p. 159. Cf. the Menomini: "God will talk to you himself. You don't need no bible" (Spindler and Spindler 1971, p. 96).
[5] Aberle 1982 b, p. 15. Revelation is here opposed to learned tradition. See also Slotkin 1956 a, p. 76.
[6] Dusenberry 1962, p. 179.
[7] Cf. Hultkrantz 1981 a, p. 227.

hands and arms – a profane rendering of the same cultural message.[8] According to the Ojibway the Christians have the Bible, the Ojibway their engraved pictographs on bark scrolls, that is, their own written sacred traditions.[9] And so on. It is obvious here that Indian culture and religion oppose white culture and religion with the latter's own arguments, but on Indian premises: according to tribal thinking tribe and religion constitute a unit, separated from other tribal-religious units. The same thinking can be traced from the seventeenth century when Jesuit missionaries noted down similar expressions of Indian religious tribalism. It seems that in more recent times Peyotists adopted the same attitude, expanding tribalism to Indianism.

However, there is also another heritage from the tribal religions among American Indians, and that is the tolerant attitude to other faiths, including Christianity. There is in Indian religiosity, a deep conviction that there are many paths to the religious mystery. While Peyotists guard their own religion they do not exclude Christianity from their horizon, and even announce their affiliation both with a Christian Church and with their own Native American Church (which of course may be interpreted as being Christian as well, as we shall see). In practice, they may turn to both religions.

The Navajo may serve as an example. They are, as Kluckhohn once pointed out, pragmatic in their attitudes, and Richard Feinberg has noted their resort to alternate religious systems in matters of disease. "Some types of illness", he says, "are thought to be most treatable by a traditional singer while others may be more responsive to peyote meetings, Christian prayer, or treatment by an Anglo doctor. If one type of treatment fails, a different one may be attempted, and it is not uncommon for all of these procedures to be used in treatment of a single illness."[10]

This inclusive religious pattern among American Indians was, strangely enough, independently observed by Slotkin, Stewart and myself in three publications which appeared in the same year, 1956. Slotkin simply stated that, "in conformity with tradition, many people participated in two of more of them simultaneously".[11] Stewart described a Northern Paiute who was both a traditional medicine man, a Peyotist and a member of the Episcopal Church.[12] "Three gods for Joe", writes Stewart, but is that correct – is it not three ways to manifest religious belief – perhaps with the same godhead in view? My own study concentrated on the religious segments in which believing Shoshoni Indians unconsciously structure their religion so that different religious configurations, sometimes even logically excluding each other, momentarily play a total

---

[8] Clark 1885, p. 12.
[9] Vecsey 1983, p. 99.
[10] Feinberg 1979, p. 244.
[11] Slotkin 1956 a, p. 20.
[12] Stewart 1956.

religious role. I have called these segments alternating configurations of religious belief.[13] Edward Spicer has coined the term compartmentalization to express the tendency (among the Eastern Pueblos) to accept certain traits from the Spanish which have remained peripheral to major cultural interests.[14] This is thus not exactly the same concept, but the term has been used to the same effect. Finally, Clyde Holler, referring to the famous Oglala holy man, Black Elk, characterizes the latter's practice of both traditional religion and Christianity as "theological bi-culturalism".[15]

It is obvious that Peyotism and Christian beliefs constitute segments, or shall we say compartments, with many Indian religious personalities.[16] In a succinct article on the Native American Church Stewart has presented a row of examples of Peyotists who have also served actively in some Christian denomination.[17] It is instructive to learn that James Mooney's guide to Peyote, the Kiowa Indian Setkopti, who became a Peyotist in 1883, was also a Methodist missionary. Stewart also mentions another Kiowa, Tsatigh, who was at the same time both a Peyotist and a full-time Pentecostal minister. The Oto Indian Jonathan Koshiway was apparently a Latter Day Saint, a Peyotist, and a sucking shaman as well. And so on. The list could be easily completed with other examples not adduced by Stewart.[18]

To Stewart, such instances show two things. First of all, that American Indians "can and do belong to several distinct religions at the same time".[19] Secondly, that the Peyote religion was from the start an "open" religion compatible with Christianity, and containing Christian ideas and symbols from its beginnings – did not Quanah Parker, the celebrated Comanche chief, pray to God and Jesus and have a framed picture of the Sacred Heart in his home? Did not Mooney observe Peyotists wearing crucifixes already in 1892?[20] However, the inclusion of symbols taken from Christendom does not necessarily mean the inclusion of Christian concepts. If Jesus and St. Mary occur among Islamic

---

[13] Hultkrantz 1956; reprinted in Hultkrantz 1982 a, pp. 28–47. For Peyotism as a configuration, see the latter work, pp. 223, 224. Cf. also Stenberg 1946, p. 132.

[14] Spicer 1954, p. 665; cf. also Dozier 1662, p. 164.

[15] Holler 1984.

[16] Vecsey however discards this interpretation. He maintains that Peyotism among the Apache originated not as a religion, but as a ritual "which added to their own religious patterns" (Vecsey 1988, pp. 198 f.). In Mexico this was definitely so. The case is more ambiguous for the situation of Peyotism in more recent times.

[17] Stewart 1980 c, pp. 193 f.; 1987, pp. 166 f. See also Ch. IV:10, VI:2.

[18] Doña Marta, one of the last descendants of the Gabrielino Indians of Southern California, was both a devout Catholic and a devout Peyotist. She quoted her grandmother as having said, "Los dos coren juntos", the two run together. "When one fails, the other helps" (Laird 1977, p. 107).

[19] Stewart 1979–80, p. 278, cf. also p. 293. See furthermore Stewart 1939, pp. 66 f., 1980 d, p. 18, 1986, p. 676, 1987, pp. 187 f., 209, 248, 279, 317.

[20] Mooney 1892.

sacred personages, this cannot be interpreted as evidence of the presence of Christian ideology in Islam. Peyotism, diffusing out of Catholic Mexico (New Spain), certainly absorbed many Catholic symbols, and in its sense of a "specific religious group" (Wach) it probably reflected Catholic organization principles.[21] However, the Peyote religion was not at the time a Christian denomination. It is another matter that some Indian-born Christian missionaries, apparently brought up with the perspective of compartmentalization we have mentioned, did not see any essential differences.

As the foregoing accounts and analyses should have shown, no doubt the Peyote religion has many qualities that make it well apt to compete with Christendom. It is Indian, it is adapted to the reservation situation, and it is easy to learn. Its simplicity rendered it victorious in many circles in its competition with tribal religion, and made it a powerful instrument against Christian indoctrination. By taking over a Christian missionary zeal and Christian forms of organization Peyotism became a serious rival to Christianity. Here was a consolidated faith, a church indeed, with a ritual, a set of beliefs and a practical ethical system, developed and run by American Indians.

The Indian character of Peyotism – which makes it easier to grasp than the foreign, complicated Christian message – is revealed in its charismatic, visionary properties. Says Hoebel, "God as preached by the missionaries has always remained a doctrinaire abstraction for our Indians, untutored in the metaphysics of the ancient Jews. Now, at last, through peyote He has taken form, for He is revealed to his worshippers through the pagan vision experience..."[22] Against Hoebel we could hold that there is an inspirational side of Christianity as well, although those missions that operate in Indian communities have often been very "institutional". However, there is no doubt that the charismatic nature of Peyotism enhances its value over Christianity in many Indian eyes.[23] In the words of the Comanche chief and Peyote leader Quanah Parker, "The white man goes into his church house and talks *about* Jesus, but the Indian goes into his tipi and talks *to* Jesus."[24]

It has been said in the foregoing that it is the Indian quality of the Peyote religion that makes it so attractive to many Indians.[25] This emphasis is made even when it should be obvious to anybody, also the most faithful Peyotist, that his religion is repleted with Christian symbolism. It is a matter of fact that elements of Christian worship and theology turn up everywhere in Peyotism, although for

---

[21] Wach 1947, pp. 111 ff.
[22] Hoebel 1949, p. 126.
[23] This could be compared with similar Indian reactions in another "new" Indian religion, the Shaker Church of the Northwest, where direct revelation is regarded as preferable to the teachings of the Bible by older believers: Collins 1950, p. 408.
[24] Simmons in La Barre 1975 b, p. 166.
[25] Cf. Newcomb 1956, p. 211.

instance La Barre devaluates their importance.[26] However, some of them are so integrated with aboriginal Indian traits that they are not recognized as Christian by the adherents of Peyote. Or Christian elements sink under the threshold of consciousness, so that the Peyote religion is represented as genuinely Indian. In some cases, again, the Peyote faith is felt to be akin to Christianity, but regarded as a separate religion, created for Indians.

The Wind River Shoshoni whose Peyote religion was presented in detail in an earlier chapter (Ch. II) offer an interesting illustration. At their Peyote meetings they pray to God (and here Christian and Indian ideas mingle completely), to Jesus and the Holy Ghost. References to Jesus' life, to Christian eschatology and the sacraments occur frequently. This does not mean that the Shoshoni ideas are identical with the Christian, or experienced as Christian by the Shoshoni. For instance, the Peyotists consider that they have a holy communion in their church, but they do not use wine, they use Peyote. The Shoshoni are somehow aware that Peyotism should have common roots with Christianity, or rather, that it was given to them as an alternative to Christianity, for it is recognized as a distinct, separate religion. To the outside observer, the Christian origins of a central part of the ideological pattern is obvious; to the believer, the outstanding feature of the Peyote religion, besides its efficacy and sacred character, is its Indianness.

Similar data could be assembled from other Peyote communities. The Omaha, for instance, attach crucifixes to Peyote fans and embroider the figure of Jesus holding a Peyote cactus on the altar cloth. Their prayers are directed in the Omaha language to the Father, the Son and the Holy Ghost. In spite of their incorporating Christian elements in their religious tissue the Omaha Peyotists consider the fundamental value of the Peyote religion to reside in its "Indian" nature, that is, its more aboriginal elements.[27]

The Winnebago founder of Peyotism, John Rave, passively accepted the Christian innovations introduced by his tribesman Albert Hensley. He thus immediately confirmed his faith in the Bible and added it to his other Peyote regalia. "To Rave, after all, the peyote was the principal element, and if Hensley chose to insist that the Bible was only intelligible to those who partook of the peyote why that naturally fell within its magical powers."[28] John Rave thought that the efficacy of Peyote was inherent in the herb and was not a result of additional circumstances. Of course, John Rave did not share Hensley's Christian,

---

[26] La Barre 1975 b, pp. 165 f., 202. Actually, La Barre provides interesting evidence of Christian symbolism in Peyotism, such as the identification of Winnebago Peyote officials with the Trinity (op. cit., p. 164), the importance of the Bible in Winnebago and other Siouan Peyote séances (p. 73), the occurrence of Christian hymns among the Iowa and Winnebago (pp. 82 ff.), and the baptism following the nightly Peyote rite among the Winnebago and others (p. 91). Cf. also La Barre 1975 b, pp. 162 ff.

[27] Arth 1956, p. 26 and note 1.

[28] Radin 1923, p. 421.

or presudo-Christian, convictions. His way of assimilating Christian elements is however instructive.

In Menomini Peyotism the tipi poles symbolize Christ and his disciples, the leader's staff is carved with crosses, and the leader makes the sign of the cross. Furthermore, the ashes are formed to look like a "dove", the Christian symbol of the Holy Ghost. Nevertheless George Spindler points out that the basic concepts are Native-oriented "though modified and perverted to meet the unique needs of the participants."[29]

Ruth Underhill, not referring to any particular tribe, makes the sweeping statement that the Indians have accepted the Christian doctrine and made a synthesis between the latter and the new religion. She adds, "Peyote, it is obvious, gives a wide range of belief, and its real unifying factor is that it is Indian, something for the Red Man alone."[30] The Christian traits then would have a pure additional value, and the fact that they have been derived from white man's religion would be accidental.

Perhaps it would be better to refrain from generalizing on this issue. The extent of Christian elements varies from reservation to reservation, and the identifications with Christianity are fluctuating. Moreover, elements that may make the impression of being Christian have sometimes actually belonged to Native religious patterns. We shall look at these points in due time.

First of all, with the risk of repeating what has been already said in an earlier context about the growth of Christian ideas in Peyotism, there has been a progressive Christian influence in the Peyote religion, a development that has had the most varying effects: in some places the Native components have been practically left untouched, in other places they share their position with Christian components, and in still other places we find a complete Christianization of Peyotist communities. For example, there is a minimum of Christian features in the Mescalero Apache ceremony, if we may believe Morris Opler.[31] Among the Delaware there is a conservative, Native-oriented fraction of Peyotists (Little Moon) and a liberal, more Christianized fraction (Big Moon).[32] Similar divisions occur among many other tribes, such as the Siouan nations, but today the Christian elements are also at home in "Little Moon" or "Half Moon" rituals. Tribes like the Menomini, Winnebago, Cheyenne, Sioux and Ute are well-known for their massive inclusion of Christian symbolism in their Peyote rituals.[33] Marvin Opler thought in 1960 that, in the future, and under conditions of further acculturation, a Christianized form of the Peyote religion would appear on the reservations.[34] Indeed, Winnebago and Ute Peyote groups early

---

[29] Cf. La Barre 1960, p. 49.
[30] Underhill 1952, pp. 143, 147 f.
[31] Opler 1936.
[32] Newcomb 1955, p. 1042. Only a few Peyotists belong to the Little Moon.
[33] See La Barre 1975 b, pp. 162 ff., and La Barre 1970, p. 301; Slotkin 1956 a.
[34] Marvin Opler in La Barre 1960, p. 57.

applied for being affiliated with local Christian denominations.[35] Slotkin reminds us that according to Peyotists the Native American Church should be understood as one among innumerable variants of Christianity. Adoption of the Trinity, he informs us, makes Peyotism a Christian religion.[36] According to Paul Steinmetz Oglala Lakota Peyotists identify themselves as Christians.[37] We may possibly conclude that there is an increasing Christianization in many quarters, but not everywhere: Washo data point in a reverse direction.[38]

Secondly, there are features in the Peyote worship which give an impression of a Christian origin but in actual fact are indigenous to North American religion. Here I am thinking particularly of the practice of making confessions which was, indeed, part of some Native religions (see above, Ch. IV:3), and the lofty concepts of God which to a certain extent were an aboriginal heritage in many American Indian religions. Of course, some Indians, like the Navajo, apparently lacked a high-god concept and in Peyotism took over the term used by the Franciscan Fathers.[39] Others, like the Oglala Lakota, changed their concept of God to conform with the one in intertribal Peyotism.[40] When some Washo and Northern Paiute declared that they joined Peyotism because to them it seemed a satisfying way to worship "the one true God" they certainly displaced a Christian attitude, in particular since most of them were also Protestants.[41] There is no doubt that Christian ideas once modelled the concept of God in Peyotism, but the foundation of the concept was certainly aboriginal.[42]

When this has been said it must however be admitted that much of both doctrine, ethics and ritual in the Peyote religion echoes Christian notions. The question then arises, is it possible to say that it is Christian precepts, ideas and customs that have helped to establish this religion as an interethnic religious movement?

---

[35] Radin 1923, pp. 395, 421; Stewart 1941 b, p. 305. Cf. also Voget 1956, p. 257.

[36] Slotkin 1956 a, p. 65. It is characteritic that a Quapaw Peyote church building is crowned with a cross (Stewart 1987, p. 114). See also Rachlin 1968, p. 103.

[37] Steinmetz 1980, pp. 164, 165. "Christianity is our motto through life", claimed a Southern Arapaho (Stewart 1987, p. 107).

[38] Merriam and d'Azevedo 1957, p. 618.

[39] Aberle 1982 b, pp. 177 f., 376 f.

[40] Steinmetz 1980, pp. 88 f.

[41] Stewart 1944, p. 86. Also the ethic rules of Peyotism are mentioned as attractive, op. cit., p. 87.

[42] It should be admitted here that in particular some protagonists of the neo-evolutionistic school in North American deny the indigenous character of the North American Indian high gods. To them the idea of a Supreme Being is the outcome of Christian missions. This is however scarcely probable. As I have remarked in another context (Hultlkrantz 1977 a, p. 421), already Torquemada and Herrera observed the existence of high gods in American religions. Later research has demonstrated that the structure of the high-god concept in aboriginal North America deviates from the Christian concept of God, and thus should be original: it trends both towards universalism (one all-pervading divinity) and pluralism (an array of spiritual beings), thus being both single and distributive (Hultkrantz 1981 a, pp. 20–27). The fact that Jesus is no part of the pantheon in traditional religion, whereas God is, seems to testify to the indigenous origin of the concept of God among American Indians. See further Hultkrantz 1979 b, pp. 15 ff.

In order to solve this question it is necessary to look again into the problem of the Christian impact on Peyotism. Opinion among researchers is divided as to whether and to what extent there was an initial admixture of Christian elements in the Peyote religion as it entered the United States (cf. above, Ch. I:2).

Three anthropologists have eagerly defended the thesis that the Peyote religion had a Christian veneer from the outset. One of them, the otherwise excellent musicologist Frances Densmore, makes the obvious mistake of postulating a Christian pattern for the ritual proceedings.[43] The other two authors make a more moderate impression by comparison, and are better aquainted with Peyotism since they themselves have been closely affiliated with it. This circumstance may however have coloured their judgments to a certain extent. In several works Omer Stewart has declared his opinion that Christian elements were integral with the Peyote religion from an early date and spread with this religion.[44] This position was vividly denounced by Marvin Opler who, like Stewart, had worked on Ute Peyotism.[45] However, as the historico-ethnological material suggests there is reason to support Stewart's opinion in the matter, although the Christian features must not be overstressed (cf. Ch. I:2).

In regard to present conditions Stewart emphasizes that most Peyotists consider themselves Christians, believing that Peyotism is the Indian version of Christianity, at the same time as they accept the Trinity and ethics of white Christians.[46] I am not sure this statement holds true however. Many Peyotists would certainly agree with Stewart, but others would probably insist that Peyotism is equivalent to Christianity, but not identical with it.

Slotkin makes a difference between "the old Peyote complex" which, before 1850, was the only existing form of Peyotism, and "the Peyote religion" which appeared on the Southern Plains about 1885.[47] The latter religion was, he maintains, a syncretistic religion from the start, with strong Christian features. Slotkin frankly states that in all essentials the Peyote religion is, for its believers, Christianity adapted to traditional Indian beliefs and practices.[48] "From the viewpoint of almost all Peyotists, the religion is an Indian version of Christianity. White Christian theology, ethics, and eschatology have been adopted

---

[43] Densmore 1941 p. 80.
[44] Stewart 1941 b, 1974, p. 220, 1987, pp. 19, 26, 51, and other works. Stewart's position was however not consequent. He writes, "It is questionable whether the addition of elements of Christian terms warrants calling the Sun Dance or Peyote, religions ... Christian religions. It appears to me more appropriate to consider them American Indian religions, to which a few Christian terms and concepts have been added" (Stewart 1980 d, p. 17).
[45] See La Barre's summary of this discussion in La Barre 1960, pp. 51 f.
[46] Stewart 1938, 1970, p. 790.
[47] Slotkin 1956 a, pp. 28, 34.
[48] Slotkin 1952, see also Slotkin 1956 a, pp. 44 f. Even more outspoken is the sociologist Bryan Wilson who – in his study of millenaristic movements – assigns to Peyotists a Christian faith, adapted to traditional American religion: Wilson 1973, chapter 13. Criticism in La Barre 1975 b, p. 262.

with modifications which make them more compatible with traditional Indian culture."[49] I think Slotkin here talks as an advocate of the Native American Church, not as an observer and analyst. His points of view on modern Peyotism come close to Stewart's. However, the two authors seem to disagree concerning the age of the Christian influence.

Other authors think that the Christian infusion occurred relatively late, as Slotkin does, but question the next to universal penetration of Christian elements presupposed by Slotkin and Stewart. La Barre, for instance, talks about a "patina of Christianity" in local Peyote circles.[50] He sees Peyotism as "a peaceful intertribal nativistic religion, in places somewhat acculturated to Christianity".[51] Some other authors like the Spindlers and Opler take a similar attitude.

Perhaps the chasm between these opinions is not as large as it may appear. Data which we have perused in the foregoing seem to indicate that in all likelihood there were Christian elements absorbed into the Peyote religion when, in the 1830s and 1890s, it spread from its Kiowa-Comanche nucleus. As we have observed, as early as 1892 Mooney noted that among the Kiowa Christ was the presiding divinity of the Peyote ceremony.[52] Stewart has clearly pointed out that whereas the Half Moon ceremony referred in particular to Indian legend and Indian supernaturals John Wilson's Big Moon ceremony more often involved Jesus, the crucifix and the Bible. Stewart adds that Wilson was of mixed Caddo, Delaware and (Christian) French ancestry and thus had a natural trend to internalize Christian concepts in his Peyote service.[53]

The Christian elements grew in number as Peyotism diffused in a milieu where only the Christian religion was sanctioned and authorized. An imperceptible Christianization took place. The Winnebago Peyote religion offers an example. As pointed out, it was introduced by the illiterate John Rave in the 1890s with, as Radin thinks, "possibly a few Christian teachings".[54] Later on a more Christian version was superimposed on the original message by the literate Albert Hensley who, among other things, instituted the reading of Bible texts. Although Hensley lost following after a few years his innovations were accepted.[55]

The Winnebago example was followed on other reservations. As in the Winnebago case, new proselytes brought in whole sets of Christian teachings. We have seen how they could be reflected in doctrine, rites and ethics. At least in

---

[49] Slotkin 1956 b, p. 64.
[50] La Barre 1970 a, pp. 281, 301.
[51] La Barre 1960, p. 45, cf. pp. 49, 52.
[52] Mooney 1892, p. 65.
[53] Stewart 1987, pp. 91 f.
[54] Radin 1923, p. 420.
[55] Radin 1923, pp. 421 f. Stewart pinpoints the following Christian innovations in the Cross Fire ritual: preaching, baptism (rubbing the forehead of the client with a dilute infusion of Peyote), singing hymns with Christian texts, presence of Bible, and the idea that roadman, drummer and cedarman represent Father, Son, and Holy Ghost (Stewart 1987, pp. 152 f., 159 f.).

the beginning, these new elements were not basic to the religion. The doctrine concentrated on the Supreme Being and Peyote, both Indian phenomena, but they had scarcely been brought together before; the rites followed Indian patterns, but had a stamp of their own; and the ethics corresponded to a new, pan-Indian and individualistic situation. The Christian elements were additive, and they reflected the new social environment in which the Peyote religion took its final form, white man's America. They therefore had no immediate deeper consequence.[56] However, they made the Peyote religion more fashionable and in this way undoubtedly facilitated its acceptance.

The intense Christian integration with Peyote in recent times corresponds more accurately to the situation depicted by Stewart and Slotkin.

These considerations have some bearing on the question whether the Christian traits in the Peyote religion facilitated its dispersion. We cannot speak of an early amalgamation between Peyotism and Christian religion. However, in a setting characterized by an increasing impact from Christian missions and a Christian surrounding the increasing amount of Christian elements in Peyotism must, as a consequence, have been auxiliary for the latter's chance of becoming accepted. That is, not accepted by the Christian missionaries who indeed always rejected Peyote in the early days (and still often do so), but by the Indians themselves. Gradually Christian missions created in the Indian mind an awareness of a new set of religious manifestations and a new structure of religious organizations. The Peyote movement combined old religious traditions with new ideas and values borrowed from Christianity. The Christian elements therefore became an important vehicle for the diffusion of Peyote.

Charles Hamilton maintains that Peyote eating serves as a "backdoor entrance" into Christianity, and he considers that it has converted many Indians who had earlier been indifferent to the teachings of the Christian missionaries.[57] This pronouncement certainly holds good today, but we may turn it around and say that, at an earlier stage of Peyote diffusion, Christian elements gave flux to the Peyote movement among persons who had lost or were about to lose their traditional beliefs.

This may sound as if some earlier arguments in this investigation were jeopardized: how could such a reception of Christian elements be reconciled with the fact that Peyote is a religion characterized by its Indianness? How could imported Christian traits pave the way for a basically Indian religion?

---

[56] Aberle who tells us that Navajo Peyotism is "explicitly Christian" nevertheless remarks that conversion to Christianity had little import for the Navajo until recently (Aberle 1982 b, pp. 176, 222). As we remember, Stewart describes a case where a Northern Paiute appears now as a traditional medicine man, now as a Peyotist, and now as an Episcopal deacon. Stewart's conclusion is that as a polytheist this man found all religions equal and serving the same ends, see Stewart 1956. A similar conclusion was reached by my Wind River Shoshoni informants, cf. Hultkrantz 1981 a, p. 227.

[57] Hamilton 1972, p. 92.

Such objections may seem reasonable, but we have to keep in mind that the inconsequences are only apparent. First of all, we must here distinguish between conscious Indian beliefs and subconscious psychic processes. What passed for Indian contents of belief may indeed have been ideas of Christian origins, or structured by Christian thoughts. Secondly, Indianness does not rule out Christian features if the latter present themselves as universal values or as compatible with Indian traditions. Thirdly, Christian features may attract Indian attention if they operate in an ideological setting imbued with or at least tinged with values and ideas emanating from Christian sources (without being recognized as Christian). It is my contention that this setting occurred on Indian reservations during the 1880s and 1890s. Christian missions were at this time established among the Indians – not all Indians, to be sure – and the general ideas and patterns of evangelization radiated out from the Mission Stations. The Christian teaching was perhaps not consciously accepted, but its general message reached the Indian tribes through a kind of "stimulus diffusion".[58]

Paradoxically, Christianity thus opened the doors for Peyotism, and Peyotism slowly developed into a conscious expression of Christian worship.

13. Ghost Dance and Peyote

It was mentioned in the foregoing (Ch. IV: 8) that in Ruth Shonle's opinion at the end of last century the Ghost Dance contributed to the dissemination of the Peyote religion. She writes, "The building up of intimate and friendly contacts was perhaps the most lasting effect of the Ghost Dance religion; its teaching of resignation was too far divorced from practical issues, its hope of relief too illusory to give lasting satisfaction. The dissemination of the peyote cult flowed easily along the newly opened channels of friendship."[1] Shonle was the first scholar to point out the Ghost Dance's role of paving the way for Peyote. However, Mooney had made such an interpretation possible by establishing that the Peyote religion was younger than the Ghost Dance among the Cheyenne Indians.[2]

This pronouncement was soon generalized into the scientific conviction that the Ghost Dance preceded the Peyote religion. Omer Stewart quotes statements in this direction from MacLeod, La Barre, Swanton, Barber, Underhill and others.[3] Stewart has objected to this kind of historiography. He demonstrates that according to documents many Texas and Oklahoma tribes – Comanche, Kiowa, Kiowa-Apache, Oto, Caddo, Southern Arapaho, Cheyenne, Pawnee,

---

[58] Kroeber 1952, pp. 344 ff.
[1] Shonle 1925, p. 57.
[2] Mooney 1907, p. 418. See also Stewart 1972, p. 27.
[3] Stewart 1972, pp. 27 f. La Barre (1975 b, p. 260) objects to Stewart that his statement properly concerns the Plains.

Tonkawa, Lipan and Mescalero Apache, Carrizo, Kickapoo, Shawnee and Osage – knew Peyotism before they knew the Ghost Dance.

A reminder of the chronologies of the two movements will immediately support Stewart's argument. The Peyote religion was, as we have seen, firmly rooted in Mexico since pre-Columbian days. It made its appearance in Texas in the 1700s, and was observed among several Indian groups in Texas and the surrounding areas in the 1830s and 1860s. The Ghost Dance religion, on the other hand, originating from westernmost Nevada, had a short flowering about 1870 and then, in a revised form, swept the western areas, including the Plains, in 1890–91.[4] The Ghost Dance was thus the younger religion. The fact that of these two revivalistic movements the Peyote religion alone survived, and the additional fact that the Ghost Dance had a spectacular outbreak before the Peyote religion had obtained its final distribution, does not allow us to postulate that the Ghost Dance religion preceded the Peyote religion in all places. The reverse is true.

La Barre contends that Peyotism spread to the Indians of the United States "mostly following the subsidence of the Ghost Dance, for which it largely substituted".[5] There is a certain, although by no means perfect, correlation between the dispersal of Peyote in the United States and the diffusion of the Ghost Dance of 1890.[6] There are important deviations, however. The Ghost Dance did not spread among the tribes of the Eastern Woodlands and the Southeast, nor did it reach the Apache; but it penetrated peripheral parts of California where Peyotism never appeared. Stewart lists several non-Ghost Dance tribes among those having Peyote in 1890.[7]

On the Plains in particular both movements were carried by tribes that had suffered from the conflicts with the whites in the later part of the nineteenth century. Many of the Peyote-eating tribes here joined the Ghost Dance, such as the Arapaho and Cheyenne, the Kiowa and Kiowa Apache, the Caddo, Pawnee and Oto.[8] On the other hand, some Northern Plains tribes were converted to the Ghost Dance before they knew Peyote.

Stewart finds no reason to accept Shonle's view that the Peyote religion followed in the wake of the Ghost Dance.[9] He rightly points out that there were, at the outbreak of the Ghost Dance, ardent Peyotists like the Comanche Quanah Parker who rejected the Ghost Dance and stuck to their Peyotism. It seems that because of his opposition most Comanche kept away from the Ghost Dance.[10]

---

[4] See Mooney 1896 a.
[5] La Barre 1960, p. 45.
[6] Cf. the distribution maps of Peyote in Posern-Zielińska 1972, p. 158 (map 1) and Driver 1961, map 13, and of the Ghost Dance in Lindig and Dauer 1961.
[7] Stewart 1972, p. 29.
[8] Cf. Mooney 1896 a, pp. 901 ff.
[9] Stewart 1972, p. 29.
[10] Stewart 1980 a, p. 184; 1987, pp. 34, 66, 74; Mooney 1896 a, p. 902.

On the other hand, a Peyotist like the Caddo John Wilson conducted both Peyote and Ghost Dance ceremonies.[11]

The whole problem of the relations between the Peyote religion and the Ghost Dance should be evaluated in terms of differences and similarities between the two movements.

The Ghost Dance was, like the Peyote religion, a revivalistic movement of a partly Christian extraction.[12] Like the Peyote religion it had deep roots in traditional Indian religion, particularly the Basin round dance, which was an annual thanksgiving ceremony of the same kind as the Sun Dance of the Plains Indians.[13] The message of the Ghost Dance was therefore recreation, but within a Christian eschatological frame. Round-dancing contributed to the restoration of the old balance of the Universe and the return of the dead. This peaceful message however became mixed up with more revolutionary expectations and was transformed on the Plains. It is possible that the warlike Northern Plains tribes, and in particular the Sioux, prepared for militant resistance against white domination, although for instance Stewart did not think so.[14] Anyhow, the white authorities lost their nerve and provoked unrest through, among other things, the arresting and killing of the Sioux Chief Sitting Bull in December, 1890. Shortly afterwards the massacre at Wounded Knee took place, with the annihilation of Big Foot and his band.

If we keep in mind that originally the Ghost Dance was a religious complex designed to cope with a new situation, an acculturated society in a state of dependence and subjugation, the parallel with the Peyote religion will become obvious. Bernard Barber, who like some other researchers took for granted that there was a succession from Ghost Dance to Peyote religion, nevertheless made a correct observation when pointing out that both movements "may in part be understood as alternative responses to a similar socio-cultural constellation".[15] With a glance at the transformation of the Ghost Dance among Plains Indians Slotkin declares that the peaceful Peyotism succeeded to the militant Ghost Dance as a more successful solution of a nativistic and national problem. Accommodation, not aggression, was the key to success.[16]

Aberle, on the other hand, rejects this equalization of the two movements. For him they are not commensurable: using his own technical terminology he states that the Ghost Dance is "transformative", i.e. aims at changing society, but the

---

[11] Stewart 1980 a, pp. 184 f., Thurman 1973, p. 283.

[12] The Christian impact is in fact lesser than has been presumed, see Hultkrantz 1981 a, p. 280.

[13] This is the reason why Burridge finds so many parallels between the Ghost Dance and the Sun Dance that he could say the Ghost Dance was "the heir" to the Sun Dance (Burridge 1969, p. 80).

[14] Stewart 1980 a, pp. 181–187.

[15] Barber 1941 a, p. 675.

[16] Slotkin 1956 a, pp. 20 f.

Peyote religion is "redemptive", i.e. aims at a state of human grace.[17] This is certainly correct, but does not rule out the fact that in both cases there was (is) an ultimate religious meaning, to restore the harmony with God, the spirits and the world.

It is therefore possible to say, with Barber and Slotkin, that the Peyote offered a similar answer as did the Ghost Dance, but one better adapted to the prevailing situations on the reservations.[18] Peyotism flowered after the disappearance of the Ghost Dance. However, it is not therefore correct to assume that the Ghost Dance paved the way for the Peyote religion. It may have done so in parts of Oklahoma, but this cannot be proved. All we can say is that the time and situation were ripe for an intertribal, modernizing religion with native roots. The Ghost Dance and the Peyote religion both filled the requirement, but the Peyote religion was better adapted to the new time and the new circumstances. It made for a sound development.

---

[17] Aberle 1982 b, pp. 317, 341 f.; cf. also above, Introduction. As pointed out in the foregoing (Ch. IV: 3) the Ghost Dance, but not Peyotism, offered salvation. However, this was salvation on a national, but not an individual, personal level. Salvation was thus not coupled to redemption, it did not make the Ghost Dance a redemptive movement in Aberle's sense.

[18] Peaceful adjustment and cooperation with white authorities may be singled out as characteristic qualities in Peyotism in contradistinction to the Ghost Dance. There are other differences as well, such as the lack of aggressive prophetism and stress on personal redemption in Peyotism. In spite of what has been said above about the reference to individualism in Peyotism, it is perhaps possible to adduce the more collectivistic spirit in Peyote séances as one of the crucial factors for the progress of Peyote. The Ghost Dance, although embedded in a collectivistic frame, favoured individualism by putting a prize on revealing personal visions from the dead and the other world. The Peyote religion, on the contrary, emphasized togetherness and common visionary experiences produced by Peyote. The strong bond of fellowship was a solace in the face of an adverse world.

V. The Religious Motivation of Peyote

1. A Question of Values

The problem of the spread of Peyote is of course intimately bound up with the problem of the personal motivation of Peyote cultists. Ideally it should be possible to separate the individual's personal motivation from the driving forces which are at work on other levels, such as social and economic factors. However, we know how intricate the relations are between personality structure, culture and society; Ralph Linton's (and Abram Kardiner's) "basic personality type" was some decades ago a measure of the close connection of all these factors.[1] At the same time there are in human society individual variations against a common background, individual preferences and inclinations. Due to physiological and psychological differences, education, roles, age and sex, occupations and personal experiences all human beings deviate from each other (and from the norms of society), and qualitative "personalities" emerge who react differently from each other. The history of Peyote is full of such personalities.[2]

It is obvious that these personalities could all mobilize different reasons for joining the Peyote Church. While the first taste of Peyote might have been a pure coincidence, or a desire to try something new and unknown, as it was, for instance, to the Winnebago John Rave (or Little Redbird),[3] the enrolement in the Peyote congregation and the systematic use of Peyote has a clear relation to its effects. These effects had a different impact on different personalities. The Comanche chief Quanah Parker, for instance, turned into a fervent Peyotist after having overcome a stomach ailment through partaking in a Peyote ceremony.[4] Radin's informant S.B. experienced a social (and religious) security through Peyote. S.B.:s story is most instructive. As a young man he had failed to acquire a guardian spirit in the vision quest. However, he nevertheless pretended to have been blessed by a spirit, and boasted about it. His false situation undermined his psychic balance, and he turned into a drunkard and reckless womanizer. Some friends made him try Peyote. To his surprise he had visions, and even fell into a deep trance. From now on he was an ardent Peyotist. Peyote had granted him the visions he had been unable to acquire earlier, and apparently visions of a more satisfactory kind – in retrospect.[5]

Now, these are conscious motivations, and a more careful investigator should

---

[1] Linton 1945, pp. 128 f. Cf. also Linton's foreword to Kardiner 1939.
[2] Cf. Stewart and Aberle 1984.
[3] Radin 1950.
[4] Cf. Jackson and Jackson 1963.
[5] Radin 1920, in particular pp. 430–449.

certainly strive to find the meaning on a deeper, latent level. Anthropologists usually refer to psychological and sociological mechanisms. It is easy to apply psychological and sociological perspectives on the Peyote religion, and some students have done so with great profit, as we have seen from the foregoing survey. Without saying so most of these investigators seem to assume that the psychological-sociological analyses of such mechanisms are real "explanations" of the Peyote religion. The present author would dispute such an interpretation. It is, in my view, arbitrarily reductionist in outlook, and a direct function of the student's own ideological outlook.

La Barre, for instance, considers the belief in a supernatural world to be "mere psychological adaptation to inner anxieties".[6] Such a psychoanalytic standpoint is certainly not new and surprising, but it is adduced here since this author has written a classic study on Peyote.

As against such cock-sure judgments of hidden contexts unknown to man I would prefer a more cautious and, to my understanding, more realistic attitude. It means that emic statements on religion should be accepted as symbolic interpretations of a *religious* content. It could be argued, of course, that such perspectives have also been applied by La Barre *et consortes,* as in the statement which was published in *Science* in 1951 by La Barre, McAllester, Slotkin, Stewart and Tax. Here we find, inter alia, the following judicial formulation: "A scientific interpretation [of the Peyote effects] might be that the chemicals in peyote diminish extraneous internal and external sensations, thus permitting the individual to concentrate his attention on his ideas of God and, at the same time, affecting vision and hearing so that these ideas are easily projected into visions."[7] Since Slotkin and Stewart have been almost believing Peyotists this paragraph apparently came about as a compromise between believers and non-believers. It does not betray La Barre's more deep-lying critical interpretation.

The problem of the basis of religion is enormous and cannot be discussed here. However, it is worth quoting Ulf Drobin's statement that both the idealism in religious studies and the social determinism of social anthropology[8] presume that their epistemology and theory reflect empirical truth. "Each perspective is, of course, governed by world view and intention and is completely legitimate."[9] One theory is as "scientific" – or, more plausible, "unscientific" – as the other. To presume that we "know" the secret of religion is a great illusion. It seems to me that many anthropologists reason from such a faulty conviction,[10] and many religionists as well.

Whether we are believers or non-believers, for our purposes there is one way

---

[6] La Barre 1972, p. 262. Cf. also La Barre 1970 a, in particular the Introduction.
[7] La Barre et al. 1951.
[8] This does not exclude that there are materialists in religious studies and idealists in social anthropology (Evans-Pritchard, for instance).
[9] Drobin 1982, pp. 270 ff.
[10] Cf. the famous definition in Geertz 1966, p. 4.

out of the dilemma: to approach the subject-matter as a phenomenon in its own right.[11] Culturally religion stands for an array of different trends and traits bound together by their reference to a supposed supernatural reality.[12] Religion expresses an existential human concern, man's effort to orient himself in the universe and create relations to what he perceives to be another dimension of existence. Whatever the truth of religion, this concern is there. It is expressed in cultural forms, and it saturates human culture, gives it directions and inspiration. I should like to call this *the perceptive approach* to the understanding of religion.

It means that religion is there as a cultural category just as is art or folklore, music, dance or science. The obsession of some anthropologists to delete religion as a cultural field, even to suppress its name, has greatly damaged our understanding of religion, and also detrimentally influenced the continued anthropological exploration of religion.[13] Such an attack against the cultural field of religion obviously springs from a conviction of religion's ultimate foundation in psychic and social processes that are easily defined. However, there is no necessary causal connection here between the description of religion as a cultural category and the belief in religion as an ontological category. Edward Sapir, for instance, wrote several papers in which he featured American Indian religions although, with Freud, he thought it possible to dismiss religion as such as "socialized compulsion neuroses".[14] If, as has been suggested here, religion is interpreted as an existential orientation towards man's integration with the universe, this makes reductionist theories less valid. The psychological and sociological interpretations may retain their meaning for some of the mechanisms involved, but they do not explain away religion. Religion keeps its place as an irreducible, unitary mental phenomenon.

It is, I think, in this light we should see the Peyote religion. It is a manifestation of man's existential concern, an effort to create relations to a wider existential context, identified as the supernatural world of Peyote. It is supernatural because it transcends the limits of the everyday comprehensible reality. In essence the Peyote religion does not deviate from Indian religious tradition, but it presents a new way of grasping and interpreting this tradition. According to this new way religious experience is released or triggered by the Peyote herb.[15] Several students studying the relation of drugs to religion have opined that it is impossible to draw a line between hallucinogens and other means to achieve trance, such as fasting, drumming, waking, flagellation or breathing

---

[11] Ninian Smart points out that, although religious nuclear concepts may be projections of our own psyche, our description of projections should not be confused with the theory about them – this is the difficulty when a Durkheimian or Freudian conclusion is aimed at too early. See Smart 1984, p. 81.
[12] Cf. Hultkrantz 1983 a.
[13] Hultkrantz 1977 b.
[14] Sapir 1949, p. 355.
[15] Clark 1969, pp. 88 f.

exercises.[16] There is possibly a difference in the nature of the ecstatic state, but this is difficult to prove. In Peyotism it is the religious experience, not Peyote as such, that is important, although due to its miracle-promoting efficacy the Peyote herb itself may become divinized.

In outlining the factors responsible for the quick acceptance of the Peyote religion one factor stands out above all the others as a frame for them all, the religious qualities of the Peyote movement. In many papers on Peyote this particular factor has been strangely overlooked. Why did the American Indians turn to a religion rather than a social or political movement in their days of distress?[17] Simply because they looked to religion as the ultimate solution of human misery and the ultimate meaning of human life. Perhaps then it is not so strange after all that the religious factor has not been duly observed, since general works on messianistic movements and crisis cults rarely mention it, or take it for granted or not for granted, depending on the author's personal idiosyncrasies. Burridge, for instance, identifies four general types of explanation, the psycho-physiological, the ethnographic, the Marxist and the Hegelian.[18] And La Barre's theories of causality are political theory, military theory, economic theory, messianistic theory, "great man" theory, acculturative theory and psychological theory.[19] With reductionist interpretation of religion as a leading light such a selection of causal factors is perhaps not so surprising. Explanations of causalities in the Peyote religion have followed suit.

In this connection I concur with the sociologist John Wilson when he criticizes the positivistic and utalitarian assumptions of most social scientists analyzing religious movements. These scientists, he says, tend to view adherents of such movements as "wishful-thinking, fantasizing people, grasping in extremis at non-rational ways of overcoming their distress".[20] Religious beliefs, he continues, are being treated epiphenomenally, as mere channels of self-interest – the only channels that are open for the expression of such interest. The symbolic dimension of religious beliefs has thus been "virtually ignored".[21]

Of course, those who cling to psychological and sociological determinism will never assign a place to religion as such in their analyses of Peyotism. They will shrug their shoulders and quietly remark that religion as "explanation" begs the question. The wealth of material illuminating the Peyotists' insistence on the central import to them of Peyotism as a religion would be dismissed as state-

---

[16] Gelpke 1966, pp. 224, 226. Similar points of view have been expressed by Aldous Huxley, Robert Masters and Jean Houston, Arthur Deikman and others.
[17] As La Barre (1970 a, p. 260, 1971, p. 14) correctly states, Peyotism has never been an anti-government uprising or a separatist national movement. It is enigmatic how Vittorio Lanternari could define Peyotism as "riposta culturale all'urto dei bianchi" (Lanternari 1960, p. 100).
[18] Burridge 1969, pp. 117–110.
[19] La Barre 1971, pp. 14–26.
[20] Wilson 1977, p. 149.
[21] Wilson 1977, p. 150.

ments on a manifestly psychological level which the researcher needs to reduce to a deeper, latent level.

To students who see religion, and in particular here Peyote religion, in this light its social dimensions will be the decisive criterion. An author like Roland Wagner, referred to in the foregoing, blames those investigators who have elaborated the visionary features of Peyote consumption for having placed an inappropriate emphasis on the purely mentalistic aspects of the Peyote religion. Against this outlook Wagner adduces "the more fundamental, down to earth, pragmatic factors which motivate people to join the Native American Church": health care, personal success, a satisfactory existence, etc.[22] Wagner admits there is some sort of mysticism present, but it is "applied", and does not resemble Christian and Hindu mysticism. "There is no withdrawal into a life of solitary contemplation as in the monastic traditions of Old World religions."[23]

Wagner overlooks the fact that there are many modalities of mysticism, and that mysticism does not rule out mundane interests. St. Teresa, for instance, alternated between extreme mystical introversion and a very active and practical daily life. It may be that Peyotists are not much for solitary contemplation, but they receive their spiritual gratification in a collective setting, the Peyote congregation. The almost complete suppression of not only mysticism but also acts of faith in some newer literature on Peyotism makes us wonder and indeed question the onesidedness of such Peyote research.

When we scrutinize the original documents on Peyotism the perspective looks different. New adherents of the Peyote religion have often expressed a *religious* satisfaction of now being settled in a safe faith. S.B., Radin's informant, had a trance in which he saw Earthmaker (God) and had a vague feeling of a *unio mystica* with him. He experienced that he knew the thoughts of others, and he went with his thought; "I was my thought", he said.[24] S.B. got over his alcoholism, and went around telling everybody "that this religion is good. Many other people at home said the same thing."[25] His fellow tribesman, John Rave, experienced a similar transformation from being a heavy drinker with murderous thoughts to a harmonious, balanced man in the Peyote Church.[26] Radin writes, "When I first met him in 1910 it was hard to believe that this mild, gentle, outgoing, self-disciplined and manifestly well-integrated man had ever been a completely torn and disoriented individual."[27]

The Winnebago dramatized such a personal transformation as a *conversion,* if we may trust Radin. It included the abstention from alcohol,[28] the discarding

---

[22] Wagner 1975 b, p. 200.
[23] Wagner 1975 b, p. 203.
[24] Radin 1920, pp, 441 f., 1923, p. 407.
[25] Radin 1920, p. 449.
[26] Radin 1950, p. 258.
[27] Radin 1950, p. 290.
[28] Apparently, many Indians and whites first thought that this was a direct effect of the Peyote ethics, cf. Radin 1920, p. 431 n. 126.

of medicines and guardian spirits, the abandoning of smoking, tobacco offerings and feast-giving, the giving up of the respectable Medicine Dance – keeping nothing holy except Earthmaker.[29] (We may wonder what became of Peyote as a spirit in this process.) Such radical turns may characterize a movement that is in direct opposition to traditional religion. However, where individuals are free to alternate between religions, as Stewart has described in *Three Gods for Joe* and I have outlined in my writings,[30] the reaction will be milder, less tumultuous, but certainly mark a transition to a new standard of religious behaviour and ethic conduct. A Navajo, for instance, confessed to Aberle how the Peyote "teaching of the Almighty" made him realize the significance of his relationships with his closest relatives. He also realized that his body was of earth and that he breathed through the rays of the sun and the air. He did not feel any fear any more, for he now depended on the Almighty.[31]

The Peyote neophyte experienced the Peyote taking as a true religious event, as may be seen from Radin's and Spindler's conversion accounts.[32] A Menomini Indian described how during the prayer meetings he could feel a presence, "just like there's somebody around"; "it's a kind of holy feeling, the presence of the Spirit of God." "It makes you want to pray deep in your heart."[33] Similar accounts can be had from several books and articles on Peyote experiences. They testify to the true religious value of the Peyote rituals.

The religio-ecstatic Peyote experiences can sometimes reach a surprising intensity. We have seen that participants in a séance could "die", that is, enter a deep trance, during which their souls made extensive journeys outside the body (cf. Ch. IV:7). Sometimes they "die" without leaving the body, but their body-control is taken over by a spiritual being, God. The classic example is, again, Radin's informant S.B. At a Peyote session, he reports, "I died, and my body was moved by another life. It began to move about; to move about and make signs. It was not I and I could not see it. At last it stood up." Then follows what the body said: it proclaimed that the Bible and Peyote cultic regalia were just ornaments(!), that the advice of the Bible should be followed, and so on. The raconteur continues, "Not I, but my body standing there, had done the talking. Earthmaker (God) had done his own talking. I would be confessing myself a fool if I were to think that I had said all this, it (my body) told me."[34] The Winnebago called this state of mind a "shaking" state, considered holy by conservative Winnebago.[35]

In his comment on this extraordinary event Arbman declares that one could

---

[29] Radin 1920, pp. 431 f., 1923, p. 393.
[30] Stewart 1956, Hultkrantz 1981 a, pp. 28 ff., 219 f., 222 f.
[31] Aberle 1982 b, p. 381. The form "Almighty" for God is typical for the Peyote Church.
[32] Radin 1920 and 1923, ibidem, Spindler 1952, p. 154.
[33] Slotkin 1952, p. 616.
[34] Radin 1920, pp. 446 f., 1923, pp. 410 f. Radin's comments, in the former work, are not quite to the point.
[35] Ibidem.

not wish for a clearer, more drastic and graphic expression for "the completely depersonalized and automatic nature of the ecstatic activity".[36] It could be debated whether the ecstatic situation should be labelled inspirational, a case of automatic speech, or truly possessional (in a psychologic sense). The paucity of instances of states of possession in North America could be an argument against such an interpretation here. Furthermore, the idea of having the Supreme Being as a possessing agent seems shocking. However we judge this incident, there is a closeness here between man and God that is quite extraordinary.

There is, on the other hand, no real evidence of a genuine mystical union *(unio mystica)* in the Peyote exaltation. Marlene Dobkin de Rios and David E. Smith have certainly pointed out that the use of psychedelic drugs may stimulate such a union; in this context they refer, among other things, to the use of Peyote.[37] So far however I have been unable to find any examples of a mystical union in the comprehensive literature I have gone through. The only possible reference I have is Slotkin's general statement on the subject. He emphatically says that there occur in some cases such mystical experiences, although they are relatively uncommon and are limited to a certain, knowledgeable type of personality with a "mystical temperament". However, these Peyotists rarely have visions and look upon them as distractions. It is evident that Slotkin thought he had these experiences in his own communion with Peyote. His description of them is however too vague to deserve the designation mystical union: "The mystical experience may be said to consist in the harmony of all immediate experience with whatever the individual conceives to be the highest good."[38] In fact, what he seems to have experienced is the sense of a sort of cosmic unity that is so typical for persons indulging in hallucinogenic drugs.

Whatever the value of such experiences, they make up part of a flow of religious sentiments and convictions saturating the Peyote movement. It is worth pointing out that the Peyote religion spread as a religion, a new configuration of religious certainty. It formed a new branch of that old tree that stretched out through history and has been man's heritage in North America since ancient times when the immigration from Asia took place. When therefore it is asked, why the Peyote movement spread as a religion, the answer is obvious: in aboriginal America all ideological movements have been religious because religion is felt to be a necessary part of the wider scope of existence. As a movement that underscored the deeper values in life the Peyote movement was and is necessarily religious.

On this point, however, there is no unanimity among scholars. Leaving different theories of the origins of religion aside we shall concentrate on the modern theory of a "biological" origin of the Peyote religion.

---

[36] Arbman 1963–70 II, p. 150.
[37] Dobkin de Rios and Smith 1977, pp. 270 f.
[38] Slotkin 1956 b, p. 69.

2. Peyote and the "Pharmacological" Theory of Religious Origins

There is of course one circumstance that at first sight may seem to jeopardize the conclusions that have just been drawn. If we decide that the Peyote movement was carried by its religious character, how are we to explain that this religion was ramified around the hallucinogenic cactus Peyote if its magic properties are not accounted for? Does not this predicament give evidence that it was the qualities of Peyote that created this religion?

Students unanimously agree that Peyote has not gained importance due to any addictive properties, for it is not habit-forming (see Ch. I:1). However, they also agree that as a hallucinogenic plant it produces effects which may invite religious interpretations, just like LSD has done in recent times (and in a largely irreligious setting). Peyote is not the only natural drug in America to be this powerful. There are many psychotropic plants in America (mushrooms, cacti, beans, seeds, leaves, barks and vines) which have influenced religious life in the same way – some say they created it.

It is probably not too farfetched to say that speculative thinkers have here, in the last decades, found a new theory of religious origins. While older evolutionary theories paid attention to spontaneous visions and dreams as primary religious factors (cf. in particular Tylor) the new program traces religious beginnings from "artificial" visions produced by the use of hallucinogenic drugs. As far as I know no anthropologist or other researcher at least has vindicated the thesis that religion sprang forth exclusively from the use of psychotropic plants; other sources have also been mentioned, or implied.

The new program would have been inconceivable without the growth of the awareness of the existence and the use of psychotropic drugs. The knowledge of these, and the discussion of their import for cultural and religious life, is rather late. For a long time they were out of focus even among students who were familiar with the use of plant stimulants. Edwin Loeb, for instance, was well acquainted with the use of *Datura* in southern California, where it played a role in initiation ceremonies and shamanic visions, but in his short survey of intoxicants among so-called primitive peoples, written some fifty years ago, he only paid slight attention to their stimulating religious effects.[1] As Michael Harner thinks, it was the interest in hallucinogenic drugs in modern western culture that opened the eyes of the anthropologists and other investigators to the importance of psychotropic plants in traditional societies.[2] Pharmacologists, botanists and anthropologists developed constructive theories. However, some discoveries of importance had already been made in the nineteenth century. For instance, the pharmacologist Louis Lewin published in 1888 an article about a

---

[1] Loeb 1943. Loeb writes primarily about intoxicating drinks.
[2] Harner 1973, p. vii.

new stimulating drug, *Anhalonium Lewinii;*[3] this was for a time the technical name for Peyote. During the first part of the present century, New World psychedelic plants came under particular scrutiny of men like Schultes, La Barre and Wasson.

The attention given the New World in this connection was not fortuitous. It was discovered that America has the vast majority of psychoactive plants and mushrooms that are used. Schultes who established this fact in 1963[4] now counts about a hundred hallucinogenic species used by aboriginal Americans.[5] As La Barre underlines it is important to say that they were used, for we do not know if the Old World, so much larger in size, has a greater store of psychedelic plants.[6] The important fact is that nowhere in the world did the aborigines know so much about making drugs from these plants as in the Americas. La Barre therefore talks about "the New World narcotic complex".[7] Although the emphasis is on the southern United States, Middle America, Amazonia and the Andean area it seems possible to say that through Peyote this complex also stretches up into Canada.

La Barre has in detail described this narcotic complex, its constituent psychotropic plants and their ethnographical use.[8] He thinks the complex dates from earliest immigration days which to him means the Mesolithic.[9] (Like all dates for the arrival of the Indian in America this date is highly conjectural.) More specifically, on the basis of ceramic representations, he attributes Peruvian Mescaline cactus drugs to the Chavin period and later (from 1300 B.C.), whereas through C^{14} dating the earliest use of Peyote may be referred to the time span 810–1070 A.D.[10] It may of course be much older in aboriginal use, but we know nothing about that.[10a]

Associating to thoughts put forward by Schultes La Barre suggests that American Indians have been culturally motivated to seek out and use psychotropic plants.[11] La Barre envisages, as a dominating cultural program, the vision quest and shamanism.[12] Indeed, he proposes that *all* our knowledge of the supernatural derives from the messages of religious visionaries, such as shamans, and that shamanic ecstasy "may be illuminated by attention to ancient

---

[3] Lewin 1887/88.
[4] Schultes 1963, p. 147.
[5] See the account in La Barre 1979 a, p. 37. Cf. Schultes 1972.
[6] La Barre 1970 b.
[7] La Barre 1964.
[8] Cf. the literature adduced in the two preceding notes and La Barre 1970 a, pp. 143–149.
[9] La Barre 1970 a, pp. 124 f.
[10] La Barre 1979 a, pp. 33 f.
[10a] The occurence of sculptures of Peyote in the art of western Mexico (Colima) from about the birth of Christ may indicate Peyote consumption from this early time, as suggested by Furst (Furst 1976, p. 9; cf. also Ripinsky-Naxon 1993, pp. 168 f.).
[11] La Barre 1970 b, p. 75.
[12] La Barre 1970 a, p. 160, 1979 b.

hallucinogens".[13] This is a generalization that can hardly be acceptable if we cling to the hypothesis that man's sense of another reality is the foundation of religious awareness. On the other hand, this awareness may be concretized in visionary experiences, and here is where shamans come in. As La Barre rightly says, they belong to the hunting culture, the oldest culture in the world.[14] It is quite reasonable to suppose that initially shamans made use of hallucinogenic plants in America. It is also possible to adopt La Barre's point of view that man's interest in psychotropic drugs in the Americas may be referred to the fact that the hunting-shamanic complex was preserved until the present time in great parts of the continents.[15] As stated by Peter Furst, shamans have always tended to use psychoactive drugs and drinks in order to facilitate the entrance to ecstasy.[16]

So far it is possible to endorse La Barre's thesis, allowing for the amendments which have been given. However, his emphasis on the culturally programmed shaman is somewhat weakened by his insistence that to an American Indian the psychotropic effect in a plant was clear evidence of its possession of "medicine", supernatural power.[17] It is La Barre's opinion that all psychotropics were sacred in America because their mind-changing abilities constituted proof of their containing supernatural power.[18] It is however difficult to see how this pronouncement ties in with the theory of cultural motivation: were shamans culturally motivated to take drugs, or were drugs taken because of their inherent supernatural potency? It seems obvious to me that the idea of the supernatural preceded the use of drugs in religion and granted them their supernatural quality.[19] To say that the use of drugs automatically brought on their supernatural nimbus is to fall into the same trap as Tylor did when he referred the origin of supernatural things to strange occurrences.[20] He failed to understand that strange occurrences became supernatural because they tallied with an already existing supernatural tradition.[21]

Among the protagonists for the "pharmacological" theory of religion La Barre has been selected here because his contributions to this theme are more nuanced and well-researched than most others. I accept his viewpoint that for cultural reasons shamans made use of psychoactive plants and mushrooms, but

---

[13] La Barre 1972, p. 261.
[14] La Barre 1970 a, pp. 137 ff., 1970 b, p. 76; Hultkrantz 1965, pp. 310 ff.
[15] La Barre 1972, p. 272. See also La Barre 1957, p. 710, and 1975 b, pp. 263 f. The Americas and Siberia originally belonged to the same hunting culture, as recognized by Nordenskiöld, La Barre and myself, and therefore still manifest among hunters the individualistic pattern of living and the religio-magic devices (shamanism) corresponding to this pattern.
[16] Furst 1972 a, p. viii.
[17] La Barre 1970 b, p. 77, 1972, p. 270, 1975 a, p. 34.
[18] La Barre 1970 a, p. 143.
[19] Cf. Stewart's statement that Peyotism helps the Indians, not just because of its psychedelic stimulation, but because it is a religion: Stewart 1979/80, p. 293.
[20] Tylor 1891 II, p. 158.
[21] Cf. my comments in Hultkrantz 1982, pp. 164 f.

cannot endorse his statement that "the psychotropic drugs ... may have been critically important in shaping shamanism, a form which may underlie in time all religions, both of the Old World and the New".[22] Still less is it possible to adopt his thesis that "the personal magic of ecstatic shamans borrowing supernatural forces from nature evolves into religious worship and placation of cosmic gods in whom the power permanently resides".[23] One gets the impression of going back into Frazer's time.

On the other hand, the use of psychoactive medicine in religion certainly stimulates the shamans to a more mechanical handling of religious notions. This has been observed by, among others, Marlene Dobkin de Rios. In close agreement with Anthony F. Wallace's investigations[24] she emphasizes the cultural conditioning of drug-induced visions which, as Wallace demonstrated, is easily proved through the stereotypic patterning of hallucinatory experiences. de Rios points out that it is cultural variables such as beliefs, attitudes, expectations, and values that structure this patterning.[25] The guide in this structuring process is the shaman who is called "stage manager for this hallucinogenic drama".[26] The author hesitates in joining La Barre in ascribing a great role to drugs in forming religious origins.[27] However, she maintains that hallucinogenic plant rituals are linked to man's capacity to manipulate and control supernatural powers, as contrasted with the religious submission to them.[28] This manipulation of the supernatural is of course another phrase for magic control. Certainly, if we retain the term magic (which many authors doubt we should), the shamanic act is basically magic. Within the shamanic complex the Peyote then functions as medicine of magic. That is, until it has become a cult object in the Peyote religion.

This is all we can say about the "pharmacological" origins of religion. As exemplified by Peyote, the drug was from the beginning probably a resource for shamanic practice, for the attainment of ecstasy.[29] However, it was therefore not a means for discovering the supernatural world. Rather it made the shamanic assistant spirits available.[30] As has been stated earlier (Ch. I:1), in the Peyote religion the consumption of the cactus enhanced religious feelings and made the Peyote a cult symbol. La Barre is absolutely right when he claims that through

---

[22] La Barre 1964, p. 138.
[23] La Barre 1970 b, p. 79. For a criticism of La Barre's reconstruction of the origins of religion in La Barre 1970 a, see my review of the latter work in Temenos 7 (1971), pp. 137–144.
[24] Wallace 1959.
[25] Dobkin de Rios 1977 a, p. 268, Dobkin de Rios and Katz 1975, p. 66.
[26] Dobkin de Rios 1977 a, p. 266. Cf. Dobkin de Rios and Katz 1975, p. 67.
[27] Dobkin de Rios 1976, p. 11, 1977 a, p. 268.
[28] Dobkin de Rios 1977 a, p. 268, 1977 b, p. 189.
[29] That the use of Peyote originated in a shamanic milieu was earlier suggested by Ralph Beals, see Beals 1932, p. 128.
[30] Cf. Dobkin de Rios and Katz 1975, p. 71.

the use of psyochotropic drugs like Peyote psychically ungifted persons were able to partake in supernatural experiences.[31] Peyote contributed in this way to the democratization of shamanism (cf. Ch. I:2).

The rise of the Peyote religion is thus the last stage of a development that leads from the use of Peyote as instrumental to shamanic ecstasy, to its use as a means of producing wonderful visions and feelings of total harmony among men. In this development the original components of magic have become increasingly overshadowed by the religious goals.

3. The Religious Factor in the Adoption of Peyote Religion

It should thus be obvious that the Peyote religion ought to be discussed as a religion, a faith, and not just as a popular movement. It is of course a nativistic movement, but its content is religious, and it fulfils the functions of a religion. This is the reason why Schultes is mistaken when he sees its appeal solely because of its medical properties. La Barre has rightly remarked that Schultes is wrong, and that Peyote medicine is part of supernatural power.[1] And supernatural power is an expression of a religious complex.

It is however one thing to say that Peyotism is a religion, and that all causes of Peyote dissemination should be seen against a religious background, and another thing to pinpoint religion as a direct cause among others in the adoption of Peyote. To be precise, an Indian who decides to attend Peyote meetings regularly does so because he believes in the power of Peyote, but he always refers this belief to some external cause, and not to a previous revelation of a supernatural being. The strange experiences during the cultic act, and the final effects of his participation in this act, in particular with regard to health and family happiness, bring about the conviction that this is a good religion. It seems that religion is there as an implication, a frame for the great experiences, but that believers seldom refer to religious factors when discussing why they turned to Peyote.

If some particular factor should be singled out it would be the extraordinary experiences during the Peyote ritual, primarily the vision. Scholars like Stewart and Howard consider visions in Peyote meetings unimportant and infrequent, but this is questionable. The believers do not always talk about their visions, perhaps because they take them for granted (particularly on the Plains). It is true that visions are scarce among the Navajo, for reasons that have been mentioned

---
[31] La Barre 1964, p. 125.
[1] La Barre 1960, p. 54.

(Ch. IV:7). However, a perusal of Steinmetz' field material from the Oglala Lakota reveals that among these Indians there is a preponderance of visions in the Peyote ritual – visions of powers that are present, visions of distant places, soul wanderings and prophetic visions.[2] Visions are communications with supernatural beings, and there is evidence that they have promoted religious faith.

Among the Navajo there is another significant value that takes precedence, man's experience of peace and harmony in conjunction with the world order.[3] According to Aberle, the Navajo found that the reduction of livestock upset the world order, so the supernaturals withheld the rain.[4] With Peyotism a set of new supernatural symbols appeared, in particular a God who was not a part of nature but an all-powerful deity transcendent above reciprocity in religious practice, and above the world order.[5]

One seeks in vain however in Aberle's material for believers who say they sustain this interpretation (an interpretation which I suspect is quite correct). Aberle conducted a long series of interviews with the Navajo Indians and is able to state that, in the vast majority of cases, initial use of Peyote was for the purpose of being cured.[6] However, he then states that other appeals grew in importance the more individuals became indoctrinated in the beliefs and values held by the Peyotists.[7] Aberle summarizes three "ostensible appeals": first and foremost, the access to supernatural power; secondly, the insurance of equality and, in some respects, superiority to the whites; and thirdly, validation through the Peyote experience of the conception of access to power.[8]

What Aberle has said here about Navajo reactions can be generalized: the initial motivations are not expressly religious, but the religious motivation dominates once the new proselytes have become indoctrinated. *Nota bene,* the ideological frame is always religious, and the seeker for Peyote blessings knows that. He tries to find his happiness within a religious complex, but he does not – usually – refer to religion as the decisive factor for his first attendance at the Peyote ritual. Once he has become a member of the congregation he refers however to religious blessings.

It is possible that the Christianization of Peyote has facilitated this secondary interpretation. We have seen how this process made the diffusion of Peyote possible (Ch. IV:12). At the same time Peyotism was an inroad for Christianity among American Indians. It was, and is, very difficult for Christianity to gain a stronghold on Indian reservations. Where Christianity has found a response among semi-acculturated Indians it has been in the form of an alternative re-

---

[2] P. B. Steinmetz, Oglala Lakota Field Material (in the present author's possession).
[3] Aberle 1982 b, p. 15.
[4] Aberle 1982 b, p. 200. Cf. König 1983, pp. 122 f.
[5] Aberle 1982 b, p. 202.
[6] Aberle 1982 b, pp. 183, 380–398.
[7] Aberle 1982 b, p. 186.
[8] Aberle 1982 b, pp. 193 f.

ligion, a religion of Sunday service, weddings and burials. The contrast is evident with many African churches which really wholeheartedly engage their devotees, although separate developments within these churches have brought them close to old pre-Christian beliefs and cults – perhaps an answer to the segregating policy of the ruling white societies.[9] The success of Christian religion in Africa has certainly a good deal to do with the similarities in sociopolitical organization and monotheism between the ancient Hebrews, the ultimate founders of vital Christian tenets, and the African peoples. The myth treasure is also partly common to Hebrews and some black African tribes. In North America, however, Christianity arrived as a very foreign religion, having very little in common with American Indian religious traditions. To find a path Christianity had to be radically adjusted to Native American religious patterns. The Peyote movement became a vehicle for such developments. We have found how for instance Slotkin asserts that nowadays the Indians regard the Peyote religion as a version of Christianity. Gusinde considers Peyotism to be a substitute for Christianity.[10] Perhaps it is sound to say that Christian ideas have in the easiest approachable way caught the hearts of the non-amalgamated Indians through the Peyote religion. Basically however Peyotism represents another religious direction.[11]

In its Christian orientation the Peyote religion is offered many possibilities to deepen its religious contents, indeed, to develop towards an advanced theology, ethics and eschatology.[12] Certainly, many reports on Lakota Peyote rituals and religious experiences make a familiar Christian impression. And yet, some concepts which sound Christian are not Christian at all but part of an old American Indian pre-Christian tradition. For example, the concept of sin. At many Peyote meetings some members of the cultic group stand up towards dawn to make a public confession of their personal offences in the past and to ask the persons whom they have injured for forgiveness. Bernard Barber characterizes such confessions as "at once a mechanism for the dissolution of individual anxieties and a mode of social control".[13] This is a partly "reductionist" interpretation. Of course such effects arise, but the basic feelings are outspokenly religious: in the Peyote way sacrality demands that a believer cleanses his relations to God and men. Only in this manner can religious blessings, harmony and safety come upon man. Any Peyote believer could supply this information. A closer historical and psychological analysis of the confessions will be found in Ch. IV:3.

The confession of sins thus corresponds to a religious ideal that stresses harmony between man and the divine world. This ideal belongs in America pri-

---

[9] Hastings 1976.
[10] Gusinde 1939.
[11] Cf. Hultkrantz 1977 a, p. 441.
[12] Slotkin 1956 b, p. 64.
[13] Barber 1941 b, pp. 674 f.

marily to a southern tradition.[14] It is realized within the Peyote religion which as we know has a southern heritage. Whether this ideal has ever functioned as a stimulus for those who sought this religion is difficult to say. Interview statements which could be interpreted in this direction may just as well bear witness to secondary readjustments of the interviewer's mental state before joining the Peyote group. We might expect that curiosity rather than mental needs would have been operative. On the other hand, in view of the disintegration of cultural and religious values at the time of the greatest spread of Peyote, and the emergent need to have an integrated world of beliefs and values to turn to, such a possibility cannot be excluded. It is just so difficult to prove it.

Therewith we face a dilemma in an investigation of the present kind. I refer to the validity of the Indians' own information on their conversion. There is in fact not much point in referring to Peyote confessions about a person's state of mind and religious direction before the conversion since memory is an unreliable source of information, and religious commitments before or after the conversion may play their part in distorting the recollections. For instance, we know that some Peyotists were Catholic catechists before they accepted the Peyote religion. How much can we rely on their information on the appeal of Peyote, how much of what they say is dependent upon established Catholic doctrine and religious sentiments? In other cases we find that people's recollections of their feelings when they became Peyotists have been coloured by their sentiments after the conversion – sentiments which, in their turn, might have been modelled on the doctrinal pattern of Peyotism.

It is therefore futile to pursue this type of inquiry any further. We may expect that religious needs have been operative, consciously or unconsciously, in the decision to join the Peyote church. As Axel Ljungdahl insists, when the foundation of a culture is religious, and a lost harmony of mind shall be restituted, this process must work within a religious frame.[15]

Like some other social movements in our time, such as Scientology, Peyote has profited from its classification as a religious movement. In this connection we may also recall Susan Budd's reminder that a protest movement survives if it has a religious foundation.[16]

It deserves mentioning in this general perspective that the Peyote religion has served as a model and source of inspiration for other religious movements and even traditional religions. Voget has demonstrated how the Crow Elk Lodge with its full-moon ceremony offers a merging of elements which have been drawn from both Plains bundle ceremonialism and Peyote religion. Thus, the use of cedar incense, canes, cigarette prayers and tea in the moon ceremony recalls Peyote ritual details, and the occurrence of a water woman and a cedar

---

[14] See Hultkrantz 1987, Ch. 2.
[15] Ljungdahl 1975, pp. 88, 90, 90 f.
[16] Budd 1974, p. 158.

man points in the same direction. Indeed, the calling of the ceremony "tipi way" refers to the name of the Peyote ritual in the Kiowa-Comanche tradition.[17] Another observer, Barbara Jackson, notes that the Chippewa of Rice Village who adopted the Peyote religion thereby also experienced the strengthening of their traditional values and behaviour.[18]

---

[17] Voget 1984, pp. 318 f.
[18] Jackson 1980.

VI. The Decisive Causes: An Assessment

1. A Scale of Causes

As should have emerged from the foregoing survey there is considerable dissidence among researchers concerning the reasons for the spreading and adoption of Peyote. Even where an investigator joins several factors together he usually deviates from a colleague who prefers another constellation. The discrepancies have their roots in our lack of knowledge of why, originally, Peyotism was accepted: the sources scarcely give the evidence. Stereotyped traditional conversion stories from individuals becoming Peyote believers some twenty or more years after the first creation of a Peyote community in the tribe or on the reservation throw little light on original motivations. What material there is from the beginning of Peyote introductions spotlights the medical factors as the basic causes.[1] However, as was pointed out in the foregoing (Ch. IV:5), behind the medical factor we discern deeper causes, the sanction of supernatural powers through visions, the need of religious assurance.

While this contribution to a solution of the problem cannot claim to be the definite word in this difficult issue it may, in any case, pretend to give a more expansive view of the range of causes. It is my intention to separate here the basic motivation in human consciousness from the strictly cultural causes which certainly are influential in forming the human mind but may primarily be identified as external factors in the making of religion. The basic personal motivation is the religious sentiment which guides and transforms all cultural expressions so that they conform with extant religious needs. The nature of this religious motivation was displayed in the last chapter. In the interpretation of this author, if there is any basic factor behind the Peyote complex it is man's religious quest.

It is no easy task to develop this point of view: the individual choices vary with time and place among the individuals. We are here reminded of Omer Stewart's observation: "It is as difficult to ascertain why Nevada Indians joined the peyote cult as it is to know why any person was ever converted to any church. Actual reasons may be as numerous as the devotees themselves, and stated reasons may not be the real ones, but there seems to be no doubt that the rationalizations given by the different Indians are sufficient to justify all observed results."[2] I am not too certain that the last statement is valid. In particu-

---
[1] Cf. Aberle and Stewart 1957, p. 2; Vecsey 1988, p. 180 f; Stewart 1987 (throughout).
[2] Stewart 1939, p. 67.

lar I think that our main deficiency is that we do not know the personal motivations of the leading personalities in bygone days.

There is another perspective also involved here. By dividing between the basic personal motivation and external factors or causes I indicate indirectly a separation in my argument between scientific explanation and historical causes. Within our present scientific "paradigm" (Kuhn) it is of course impossible to attribute in scientific terms an existential value to religion. In Melford Spiro's words, "a testable, i.e. scientific, theory of religious origins will probably always elude our explanatory net".[3] All we can do is to reserve the place which would be taken by a scientific explanation to the ubiquitously valid observation of man's religious disposition. On the other hand, cultural and historical causes are not scientifically explanatory, but may be accounted for.

In the following it is these causes, as far as they can be identified in the case of Peyote dissemination, and to the extent that the author finds them particularly meaningful, which will be presented in their context.[4] We should of course preferably distinguish between psychocultural and historical causes, but they are often intertwined and are therefore less amenable to a distinctive treatment. The program preferred here is to outline the general preconditions for the reception of the Peyote religion, and then to indicate the factors primarily responsible for its extension, and the factors impeding it extension. All these factors are of course culturally variable, and their change with time should be observed. What matters here however is the general picture, not the specifics. It is an effort to assess the collected assemblage of causes.

In the preceding discussion of the research opinion some of the possible causes have been presented. Some of them were, more or less, refuted, others were approved. The arguments developed in this connection need not be repeated here. On the other hand, some other proposed causes of less importance were not listed, but will be mentioned here if they seem tenable. Finally, the author will produce some additional causes which may appear reasonable. In these cases it will be necessary to expound the matter in more detail.

---

[3] Spiro 1966, p. 99.

[4] Some of the "causes" apostrophized by researchers on Peyotism are so general and meaningless that they have not been mentioned in Chapter IV. For instance, Stewart refers to such arguments as the desire for prestige as cult leaders, the reception of payment for shamanic services, the longing for social contact, and marital ties (Stewart 1944, pp. 88 f.) Other "causes" are really consequences of a Christian re-orientation, such as an appealing ethics and eschatology (cf. Slotkin 1956 a, pp. 44 f.)

2. The Growth and Development of the Peyote Religion

In order to understand the emergence of the Peyote religion we have to realize two characteristics of tribal, or "primal" religions, their relative tolerance to other religions and their ethnic and cultural confinement. This double tendency may appear as a contradiction. However, the tolerance is enacted on a spiritual level, the cultural enclosure is a more or less unconscious process in man directed by the cultural mechanism.

The open attitude to other religions among North American natives is clearly established in the source material, and need not be elaborated upon here.[1] Some further observations need, however, to be added. We notice that this tolerance is limited in two respects: a foreign religion, in particular a mission religion, is not allowed to impinge upon one's own cults and cultic activity – scholars of comparative religion talk here about "cultic exclusiveness";[2] and tenets of a foreign religion are not accepted unless they are built on (supernatural) personal experiences. The history of Christian missions in North America is filled up with examples of clashes between clergymen and tribesmen on account of Christian transgressions and bans on Indian cultic executions. The Peyote cult has of course fallen under the same curse, whether the Peyotists have been accused of narcotic indulgences or not.

There are excellent examples in the famous Jesuit Relations three hundred years ago of the contempt and impatience of north-eastern Indians when they were confronted with the beliefs and dogmas of the white people. "Thou hast no sense" was their reproach to the missionaries when the latter asked for Indian ideas of the afterlife, without paying attention to their other-world experiences. This was certainly in their eyes a despised credulity.[3] I am also reminded here of the angry criticism a Shoshoni gave me when I tried to uncover his ideas of the Supreme Being: why did I not myself pray and meditate to see how God is?[4]

If we keep these hesitations in mind it is obvious that the Peyote religion had the chance to develop, provided the right circumstances prevailed (see below). Peyotism did not always oust traditional worship, it added to it. It referred its truth to the experiences of individual Peyotists, and to collective experiences in the Peyote group. It is interesting to repeat again what Stewart has to say about the tolerance of Peyotists (Ch. IV:12). He emphasizes that Indians are not raised in one religion exclusively, but can belong to several religions at the same time.[5] He gives many examples of Peyotists who have taken part in several religions

---

[1] See further above, Ch. IV:12.
[2] The opposite is, according to Helge Ljungberg, "doctrinal exclusiveness".
[3] Kenton 1954, pp. 57 f.
[4] Hultkrantz 1981 a, pp. 233 f.
[5] Stewart 1980 d, p. 18.

at the same time, and who have visited an assortment of churches of different denominations. He maintains that it has been characteristic for the Indians not to throw away old religious traditions when accepting new ones.[6]

As always in American Indian religion there is no rule without exceptions. There are, says Stewart, Indians who criticize the mixture of Christianity and Peyote, or who, although Peyotists, declare that "Christianity is our motto through life".[7] In the latter case the speaker obviously looks at Peyote as a form of Christianity. As we have seen, this seems in many circles to be the final destination of the Peyote movement.

Most students of the Peyote religion have seen personal and social crisis situations as the triggers of the Peyote religion (Ch. IV:2–3). It is difficult however to list these factors as general preconditions and, moreover, they cannot be regarded as the main sources of the Peyote religion (cf. Ch. V). They will be dealt with in the next sub-chapter.

The scenario of religious change is usually, but not always, cultural change. This should not be understood to mean that religion is just an epiphenomenon of culture; what it means is that the expressive forms of religion are not operative if they do not correspond with cultural and social values. Peyotism is a good example of this rule: when tribal religions became weakened as a consequence of the downfall of Indian tribal culture and society the Peyote religion tended to take their place. Expressed in another way the original Mexican Peyote rituals were transformed into a religion of their own.[8] At the same time attitudes and ritual forms were adjusted to Native North American patterns.[9]

We are here primarily concerned with Oklahoma and Plains Indian religions. A map of the distribution of Peyotism in North America shows convincingly that the Plains area was the nucleus of the Peyote religion.[10] The instances from the Eastern Woodlands are occasional and mostly represented by tribes which during the nineteenth century had been allotted reservations in Oklahoma – the former homelands of some Plains tribes (Kiowa, Kiowa Apache, Comanche and Wichita). The Peyotism of the Great Basin is late and can be referred to a time when the Plains culture had largely transformed the indigenous Shoshoni, Bannock, and Ute cultures.[11] Whereas so many features of Plains culture and religion can be found in Peyotism – despite Stewart's denials – he is right in his insistence that there is very little place for aboriginal Great Basin beliefs in the ideology of Peyotism.[12] The Southwest, particularly the Pueblos, constituted a barrier against Peyote. We shall soon return to the question of why this was so

---

[6] Stewart 1987, p. 67.
[7] Op. cit., pp. 96, 107.
[8] Cf. Hultkrantz 1992, p. 139. Cf. also Vecsey 1988, pp. 198 f.
[9] Hultkrantz 1992, p. 2.
[10] Driver and Massey 1957, p. 269, map 76.
[11] Gunther 1950, pp. 174–180.
[12] Stewart 1944, p. 81.

(Ch. VI:4). The main result of this quick survey is that the Plains Indians have been the main carriers of the Peyote religion.

This is in conformity with the general profile of Peyotism as demonstrated in preceding chapters. The Plains colouring of so many features of the Peyote religion makes it probable that the latter received its stable form in the Plains setting. This also seems logical in view of the fact that the Peyote-growing area was closest to the Southern Plains Indians of pre-reservation times. The Lipan Apache, the Coahuiltecan tribes, the Caddo are precisely those tribes whom we meet as Peyotists in the early eighteenth century.

Such a perspective does not of course outrule the legacy of early Mexican traditions. It was demonstrated before that quite a few ritual elements are common to Mexican and Plains Peyotism (see Ch. I:2). It is even possible that these common elements once belonged to a coherent pre-Columbian Peyote area comprising the "cultural sink" of northern Mexico and the southernmost Plains. A southern Texas tribe like the Tonkawa might have taken part in this spiritual community, perhaps also the Caddo. With the exception of the latter and the Coahuiltecans, other tribes mentioned above were newcomers to the Southern Plains about 1500 A.D.[13] However, beyond this conjectural area of intensive Peyotism we perceive another, coinciding with the ancient civilization of Mexico, where Peyote was probably used to intensify religious experience.[14] It is reasonable to see the Aztec Peyote consumption as an outgrowth of the Peyote use on a more popular, "shamanic" level over the whole of Northern Mexico and parts of Texas.

The changes that Peyote ritualism underwent on its way from the Mexican borderland to the North American Plains have been described in the foregoing (Ch. I:2). In particular it was emphasized that a tribal anniversary ceremony for the benefit of the vegetation and man, turned into a private ritual for man's wellbeing, and that the "shamanic" character of the proceedings gave way to a more democratic pattern. At the same time, Peyote itself became the center of ceremonies, and a heretical religion. The change was motivated by the new cultural situation on the Plains.

Here we meet the *first adaptation* of Peyote to Native North American culture. Some factors in the Southern Plains cultural situation seem to have determined the course of adaptation:

(1) The "democratization" of shamanism in the vision-quest pattern. It is a fact that on the Plains the import of shamanism has given way to the general rapport with supernatural beings through the vision quest (Ch. IV:7). Indeed, Shonle goes so far that she says the vision-quest pattern killed shamanism.[15]

---

[13] Coahuiltecan seems to have been a collective term for several unrelated groups. See Newcomb 1961, pp. 32 f., Hale and Harris 1979, p. 170, Goddard 1979, pp. 355, 375 ff.
[14] On the use of Peyote in Aztec Mexico, cf. La Barre 1975 b, pp. 35 ff., Slotkin 1955, pp. 205, 209.
[15] Shonle 1925, p. 59.

This is not correct, however; until modern times medicine men have been distinguished from other visionaries by their possession of a multitude of spirits, and by their ability to heal sick people. In the Peyote ritual, a trusted man, sometimes but not necessarily a medicine man, presided over the ceremonies. (The Mescalero constitute, as we have seen, an exception, the shaman always being the ritual leader among them.) In Mexico the shaman had extraordinary experiences of Peyote visions, while his profane tribesmen just followed suit. On the Southern Plains, the amount of Peyote intoxication and not professional status determined the depth of psychic, in particular visionary experiences.

(2) The society setting. Plains culture is famous for its many societies – cult associations, military societies, and age-group societies. The cult associations are often organized around a central cultic symbol, such as a tribal bundle containing a sacred pipe or other sacred object. Peyote was incorporated into such an organization as a cult symbol, or rather, a society was formed around the consumption of Peyote. In both cases, the pattern of ritualism was set by Plains traditional heritage. Also the application of Plains ritualism affected Peyotism: the old documents tell us that luck in war was promoted by Peyotism. Typically, in contradistinction to Mexican Peyotism women were excluded from the ritual.

(3) Possible transference from earlier drug consumption. As we have seen in preceding chapters, some anthropologists consider it probable that the taking of Peyote has supplanted the earlier use of intoxicating or cleansing drugs, such as the black tea of the Southeast, or the mescal bean of the Southern Plains. This is quite possible, but difficult to prove. It seems certain however that the ritual pattern of Peyotism qua a Southern Plains ritual pattern has been similar to the Mescal Bean ritual pattern. It is probable that the ritual consumption itself owes some of its outlines to the mescalism consumption pattern. The Peyote took over from the Mescal Bean because of its milder physiological consequences.

(4) Peyotism as a means to individual achievement. The Mexican character of Peyotism as a collective seasonal experience in a milieu of plant collectors or horticulturists was, north of the Rio Grande, transformed into a more frequently occurring personal experience in a sectarian group of individualistic hunters. Although the feeling for the welfare of the group was in focus more emphasis was laid on personal feelings, personal luck and personal care of one's own family.[16]

This process of adaptation belonged to the post-Columbian times up until the 1850's. Our source material for this change goes back at least to the 1700's. The reasons for the adoption of Peyote in those days are of course little known. My own hypothesis would be that the cultural situation itself on the Southern Plains demanded an absorption of available "medicines" into the pattern of visionary experiences and tribal-bundle organizations.

---

[16] The collective spirit of the Mexican age was at the same time preserved in the intense common experiences of sympathy, affections and coherence in the ritual group.

The spread of Peyote after the 1870's, coincided with what I shall call here the *second adaptation*.

I think the date for a new development can be set at the end of the Indian wars, which overthrew the old Plains Indian cultures. The same opinion has been presented by Shonle and Slotkin (cf. above, Ch. IV:2). Driver and Massey sum up the discussion adequately in the following well-balanced statement: "Anthropologists are not in complete agreement as to the reasons why peyote spread where it did when it did. However, one explanation recurs again and again in the literature. During the last hundred years in the United States, the Indians have been fighting a losing battle against the encroachment of our culture. Anxieties have multiplied to the point of despair. A new drug associated with a new religion which promised to improve the individual's plight had strong appeal."[17] The culmination of the Indian wars took place in the 1860's and 1870's. They ended on the Southern Plains with the capitulation of Chief Quanah Parker in 1875, and on the Northern Plains with the surrender of Sitting Bull and his Hunkpapa Sioux in 1881. It is certainly no coincidence that thereafter the Comanche war leader, Quanah Parker, became a protagonist of the Peyote religion.

The long-range causes of the Indian defeat were devastating epidemics, introduced by the whites, the annihilation of the buffalo, the staple food of the Plains Indians, and the growth of white settlements and communication links. Of course, the military supremacy of the numerous and well-equipped American troops decided the outcome.

It is important to observe that all these events took place on the Plains. There were certainly wars of resistance at the same time in other parts of the continent, among the Modoc in the 1870's, among the Apache in the 1880's;[18] but these wars were more marginal to the general course of American civilization (this said with all respect to Captain Jack, Victorio, Mangas Colorados and Geronimo!), and they had less profound consequences for the religious situation – in any case for the diffusion of Peyotism. Again, then, the Plains Indians are the key to the development of Peyote religion. What this meant to the elaboration of the Peyote religion will be obvious in the next sub-chapter.

The military defeat of the Plains Indians was followed by their forced resignation of sovereignty and political independence. The tribes became wards of the Washington Government. They were moved to reservations, situated in most cases within their ancient hunting grounds, but away from areas that were or could be attractive to the expanding white population. In Oklahoma, (Indian Territory), the key-country for the spread of Peyotism, tribes from the Southeast, and some tribes from the Northeast, had been collected on reservations since the 1820's. The Southern Plains tribes were concentrated to Oklahoma,

---

[17] Driver and Massey 1957, p. 271.
[18] Some other wars between the 1870's and 1890's, like the Ute uprising, the Nez Percé war, and the Bannock war, may be counted as peripheral Plains wars.

becoming close neighbours of these other tribes, and apparently spiritually influencing them. The Southeastern Creek and Chickasaw, the Northeastern Delaware and Kickapoo had already changed their dress and way of living to the demands of Plains existence and the fashion of Plains Indians; now they were imbued with spiritual values imparted by their new Plains Indian neighbours. Peyotism was one of these values.

Most of the Southern Plains Indians, and some of the Northern Plains tribes, were moved to reservations that were situated far away from their sacred places. For instance, on their reservation in Montana the Cheyenne were hundreds of miles away from their sacred mountain in the Black Hills (Inyan Kara in Sioux, Bear Butte in English) where they used to receive visions.[19] In the long run such conditions undermined the main religious expression of the Plains Indians, the vision quest.

The arrival of Christian missions constituted another threat to traditional religions. The Indians were, superficially at least, forced to accept a new, foreign religious ideology. As we have seen (Ch. IV:12), the result was a split religious situation, where traditional religion kept its hold over the individual in different degrees, and Christianity was resorted to in sacred situations that had been introduced by the whites (Church-going on Sundays, baptisms, weddings, funerals, etc.). Some Indian thinkers tried to reconcile the two religions, interpreting them as different ways to the same religious truth, or assigning to Christianity a lesser value, in any case from the Indian point of view. As acculturation set in, more Indians were inclined to accept Christianity, or at least to reassess their Native religions as being in conformity with Christianity (cf. for instance the symbolic reinterpretation of the Sun Dance).[20] Peyotism took part in this development. However, Christianity has never been wholeheartedly accepted by the Plains Indians (or other North American Indians) in the same way as was the case among the peoples of Africa. African social structure, African mythology and African concepts of God have been closer to the Jewish-Christian ideals.

Perhaps the worst manifestation of missionary activities – which stretched from the ways of dressing to the teaching of sin and grace – was the prohibition of traditional religious ceremonies. To these belonged certain dances, considered to be indecent, the celebration of tribal bundles, and, first of all, the annual thanksgiving ceremony, the Sun Dance. The Sun Dance was forbidden in different tribes from the beginning of the 1880's, and in several tribes it was stopped for ever.[21] In other tribes the Sun Dancing continued, but only occasionally, and in secret. Indeed, as Bea Medicine has said, the celebration of the Sun Dance became a resistance movement against white supremacy and white intrusion.[22] In a religion as dependent on religious practice and ceremonialism

---

[19] See Powell 1969, vol. I, pp. 18 ff., 279.
[20] Hultkrantz 1981, pp. 231 ff., 258 ff.
[21] Cf. Liberty 1980, appendix pp. 173–175.
[22] Medicine 1981, pp. 277–286.

as the Plains religion is, their absence meant psychic deprivation, disillusionment and anxiousness (cf. above, Ch. IV:2, 3, 4). As always in situations of cultural-ideological conflict, religious doubts ensued in many individuals.

The shocking acculturation had, however, some positive traits. The reservation system meant – at least in the long run – that inter-tribal warfare ceased, and old enemies could meet to concerted action over the tribal boundaries.[23] The railroads opened new communication facilities. A network of railroads crossed the Plains and joined it with other areas.[24] The construction of roads, and the development of the postal service were other instruments for quick communications between Plains Indian and other more remote reservations.

The communication between distant places and the use of mail service presupposed of course a mutual understanding. Within the Plains area, the sign language could still be used to some extent.[25] However, the need for a common language made itself felt (cf. Ch. VI:3).

The reservation system which freed the Indians from wars and work for subsistence allowed them – that is, the men – much leisure time. As had been the case traditionally, such time could be used for religious ceremonies. But which ceremonies?

This was the situation in the 1880's when Peyotism started to spread. It marched right into the spiritual vacuum that the end of the Indian wars and the take-over of the whites had created.

3. Factors Enhancing the Diffusion of the Peyote Religion

Our main object in this investigation is, as was said in the Introduction, to try to reveal the factors behind the acceptance and diffusion of Peyotism. It has been demonstrated, in Ch. IV, how different writers have understood these factors. The following analysis is the present author's own interpretation which, of course, in many aspects builds on the previous survey. For a scholar dealing with the anthropology of religion it should be principally important to make a distinction between factors and ulterior motives. The former are focussed on the external conditions, whether they are instruments or traditions, the latter refer to the mental, in particular religious, conditions. It has been shown above (Ch. V) that, according to the author's understanding, these conditions are of an intrinsic religious nature. In practice however, it is very difficult to apply this

---

[23] Hartmann 1973, p. 256.
[24] Webb 1931, pp. 270 ff.
[25] Clark 1885.

distinction, for the religious motivation pops up here and there.[1] The review of opinions in Ch. IV is illustrative in this regard. The following exposition will, unfortunately, suffer from the same weakness.

In this sequence we shall thus look upon the major co-operating factors which promoted the rapid diffusion of the Peyote religion at the end of the last and the beginning of this century. The opposition against Peyote, and its particular fate in the Southwest, will be dealt with in Ch. VI:4. The later contributory causes of Peyote diffusion will be presented in Ch. VI:5, together with a general summary of the results of this investigation. The reader should be aware of the restrictions of the scope of investigation pointed out in the Preface, in particular, that local causes and developments can be more closely discussed only in exceptional cases.

The outlines of the preceding sub-chapter brought us to a point where, to quote a Biblical expression, the time was fulfilled. The old Plains culture lay in shambles, ethnic freedom was gone, religious values were in doubt when the cultural existence to which they were integrated only randomly survived. Four possible religious solutions seemed to be at hand: to give up religion completely; to turn to Christianity; to revive and perpetuate traditional religion; to seek a new religious way. We cannot tell how the individuals of those days fought their mental battles, but we may with Radin suppose that some of them were highly aware of the choice they confronted, while others more or less anxiously followed the path of their spiritual leaders or were indifferent as to the outcome.

The first possibility, an agnostic or even atheistic stand, was mostly out of the question. As has been emphasized in the foregoing, the religious interpretation of life was and is a most basic part of Indian consciousness, so much, indeed, that it relates to Indian nationalism. I have experienced how Indian nationalists have delivered their messages in uncompromised religious terms. On the other hand, I have found very few Indian agnostics, and only one confirmed atheist.[2] Other field researchers may have come to other figures, but I doubt that the results differ very much.

Christianity's difficulties to establish itself and to oust traditional Native religion has also been discussed in several connections. Besides the structural obstacles, mentioned in the last sub-chapter, it has against itself the fact that it is a foreign religion, not Indian, and that it lacks the charismatic and experiential character (except in certain sectarian movements, such as Pentecostalism) which is so typical for Indian religions.

Traditional religion could survive, and did so in spite of the persecution of old ceremonies, until with the Collier administration of the 1930's it received a

---

[1] There is the further complication of religious motives changing in time and space – of which we know very little.
[2] My field experiences are not limited to the Wind River Reservation but also relate to discussions on other Plains Indian and Basin Reservations.

reinstatement. It was, however, a modified tribal religion that now appeared: many of the old knowledgeable religious authorities were gone, and had taken their secrets with them to the grave, and the ceremonies that remained changed or had already changed character. For instance, the Sun Dance lost some earlier features, such as the symbolic fight at the bringing home of the center tree, or the self-torture (until the 1970's), but absorbed other elements from minor rituals; indeed, in some places the Sun Dance overtook most of the traditional religious traits, for instance, the vision quest.[3] However, at the time of the Peyote explosion the Sun Dance was banned as emasculated.

What remained was the possibility of finding a new religious synthesis, a religion which stood for the most crucial life values, conserving a heritage from the past and joining it with ideas and behaviour orientations which befitted the new, broken cultural situation. There were two answers, the Ghost Dance and Peyotism, alternative responses to a similar socio-cultural situation.[4]

The Ghost Dance of 1889–90 failed partly because it coupled religious rejuvenation with old-fashioned military action or, at least, ideas of such actions,[5] partly because its prophecies of an immediate eschatological change were not fulfilled. The relations between the Ghost Dance and the Peyote religion were discussed in Ch. IV:13. Peyotism was, as we have seen, much older and managed to survive the Ghost Dance crisis due to its better adaptation. There could be some doubt as to Peyotism's ability to conform to a military pattern in modern times. In any case, like the Sun Dance which turned into a peaceful Dance Peyotism re-orientated itself in a more peaceful direction after the Ghost Dance or thereabouts.[6] The association between warfare and Peyote religion, so common in the past, had of course no actuality in the new times.

Peyotism was on the whole a better answer to the needs of the Plains Indians at the time. It referred to traditional patterns of religious expression, and it mediated an immediate relation to the supernatural. At the same time it was able to integrate important aspects of the new value systems and organizational forms promoted by Christianity and white civilization in general. It represented a middle way between traditional tribal religion and Christianity. And it had a flexibility and simplicity that made it easy to adopt and to adapt to different cultural systems – it became the herald of pan-Indianism, as we have seen (Ch. IV:8).

The factors which the majority of anthropologists have presented as causative to the diffusion of Peyote have too often missed the salient points in the process.

---

[3] Cf. Hultkrantz 1981 a, pp. 244, 248, and Jorgensen 1972, pp. 191 f., 212 ff.
[4] Barber 1941 b.
[5] There is little doubt that whites provoked such actions through their policy and military dispositions, cf. Stewart 1980 b.
[6] The Sun Dance, once integrated with the Plains war pattern, changed among the Shoshoni about 1890 to a Dance for health, peace and well-being. Cf. Hultkrantz 1981 a, pp. 219, 229 f., Jorgensen 1972, pp. 18 f., 77, Shimkin 1953, pp. 435 ff.

A common idea is that cultural shock, personal suffering and economic deprivation – all due to cultural acculturation, if this concept is accepted (sometimes it is not) – have called forth a nativistic reaction which, in its turn, has favoured the acceptance of Peyotism (cf. Ch. IV:2–4). Aberle's account of Navajo Peyotism is here demonstrative: a great reduction of the livestock (sheep) took place in 1933–1935, and in 1936 and the following years there was a rapid spread of the Peyote religion.[7] There is no reason to distrust this description of the historical course, but it would be wrong to consider the deprivation as such as the primus motor of the religious development: here it was a question of finding a more satisfactory answer to the sufferings in life than the traditional ritual, *a search which entirely took place within the religious setting*. No doubt deprivation paved the way for Peyotism, but only in the sense that it made it possible for the Navajo to more generally adopt a religion which already existed among them (see Ch. IV:2, 3).

It is another matter that, as was pointed out above (Ch. IV:4) this change of religion, or addition of a new religion, could be associated with feelings of uncertainty and anxiety. As I have mentioned, such anxiety is the reaction of a religious person when his or her religious values are at stake (Ch. IV:4). In the Peyote movement confessions of committed offences – according to old traditions in aboriginal America – might have eliminated personal disturbances and thus facilitated personal adjustments.[8]

Other arguments for the diffusion of Peyote, such as social prestige and economic gain for the Peyote propagandist, can be easily disregarded. It is true that some individuals benefitted from their active roles, but it was always a gamble whether they should win or lose. Considering the fact that the Peyote religion challenged traditional religious customs it seems more to the point to presuppose that religious conviction was a decisive motive for most converters. Only in exceptional cases could other motives have been operative (cf. Ch. IV:10).

At the same time we must not ignore the fact that basically the inclusive religious pattern, or religious tolerance, of the American Indians made the spread of new ideas easier here than in, for instance, dogmatic religions in the Old World. This factor was dealt with in Ch. VI:2.

Many researchers have, as has been shown in the foregoing, emphasized the simple religious structure of Peyotism – simpler than any traditional tribal religion, and of course simpler than Christian religion (Ch. IV:9). The Peyote movement contains as it were a "gist" of Indian religion, a pan-Indian quality that made it possible to transcend tribal boundaries (Ch. IV:8). When in Reservation times old tribal religious patterns increasingly passed away Peyotism remained, an Indian religion available to the uprooted individual who found his trust in resistant common Native American values.

---

[7] Aberle and Stewart 1957, pp. 105 ff., 1909.
[8] Cf. La Barre 1947.

In this connection we are reminded of the fact that Peyotism throughout the centuries was influenced by other religions. It brought along much Mexican ideology, both mythological and ritual,[9] and some ritual symbolism was found in the Plains Indian religion.[10] The Mescal Bean cult obviously had an impact on Peyotism (Ch. IV:6, VI:2). Among the Delaware Peyotists Petrullo found ritual traits which obviously were derived from the old Delaware (Lenape) tribal annual ceremony, the Big House Ceremony.[11] And then, of course, Christianity made a deep impact on Peyotism. The outcome of all this penetration by outside religious influences was that Peyote was more easily adopted among Indians of the regions where the impact, assimilation and – sometimes – fusion took place.

The processes through which these changes were enacted are mostly called acculturation (or, particularly in the Great Basin, culture contact). Much has been written about acculturation since Redfield, Herskovits and Linton wrote their *Memorandum* in 1936,[12] and some criticism has been delivered. In particular the aspect of acculturation has been attacked as a finished situation. Edward Spicer, for instance, defined acculturation as a process inaugurated by many types of contact and differential processes of change.[13] His view that there are persistent symbolic references which withstand change has been accepted by scholars such as Armin W. Geertz[14] and was in fact independently developed by Verne Dusenberry.[15] Personally I should prefer to talk about "traditional frames" which better interpret the situation of wholeness in which new elements are caught up.

It is my contention that through such an acculturative process the decisive factors in the formation of Peyotism were and are at work, a process that is still going on. Open and covert nativism have given the process its direction. As far as this author can see the dominant factors are the following:

(1) The therapeutic value of Peyote. With the possible exception of some Kickapoo and Caddo groups, referred to by La Barre, medical treatment seems to be the most common reason given for calling a Peyote meeting.[16] This is at least what the people themselves say. We have noticed how indications of a shamanic ceremonial lead appear from several corners, although it is stated that not the shaman, but Peyote, heals a sick person (cf. Ch. IV:5, 8, 10). It is also possible to point out that the first "missionaries of Peyotism" were men who had

---

[9] For a short survey, see La Barre 1975 b, pp. 35 ff., 54 ff.
[10] Op. cit., pp. 57 ff.
[11] Petrullo 1934, pp. 26 ff.
[12] Redfield, Herkovits and Linton 1936.
[13] Spicer 1961, pp. 517 ff.
[14] Geertz 1992, pp. 15 f., 161 f., 170.
[15] Dusenberry 1962.
[16] La Barre 1975 b, pp. 58 f. However, there is evidence of doctoring at Caddo meetings, see Stewart 1987, pp. 91 f.

been cured from a disease by Peyote.[17] As was demonstrated above, however, it is not a question of medicine in our restricted sense, but of medicine as a supernatural quality (Ch. IV:5). The medical effects are biphenomena of Peyote's general supernatural character. The medical effects were more important than other effects because, in the century after the cessation of the Indian wars, health problems became a main issue in Native American ritual. There is no certain information about the medical properties of Peyote in ancient times.

(2) Expansion of Plains cultural patterns. A closer study of Peyote history reveals that Peyotism was closely bound up with Plains Indian culture during the past two centuries. With the expansion of the latter Peyotism could also expand its domains.[18]

We have seen that Peyotism, in spite of its ultimate origin in more southerly quarters, was well integrated with Southern Plains cultural values and ritual symbolism. This means that it had not changed the patterns of Southern Plains religion. As Elizabeth Colson has emphasized, although everything in a culture is in perpetual change people's models of how things should be are static.[19] New religious elements may pour in, but through their adaptation to existing models they are not experienced as changes. Only a major confrontation may alter this picture. Peyotism, apparently, was well adapted on the Southern Plains. Howard was of the opinion that the Peyote instruments are felt to be general Indian on the Southern Plains, but are distinguished as particularly pertaining to Peyotism on the Northern Plains.[20] This observation is interesting and could indicate that the northerners perceived the alien flavour of Peyotism as it spread northwards.

And yet, as Raymond Wood has pointed out, the Plains culture portrays a striking uniformity. "There were a number of mechanisms which moved cultural elements from one Plains group to another, thus contributing to areal homogeneity", he states. We can speak of mechanisms for moving ideas, or mechanisms for moving individuals from group to group. Such passage of ideas could be favoured by trade, warfare and visitation, whereas the passage of individuals found place via marriage, slavery and adoption.[21] Several Peyote researchers, for instance Slotkin, mean that the similarities of ritual paraphernalia

---

[17] Hultkrantz 1992, p. 143.

[18] Vecsey points out that Peyotism "flowered on the Plains because Plains culture was already homogenized to a large degree. Peyotism should thus be considered a Plains religion growing out of an areal culture, coalescing many Plains features, although carried beyond the Plains by missionaries" (Vecsey 1988, p. 189). Vecsey opines however that there was an important difference between Peyotism and traditional Plains religion: the latter shows emotional restraint, whereas Peyote meetings display an "overt emotionalism" (Vecsey 1988, p. 193, Spindler and Spindler 1971, p. 104). This is a doubtful statement, however. The present author has seen a Shoshoni medicine man praying to his guardian spirit, represented by a big doll, while his eyes were streaming with tears. The medicine man was not, and never had been, a Peyote man.

[19] Colson 1976, p. 264.

[20] Howard 1976, p. 256.

[21] Wood 1974, pp. 9 f.

in traditional Plains ceremonialism and in Peyotism have been important for the acceptance of the latter.[22] As Plains culture spread among Indians outside its nuclear area – Southeastern Indians and Middle West Indians concentrated in Oklahoma, Bannock and Ute Indians of the Great Basin – the Peyote religion could come along, as an outgrowth of this Plains culture.

This conclusion is important. However, with Stewart we must also consider that similarities of this sort cannot solely account for the diffusion and adoption of Peyote. But they certainly would pave the way.

(3) The continuity of visionary experiences. Since Peyotism was part of the Plains religious pattern it was also integrated with the visionary complex dominating this pattern. It should again be stressed here that the vision channelized supernatural experience, it was the Plains Indian's medium for making contact with the supernatural world. Peyote visions became crucial when the vision-quest ritual had to be abandoned. It was not only the loss of sacred places where visions had been sought that motivated this abandonment. The zoomorphic guardian spirits achieved in the visions were guarantors of, primarily, hunting luck and success in warfare, and both these pre-occupations had lost their importance in the reservation situation. Health, happiness in family life now meant more, and also security against the dangers of white supremacy. The old guardian spirit did not adequately provide for these securities. At the same time, visions as channels to the supernatural had to remain. The Peyote religion here offered a time-bound answer. Its visions supplied general safety, medicine against diseases, and happiness.

Besides, these visions could be obtained in an easier way than those of the vision quest. To quote La Barre, they are a "shortcut" for groups which value visions.[23] Long fasting periods were no longer needed, nor of course self-torture. The sometimes painful loneliness in the wilderness was replaced by the joyful togetherness in the Peyote tipi. Everybody could receive visions, not just the few favoured by the spirits, or strong enough to withstand the attacks of wild animals or bad spirits. Faith was restored to those whose religious stability was shaky after the loss of guardian spirits in the vision quest. Indeed, some Peyote visions seem to have been stronger and more compelling than their vision-quest counterparts.[24]

The character of the visions deviated considerably from the sought visions of the past. With few exceptions, the guardian spirits were gone. They could be replaced by Peyote or (later) Christ, but the figures of the supernaturals now mattered less. Also, the conferring of power was no longer specific, but general, in most cases. The vision mediated a direct experience of the spiritual sphere of existence. It imparted a general consciousness and feeling of divine power, or it

---

[22] Slotkin 1956 a, p. 33.
[23] La Barre 1947, p. 295.
[24] Cf. Hultkrantz in La Barre 1960, p. 57.

showed in symbolical form a spiritual way of living.[25] Sometimes the vision told the future, as in the old days, by symbolic representation.

The continued weakening of the old Plains culture meant in the long run, however, that the vision pattern lost its grip. New adepts did not join Peyotism to experience visions any more, but for other reasons, such as medical help. Some Peyote missionaries on the Plains, like the Caddo John Wilson, even suggested that visions indicated that the mind had wandered away from Peyote.[26] The visions receded for the gifts they brought, but, at least among Plains Indians, they have never disappeared as a possible resource, or as a frame of extraordinary experiences.

(4) The ceremonial function of Peyote. It has been repeatedly pointed out that Peyotism supplied a ceremonialism that was much more easy and simple than traditional Plains ceremonies. At the time of the Plains culture showdown it replaced much of the older ceremonialism which, like the Sun Dance, was forbidden or suppressed. There is much that speaks in favour of the hypothesis that the Peyote religion spread because the older ceremonies no longer had a free sway. Because of its smaller scope, non-tribal character and peaceful intents Peyotism may have had a better success, although both administrators and clergymen branded its supposed use of narcotics.

(5) Christian re-orientation of Peyotism. As noted already by Shonle, the impact of Christian symbols in the Peyote religion increased with time.[26a] The presence of Christian elements was observed in the 1880's and 1890's, and no doubt goes back to Catholic influences on Northern Mexican Peyotism in relatively early post-Columbian times (cf. Ch. I:2). The non-tribal, finally pan-Indian character of Peyotism facilitated its assimilation of Christian traits. Christianity offered new values which at least partly corresponded to the new situation about 1890–1900, and which became increasingly topical with the growth of acculturation. Moreover, the Church organization served as a model for the Peyote movement.

Christianity contributed in many ways to influence Peyote, and thereby provided Peyotism with qualities which made it more acceptable in a more modern, wider world. It gave models for proselytism and institutionalism (Ch. IV:10), suggested the independent identity of a religion divorced from society, served as a model for an ideology that could be imitated in Peyotism (Ch. IV:11), showed exemplary ethics that could be accepted by Peyotists (Ch. I:3, IV:3, IV:9), and opened the possibilities for the Christianization of Peyote (Ch. IV:12).

The last development has been underlined by Fred Voget who sees Peyotism as an illustration of a transitional religion where we find a combination of old ceremonial statuses with new, largely administrative statuses which have been

---

[25] Cf. Hultkrantz 1975, pp. 80 f.
[26] Stewart 1987, pp. 91 f.
[26a] Shonle, op. cit., pp. 66 f.

modelled on the dominant society.[27] Voget thus finds that the old Indian role of roadman, or Peyote chief, has been completed with that of minister, "employing lengthy sermons on morality and calling upon members to rid themselves of their sins".[28] Voget also refers to the Oto Indian Koshiway who used ceremonies for the wedding, baptism and funeral of Peyote members.

J. S. Slotkin, himself a Peyotist, wrote forty years ago, "From the viewpoint of almost all Peyotists, the religion is an Indian version of Christianity. White Christian theology, ethics, and eschatology have been adopted with modifications which make them more compatible with traditional Indian culture."[29] This pronouncement gives *in nuce* the nature of the process that has taken place. Christianity was at the time too foreign to conquer Indian hearts – such of its inherent values which could find fertile soil in the Indian mind had to emerge on by-roads, and was transformed into the program of the Peyote religion. These values, and the Church organization taken over from Christianity, rendered Peyotism a solid strength. At the same time Peyotism preserved Indian religious qualities that Christianity lacked, such as the vision complex and (generally) charismatic experiences.

(6) Peyote as a means of furthering pan-Indian unity. It is obvious that the Peyote religion was well adapted to reservation life with its growing inter-tribal relations. It could be considered the religion *par préférence* of pan-Indianism (Ch. IV:8). An interesting fact is in this connection that Peyotism furthered the use of English as a Lingua Franca.[30] For instance, at intertribal Peyote meetings where Shoshoni, Paiute and Washo come together English is the principal language spoken. Indeed, some people even learn English by joining the Peyote religion.[31] Students of Navajo Peyotism report that their informants claimed their knowledge of English had increased considerably since they began attending meetings.[32] For the intercommunication between tribes who lived far away from each other, or who belonged to different linguistic families, the English language was the appropriate channel.

(7) The institutionalization of Peyote in the Native American Church. The creation of this organization in 1918 (and with a more regional beginning in "The Firstborn Church of Christ" in Oklahoma, 1914) was implemented on the initiative of the well-known anthropologist James Mooney.[33] It corresponded, however, to the wishes of Native Peyotist elders. The background of its coming into being was the strong pressure from anti-Peyotic forces like the Bureau of Indian Affairs. By uniting Peyote groups in an organization of a Christian

---

[27] Voget 1956, p. 256.
[28] Op. cit., pp. 256 f.
[29] Slotkin 1956 b, p. 64.
[30] La Barre 1975 b, p. 113.
[31] Stewart 1944, p. 83; Downs 1966, p. 104.
[32] Wagner 1975 b, p. 202; Aberle 1982 b, p. 413.
[33] Moses 1984, pp. 206 ff.; Slotkin 1956 a, pp. 57 ff., 137; Stewart 1961 b, 1987, pp. 222 ff., 239 ff.

model, a Church, Peyotists hoped to ward off the dangers. It is true that in reality this Church was rather a toothless organization, "with no bishops, no dogma, no heresy accusations, and no synods, despite its legal super-structure".[34] Nevertheless, there is every reason to presume that this institutionalization not only meant a feeling of security for most Peyotists, and enhanced the status of Peyotism as a religion. It certainly also allured many American Natives to join this religious organization which in prestige and "modern" structure could be considered to compete with the Catholic Church. As a matter of fact, Peyotists could now better present their creed as a true religion, not just as a bag of aboriginal superstitions.[35] It is reasonable to expect that this institutionalization of Peyote religion was one of the factors behind the acceptance of Peyotism, although it is most difficult to present definite proof.

There are many causes of why the use of Peyote spread. Those mentioned above seem to have been the crucial ones during the last hundred years. They have changed during different epochs and from place to place, but in one form or another they have given impetus to the diffusion of Peyotism.

4. Factors Restricting the Acceptance of the Peyote Religion

The obstacles to the diffusion of Peyotism have mostly been referred to the conservatism of tribal Indians. There is no doubt that this has been the case in many places.

Among the Winnebago for instance, around 1907, conservatives were frightened when the new Peyote religion started to affect people. They warned newcomers against the dangerous effects of eating Peyote.[1] Even in our time a visitor to Indian reservations on the Plains has soon found out that there is a religious factionalism between traditionalists and Peyotists.[2] The case study of Shoshoni Peyotism presented in the foregoing illustrates the point (Ch. II:1). In particular, the foreign, non-tribal extraction of Peyotism has been adduced as being damaging to the common good. In anthropological terms, with some exceptions, Peyotism has not been integrated with traditional society and culture like the tribal religion. Its detrimental effects on the latter are sometimes obvious.

---

[34] Vecsey 1988, p. 198.

[35] Religion is among American aborigines primarily a church-like organization, not a tribal set of conceptions, myths, and rituals.

[1] Radin 1920, p. 431 and note 124.

[2] Conservative opposition against Peyote has been reported from several Plains tribes, such as the Kiowa and the Kickapoo, cf. La Barre 1975 b, pp. 112, 116.

Scholars have found among the Navajo that where Peyotism has gained ground the old ceremonialism has decreased, particularly the curing ceremonials.[3]

However, the conservatism must not be exaggerated. The history of Peyotism tells us that it was often accepted by the fullbloods and conservatives. This in itself is a sign that it was understood as a movement which renewed and intensified old values. Moreover, when there were difficulties to continue old ceremonies, here was Peyote to take their place. We must also consider that Peyotism has originated and spread to polytheistic, religiously tolerant societies. It should be noted that among the Shawnee Peyotism is not seen as breaking against their traditional ceremonialism, in fact, all ceremonial dance leaders are also Peyotists.[4]

In several respects the Peyote religion perpetuated old religious customs and ideas, not only in its general outlines – as a ceremony among other Plains ceremonies – but also in its specific tribal connections. For instance, among the Wind River Shoshoni Peyotists arrange a Sun Dance, coinciding with the traditional Sun Dance except in the practice that dancers wear Peyote talismans around their necks (Ch. II:1). It is interesting to find the same sanction of tribal values in Peyotist ceremonialism outside of the Plains area. Referring again to the Shawnee we notice that children are given their names after a nightly Peyote meeting.[5] Shawnee Peyotism is anchored in a prophecy made by the famous Shawnee prophet Tenskwatawa at the beginning of the last century.[6] A very remarkable link between Peyotism and old Shawnee religion appears in the belief in the Supreme Being. Until about 1824 the latter was a male divinity, but from then on he was overshadowed by a female deity which usurped his place.[7] Today only Shawnee Peyotists pray to the old Supreme Being whom they have revived, identifying him with the Christian God.[8] No doubt it was the Christianized Peyote concept of God that demanded this regressive theology.

Some other examples: The famous Peyote leader among the Winnebago, John Rave, identified himself as a traditional shaman, because to him Peyote was primarily a curative medicine.[9] As a shaman he offered tobacco to Peyote, in the old style.[10] Until the 1950's the Lakota Indians of the Pine Ridge Reservation excluded women from attending Peyote ceremonies. George Morgan refers this to the old Indian taboo against allowing menstruating women to be near medicine, as a transgression of this taboo threatened the health and life of other Indians. "Recently", he reports, "a woman who had a child ignored warn-

---

[3] Aberle 1982 a, pp. 225 f. (quoting a dissertation by Stephen J. Kunitz).
[4] Howard 1981, pp. 228, 301.
[5] Op. cit., p. 93.
[6] Radin 1923, p. 73.
[7] Cf. Hultkrantz, 1983, pp. 210 ff.
[8] Howard, op. cit., pp. 163 f.
[9] Radin 1923, p. 423.
[10] Op. cit., pp 419 f.

ings and entered a Peyote meeting; all the men at the meeting became violently ill, and many of them vomited".[11] The same ritual observances hold for the Northern Ute Peyotism.[12]

There is apparently a retention of old tribal values even in a religion that breaks as much with the past as Peyotism. Although there are deep-lying differences between traditional Potawatomi religion and the Peyote religion,[13] old tribal patterns continue in the behaviour of the Potawatomi Peyotists.[14] The same could be said for the Navajo whose Peyotism has been formed after their traditional ritual patterns.[15] Indeed, if we may believe Morris Opler the Navajo incorporation of Peyotism meant an intensification of old tribal religious values.[16]

It is therefore doubtful if conservatism as such, in an unqualified sense, has been the obstacle of Peyotist expansionism. We have rather to seek for more specific factors.

One of these factors is the resistance from professional medicine men. Medicine men in particular have reasons to counteract Peyotism: it threatens their authority as trance specialists and healers. Within the Plains area where medicine men were not so different from other visionaries there was little tension. We have seen how one Shoshoni medicine man belittled the powers of the Peyotists (Ch. II:1). Where medicine men had a more prominent position (as they did outside the Plains and Pueblo areas) they objected to the competition from the Peyotists who were both visionaries and administrators of medicine. Slotkin rightly emphasizes that the Peyote ritual ousted the shaman as an intermediary between man and spirits, making shamanic curing rites unnecessary.[17] Among the Washo of the western Basin, for instance, medicine men have found their influence weakened, and therefore have attacked the new religion.[18] Peyotists have taken over the medicine man's eagle feather "fans" – which indeed are so powerful that only very skilful roadmen can use them; all power is claimed to belong to Peyote, and shamanic power is depreciated as bad. The arts of the medicine man, including the removal of disease objects and the fanning of afflicted body parts with eagle feathers, have been usurped by the roadman.[19]

Another obstacle has certainly been the difficulty of promoting a Plains ceremony outside the genuine Plains culture. It has been stressed here again and again that the Peyote religion both in its charismatic, visionary type and in its

---

[11] Morgan 1983, p. 93.
[12] Smith 1974, pp. 168, 170.
[13] Bee 1966, p. 202.
[14] Op. cit., pp. 194, 200; cf. also p. 204.
[15] Wagner 1975 a.
[16] Opler 1936.
[17] Slotkin 1956 a, p. 47.
[18] Merriam and d'Azevedo 1957, p. 616.
[19] Merriam and d'Azevedo, op. cit., pp. 617 f.; Stewart 1944, p. 84; Hultkrantz 1992, pp. 140 ff. This is in opposition to Slotkin's statement (1983) that Peyotists denounced medicine men's roles as religious leaders.

ritual elaboration is basically a Plains Indian phenomenon. Shonle, in particular, but also La Barre have linked the diffusion of Peyotism with the extension of the Plains vision-quest area.[20] It would not be correct to say, with La Barre, that here we have the boundaries of Peyote's optimal diffusion. However, it is possible to say that Peyotism for a long time was best adapted to this area. Only when visions became less topic in Peyotism, or roughly after 1910, did Peyotism find converts also outside of the Plains (or Eastern) area.[21]

Peyotism could win proselytes in the Great Basin area, particularly in its eastern parts where the Plains culture had made inroads, and where a vision quest similar to that on the Plains could be found. However, as Stewart has demonstrated, obstacles for diffusion appeared in the western and southern parts of the Great Basin where – for instance – the vision quest was less pronounced.[22]

There was, however, another obstacle to Peyote's penetration of the Far West, the use of *Datura*. In the southern parts of California, from the Chumash Indian area in the north and southwards, this strong psychoactive plant was imbibed by Indians to achieve goals compatible to those of the consumption of Peyote: Diegueño, Luiseño, Gabrielino and Serrano Indians used it in their puberty rites to facilitate the supernatural visions of their novices, and Chumash medicine men used it in order to attain ecstatic visions of supernatural powers.[23] The presence of this drug made Peyote superfluous. The diffusion maps of Peyote and *Datura* (toloache, jimsonweed) show that they are mutually exclusive in the Indian use of them. Indeed, there is even information to the effect that Great Basin Indians who know *Datura* counteract the spread of Peyote.[24]

Besides, many Californian Indians have possibly been far too acculturated to feel attracted by Peyotism.[25] The only truly Californian group which, to my knowledge, makes use of Peyote is the Modoc. However, they were transferred to Oklahoma after Captain Jack's unfortunate war in 1872–73, and learned Peyotism from the Quapaw on whose agency they had become settled.[26]

There was still another hindrance, in the Northwest. Here, John Slocum's Shaker movement had gained ground in the 1880's.[27] Robert Newberne and

---

[20] Shonle 1925, p. 59; La Barre 1972, p. 277 note.

[21] By Eastern is meant here those Indians from the Eastern Woodlands who had been concentrated in Oklahoma during the nineteenth century.

[22] For an orientation of vision patterns in the Great Basin, see Spier 1930, pp. 249 ff.

[23] See for example Du Bois 1908, (and the Introduction, above, note 16); Furst and Furst 1982, pp. 777 ff.

[24] Driver and Massey, op. cit., pp. 271 f., and maps 76 (peyote) and 77 (jimson weed). A parallel can here be drawn to the Southeastern Indians who, because of their dedication to the emetic black tea were arrested in their acceptance of the Peyote religion. See above, Ch. I:2.

[25] In the new Handbook of North American Indians, vol. 8: California (Washington 1978), there is no reference to the use of Peyote. Cf. also Stewart 1987, p. 149: map of Peyotist communities in western United States.

[26] Cf. Wright 1951, p. 185, and La Barre 1975, pp. 116, 122.

[27] Amoss 1990, Barnett 1957, Gunther 1949.

Charles Burke state, "Where Shakerism thrives Peyote is not popular, for the former seems to give the Indians an avenue for the outlet of their emotional nature and satisfies their pride in the possession of a distinctive Indian religion."[28] Also the lack of psychoactive drugs, partly also tobacco, in Northwestern culture may have impeded the diffusion of Peyote here.[28]

The great lacuna in the dissemination of Peyote is however, as has been pointed out in the foregoing, the Southwest (Ch. I:2, Ch. IV:7). This area which is so close to the nuclear area of Peyotism has constituted a formidable impediment in Peyote's way. General references to the conservatism of the Pueblo Indians, or the fright of visions of the dead among Athapascans, are of little avail. We shall peruse the evidence.

To start with the Athapascan Indians, the Apache and Navajo, we have seen that the Lipan Apache were Plains Indians who played an important role as transmitters of "basic" Peyotism. The Kiowa Apache, also on the Plains, have contributed to the development of Peyote ritualism. However, the Mountain Apache to the west differed in being less open to Peyotism, with one exception, the Mescalero Apache. Their shaman-guided Peyotism, an outgrowth of Mexican Peyotism, has been discussed in the foregoing. After 1910 it has been fading, apparently due to witchcraft fears.[30] The case of the Mescalero was brought up by Ralph Linton when he illuminated the concept of cultural conflict in his classic *The Study of Man*.

In this work, Linton defined three facets of the diffusion of cultural elements, their presentation, acceptance (or rejection) and integration.[31] In this connection he called attention to the rejection by the Apache – he obviously means the Mescalero Apache – of Peyote, "a narcotic cactus used by many Indian tribes to induce visions and through these to put the individual in closer touch with the supernatural".[32] Linton maintained that the Apache attached great importance to visions. However, each individual hoarded the power, fearing that it might be stolen by a medicine man. This fear accumulated in the Peyote assembly where the individuals under the influence of the drug might be off guard and thus were likely to lose more power than they could gain. Peyotism therefore became infrequent or was rejected.[33]

The stealing of medicine is tantamount to witchcraft. Fears of witchcraft have been common in the Southwest, particularly among the Apache and the Pueblo Indians.

---

[28] Newberne and Burke 1922, p. 12.
[29] It is also possible that Northwestern Indians were not reached by the apostles of the Peyote movement during its period of intense mission.
[30] This according to a testimony given to me by Ines Talamantez. Cf. Ch. I:2. Cf. La Barre 1975 b, p. 259: Mescalero Peyotism is extinguished.
[31] Linton 1936, p. 334.
[32] Linton, op. cit. p. 342.
[33] Linton, loc. cit.

As should have emerged from our earlier discussion the Navajo present a special case in their reactions to Peyote. Their initial opposition to Peyote was, as we remember, founded on its non-Navajo origin and its supposed damage of the mind. Only the deprivation of the 1930's could overcome Navajo resistance to Peyote (above, Ch. IV:2). Guy Cooper who watched Navajo Peyotism about 1980 observed that Peyotism has been most efficiently opposed in the richer areas of the Reservation. In general, there is an eclectic attitude towards ritual, but all ceremonial singers draw a clear line between traditional Navajo religion and Peyotism. Many singers "profess no knowledge of Peyotism and do not want to know about it, as they feel it would interfere with the clarity of thought required for performing traditional ceremonials".[34]

The resistance against Peyote among the Pueblo Indians has intrigued scholars. Shonle maintained that the seasonal division of ceremonies in the Southwest (she probably meant the Pueblo Indians) constituted a hindrance for the adoption of Peyotism.[35] La Barre attributes this resistance to the complex religious systems of the Pueblo Indians,[36] and to their repugnance to pshychotropical substances.[37] Driver and Massey emphasize that the cultural shock suffered by the Plains Indians after the Indian wars had no counterpart among the Pueblo Indians. The latter could continue their old formal existence. Their religion was highly socialized, their personal expression of this religion moderate.[38]

It seems that all these arguments are correct, and that they have one common denominator: the quality of Pueblo culture. Ruth Benedict has, perhaps a little too generalizing, characterized its ethos as "Apollonian" in contrast to the "Dionysian" Plains culture.[39] Pueblo culture owes its pitch to the intense collective ceremonialism developed in an horticultural setting.[40] The co-ordination of all powers, supernatural and secular, was essential in this society. Personal religious experiences had to cede for ceremonial commitments within a strictly ordered collectivistic frame. Each individual spent his lifetime playing his appointed role in religious organizations. The vision had little function in this type of culture, and the guardian spirit as well. They had no use of ecstatic experiences, they shunned psychotropical drugs and avoided alcohol. Only Zuni rain priests and fraternity leaders would handle *Datura*.[41]

Besides, the Pueblo were really never conquered. Until this day they have guarded their relative autonomy and their religious secrets. They did not suffer the deprivation of the Plains Indians or, for that matter, the Navajo. White expansion has only slowly infringed upon the Pueblo Indian traditions.

---

[34] Personal letter from Dr. Guy Cooper, November 28th, 1981.
[35] Shonle 1925, p. 58.
[36] La Barre 1975 b, p. 40.
[37] La Barre 1972, pp. 277 f.
[38] Driver and Massey, op. cit., p. 271.
[39] Benedict 1935, pp. 56 ff.
[40] Although a setting which ecologically seen was sometimes little apt for agrarian cultivation.
[41] La Barre 1972, pp. 277 f.

There was one exception, however: Taos Pueblo. As we have seen, its proximity to the Plains culture, and the participation of the Taos Indians in the buffalo hunting on the Plains, made them receptive to a more individualistic way of life (Ch. IV:7). Not unexpectedly therefore, Peyotism was introduced here about 1909–1910, after some preliminaries in 1907. It made, however, slow progress.[42] The local religious hierarchy was bitterly opposed, and Peyotists were deprived of their Kiva membership. The over-riding fear was that the Peyote religion would stop the rain, but the Peyotists retorted that their ceremonies would bring the rain.[43]

In the long run the Peyotists won the race. As Parsons has pointed out, at Taos no powerful curing societies and no Kachina organization existed, as it did in other pueblos, and therefore there was no effective objection to the inclusion of Peyotism in the religious pattern.[44] Quite against Parson's expectations, however, the Peyote religion has grown among the population of Taos and today embraces about a third of their number.[45] It has been labelled "the uniting religious mechanism at the present time".[46] Members of other Pueblo groups take part nowadays in the Taos Peyote meetings.[47]

Perhaps the ban on Peyote is about to lift in the Southwest. The fast, modern spread of Peyotism among the Navajo and Taos may suggest that the Southwestern Indians are making up for a delayed development.

There is, finally, all the obstruction to the use of Peyote that emanates from the white authorities. Supported by both military and civil superiority of force anti-Peyotists appeared as political and religious activists. Leading politicians and military men of the United States fought against Peyotism because it was a religion that, in their eyes, prolonged the doomed "heathenism" and also withstood the official politics of assimilation.[48] This was not the vision of other white authorities, such as the ethnologist James Mooney, for instance. Peyote, he stated, "is not a Christian religion, but it is a very close approximation, and, in my opinion, as Indian religions and Indian psychology go, it is as close an approximation to Christianity and as efficient a leading up to Christianity as the Indian, speaking generally, is now capable of".[49] Mooney was one of the foremost instigators in chartering the Native American Church which came about on October 19th, 1918.[50] We may thus consider this institutional frame of the Peyote movement as a response to the persecutions of the public authorities.

---

[42] Lasswell 1935, p. 237.
[43] Dustin 1960, p. 10. Cf. Parsons 1936, pp. 66 f.
[44] Parsons 1936, p. 118.
[45] Cf. Dustin, op. cit., pp. 11, 12, and Collins 1967, pp. 183–191.
[46] Collins, op. cit., p. 190.
[47] Collins, loc. cit.; La Barre 1975 b, p. 213.
[48] For a survey of prohibitions and legislation on Peyote, see Stewart 1991.
[49] Moses 1984, p. 191.
[50] Moses op. cit., pp. 206 ff. For further charters see Slotkin 1956 a, pp. 60 f.

5. The Appeal of Peyote

Our investigation has brought us to a point where it is possible to have an overall view of the attraction of Peyotism up to our own time. In retrospect, the following remarks can be formulated, serving as a point of departure for the argumentation:

(1) Whatever causes we can mobilize for the understanding of the spread of the Peyote religion, the deepest motivation is religious. The balance between man and a spiritual universe lies behind the North American Indian's perspective on himself and his own life. He is part of a spiritual context where the spiritual world, the human beings and all other living beings on this earth belong together. The Peyote religion is a feasible interpretation of this world order. In Indian fashion it cultivates the experiential way to the supernatural, through the effects of Peyote consumption.[1]

(2) Diverse historical factors have promoted the spread of the Peyote religion. As Robert L. Bee has pointed out, all factors are not of equal relevance in explaining the individual cases of Peyote diffusion. He regrets that the arguments between scholars over the primacy of single factors have disregarded the shifting cultural contexts. "To determine general factors operative in peyote diffusion, *and* to assign them a relative position of cross-cultural importance, requires much more than the example of one or two Basin *or* Plains groups for support."[2] In the present investigation the different factors have been related to some particular contexts of place and time which have been relevant. A complete co-ordination between factors and ethnic groups is impossible to reconstruct because of the detailed dynamics of cultural development.

(3) The Peyote religion has undergone an historical process, correlated with major cultural changes, and different factors of diffusion have been operative from time to time. We may roughly indicate the following phases and factors:

(a) A pre-Columbian tribal and shamanic Peyotism, integrated with the harvesting year among seed gatherers and horticulturists, but originally designed in a hunting-and-gathering milieu. This is the antecedent of the Mexican–South Texan rite. After the conquista Catholic traits, for instance, the veneration of the Virgin Mary, were adopted into the cult system.

(b) Basic Peyotism in North America. This involved a strengthening of the hunting pattern ingredients in the Southern Plains milieu. However, shamanism gave way to a democratic pursuit of visions, and a privatization of Peyote ceremonialism in a Peyote lodge supplanted tribal ceremonialism. The new ceremonial was structured on earlier Plains (mescal?) ritual patterns. Personal and individual, not tribal horticultural gains were at the center of interest. Peyote

---

[1] Vecsey reminds us that Peyote myths "describe dimensions of religious life that surpass the notion of peyotism as an 'escapist', 'accommodationist', 'crisis cult'." (Vecsey 1988, p. 165).
[2] Bee 1965, p. 32.

worship became a religion in its own right, separated from traditional tribal religion.

(c) The Peyote religion of the first reservation time, the era of rapid Peyote diffusion. This is the time to which most investigations of Peyote causes relate. The setting is again mainly the Plains after the Indian wars. Removal from ancient tribal grounds, missionary decrees, acculturation, deprivation and despair terminated older ceremonialism and, most important, the common vision quest. The religious vacuum, the change of the general situation and the new communication systems facilitated the spread of Peyotism. As particular factors behind this diffusion we notice the expansion of Plains cultural patterns, a restricted continuity of vision experiences within the Peyote frame, the simple but attractive, pan-Indian character of the Peyote ceremony, and the growing Christianization of Peyotism.

(d) The modern Peyote development. This is characterized by the institutionalization of Peyote religion into the Native American Church, the weakening of the import of visions in favour of the gifts contained in visions (medicine, health, family happiness), the strengthening of pan-Indianism, and the continued diffusion of Peyotism to tribes outside the Plains area.

This general scheme shows that different factors have at different times sponsored the spread of Peyote. It is impossible to refer this diffusion to one or a few preferred factors; it makes no sense to reduce Peyotism to the operation of demands on just medicine or economic well-being. Peyotism is a structured religion and as such is exposed to the changes in history. The particular aspects of this religion hold different weight in different cultural situations. However, because of its religious character in an American Indian setting the initial successes of Peyotism owe much to the vision-producing power of the Peyote cactus. Much, but not everything.

The declination of visions is clearly perceptible in modern Peyotism. It is part of the general eclipse of Plains elements in the Native American Church. Many contemporary Peyotists ascribe little importance to visions. This depreciation of visions has no doubt furthered the diffusion of Peyotism to places where visions were less essential, as among the western Basin Indians and the Navajo, or where visions only sparsely occurred, as among the Taos. It remains to be seen if the other Pueblo Indians, with their negative view of visions, are now ready to accept a reformed Peyote religion without visions.

Pan-Indianism is a natural outcome of the present situation. To quote William Newcomb, writing on Delaware Peyotism: "The modern attractions of the peyote cult are particularly strong in its aspects as an *Indian* ceremony and as a rallying point for Pan-Indianism."[3] Dustin, speaking of the Taos Indians, tells us that "the pan-Indian nature of Peyotism is clearly recognized by the members of the cult".[4] However, also traditional religions are seen today by their repre-

---

[3] Newcomb 1956, p. 211.
[4] Dustin 1960, p. 14.

sentatives as manifestations of a united American Indian religion. Conferences of medicine men and other spiritual leaders consolidate this vision.

It is difficult to tell what the future of Peyotism will be. Perhaps it will develop as an Indian way to Christianity, something similar to the role of African indigenous churches.[5] Or perhaps the new nationalism will turn the tide from the Peyote religion, organized as it is as a Church on the Christian model, to a renewed and simplified concept of traditional religion (cf. Ch. I:2).

Concerning the indefatigable fights for Indian religious freedom, Vine Deloria, once asserted that Peyotism appears to be "the religion of the future" among American Indians. He even thought that "eventually it will replace Christianity among the Indian people".[6] This pronouncement reflects the author's conviction some twenty five years ago. However, it we want to read the future it would seem to be more realistic to look at the modern tendencies in different ethnic groups.

This is not the place for a full coverage of these tendencies, but some observations from nuclear areas should be communicated. The picture that emerges from Hurt's data covering the Northern Plains and adjacent areas in the late 1950's is very varied. The Winnebago are active Peyotists since their tribe in Nebraska is small and therefore homogeneous ("transitional types of Indians"), and some of their leaders are members of the Peyote religion.[7] The Santee of Nebraska have had Peyotism, but it was apparently repressed by intense Christian mission.[8] The Yankton of South Dakota have Peyotists among lower class Indians, but these meet strong opposition.[9] On the Pine Ridge Reservation, the number of Peyotists is slowly increasing. Hurt attributes this to the large population, the lack of organized opposition, political factionalism and variations in acculturation.[10] Morgan, however, considers that Peyotism is growing because of an increase of children in Peyote families, whereas the acquisition of new members from outside is negligible.[11] On the Rosebud Reservation, however, tribal leaders have succeeded in diminishing Peyotist activities through an old Sioux technique of social control, ridicule.[12] And so on. Like Barber and Aberle Hurt suggests that the economically depressed members of a tribe tend to turn to the Peyote religion.[13] Factionalism and half-way acculturation seem to be important causes for the stabilization, but not spread, of the Peyote religion.

---

[5] Sundkler 1976.
[6] Deloria 1970, p. 116.
[7] Hurt 1960, p. 18.
[8] Op. cit., p. 19.
[9] Op. cit., pp. 19, 20.
[10] Op. cit., p. 21.
[11] Morgan 1983, p. 91. Surprisingly, and certainly in conflict with data supplied by Steinmetz, Morgan says that the Peyotists amounted to only 2% of the total population of 15000 souls in 1980.
[12] Hurt, op. cit., p. 22.
[13] Op. cit., p. 25.

In outlying regions of the Plains the advance of Peyotism seems to be very slow. The new nationalist political consciousness and the resurgence of traditional tribal religions are factors which should not be overlooked in this connection. The Stoney (Assiniboin) of western Alberta, for example, stay clear from [American Indian Movement agents as well as from] Peyote. One otherwise well-informed Stoney told me that he did not know what Peyote really is. "It does not belong to the Stoney people."[14]

Hurt's conclusion coincides with my own observations on the Wind River Reservation. It also tallies with Spindler's and Wagner's opinion that Peyotists belong to an intermediate acculturative group (cf. above, Ch. IV:4). What should be observed in particular is that Hurt speaks about persistence, not expansion. While there is some expansion going on in Canada the Plains Indians on the whole do not today seem more motivated for Peyotism than for other religions. Certainly, the comfort and persuasion of the Peyote experience is there, but the enthusiasm and challenge of the past is gone. Gone with the vision?

In the Great Basin the Peyote religion has apparently come to a standstill. Indeed, I was told by Dr. Warren d'Azevedo that Peyotism is decreasing in Nevada.[15]

The situation in the Southwest remains fairly constant. The Pueblo Indians refrain from Peyote, except in Taos. The Mescalero Apache who tried Peyote between 1870 and 1910 now despise it as an expression of witchcraft, says Dr. Inés Talamantez, herself one of the people.[16]

In contrast to the Plains Peyotism, Navajo Peyotism is still spreading. The diffusion is however uneven, apparently depending upon available contacts and individual preferences.[17] As pointed out previously, the simplicity of the Peyote ritual in comparison to traditional Navajo nine-nights rituals is certainly attractive to many religious persons (Ch. IV:9).

Dr. Guy Cooper has this to say about the present-day Navajo: "Peyotism is on the increase on the Navajo Reservation, particularly in the poorer areas of the Reservation (richer areas tend to be more conservative) and among the youth. The young (and older people too) are attracted to it because the ritual is simpler than traditional ceremonials, more easily learnt and because a peyote ritual offers more instant (and cheaper) relief in the event of illness than the longer, more expensive traditional ceremonials."[18] Also Dr. Talamantez testified to the spreading of Peyote among the Navajo, and also emphasized that the elementary character of the Peyote ritual, as compared with traditional cere-

---

[14] Hultkrantz, Stoney Field Notes, Ms. (1977).
[15] Information in October, 1977, in Reno, Nevada.
[16] Information in January, 1980, in Santa Barbara, California.
[17] Aberle and Stewart 1957, p. 111.
[18] Personal letter from Dr. Guy Cooper, November 28th, 1981.

monies, saves time for Navajo wage-workers.[19] However, Aberle reports on a growing conversion to charismatic Protestant missions since the end of the 1970's, a process that has taken place at the expense of both traditional Navajo religion and the Native American Church. Still, he thinks that today about 50% of the Navajo are Peyotists.[20] And Stewart concludes that "Peyotism today finds its strongest expression among the Navajo".[21] It is of course possible that the Peyote religion increases in some Navajo quarters, and decreases in others.

The picture is thus varied, but the pervading characteristics are the same: no more Peyote expansion, but increase or decrease of Peyotism within the reservations.

The Peyote religion is still a very important religion, and the most impressive pan-American religion. However, the tuning down of its ecstatic capacities have, it seems to me, reduced its power to inspire and engage. The lure of Peyote is still there, but it is weaker and less attractive. We receive the impression that the heyday of Peyotism is over. Whatever the future holds, the Peyote religion keeps its rank as the dominant Native religion in North America.

---

[19] Information in January, 1980, in Santa Barbara, California.
[20] Aberle and Stewart 1957, p. 111; Aberle 1982 b, pp. xliii ff.; Aberle in Lynch 1984, pp. 179 f.; Stewart 1987, p. 293.
[21] Stewart 1987, p. 317.

Bibliography

Aberle, David F.
    1966 The Peyote Religion among the Navaho. Viking Fund Publications in Anthropology 42. New York.
    1982a The Future of Navajo Religion, pp. 219–231 in Navajo Religion and Culture: Selected Views, ed. by David M. Brugge and Charlotte J. Frisbie. Santa Fe: The Museum of New Mexico Press.
    1982b The Peyote Religion among the Navaho, 2nd ed. Chicago: The University of Chicago Press.
    1982c The Peyote Religion among the Navajo and Its Competitors, p. 301 in Abstracts, 44th International Congress of Americanists. Manchester.

Aberle, D. F., and O. C. Stewart
    1957 Navaho and Ute Peyotism: A Chronological and Distributional Study. University of Colorado Studies, Series in Anthropology No. 6. Boulder, Colorado.

Alvarsson, Jan-Åke and Åke Hultkrantz
    1995 Psychotropic Plants in the Americas – An Introduction. Acta Americana 3 (3): 5–23.

Amoss, Pamela T.
    1990 The Indian Shaker Church, pp. 633–639 in Handbook of North American Indians, ed. by William Sturtevant, vol. 7. Washington D.C.: Smithsonian Institution.

Anderson, Edward P.
    1969 The Biogeography, Ecology, and Taxonomy of Lophophora (Cactaceae). Brittonia 21 (4): 299–310.
    1970 Structure, Development and Taxonomy of the Genus Lophophora. American Journal of Botany 57 (5): 569–578.
    1980 Peyote, The Divine Cactus. Tucson, Arizona: The University of Arizona Press.

Arbman, Ernst
    1963–1970 Ecstasy or Religious Trance. 3 volumes: Stockholm: Scandinavian University Books.

Arth, Malcolm J.
    1956 A Functional View of Peyotism in Omaha Culture. Plains Anthropologist 7: 25–29.

van Baaren, Th. P.
    1975 Religions of Faction and Community-Religions, pp. 25–28 in Explorations in the Anthropology of Religion, ed. by W. E .A. van Beck and J. H. Scherer. The Hague.

Barber, Bernard
    1941a Acculturation and Messianic Movements. American Sociological Review 6 (5): 663–669.

    1941b A Socio-Cultural Interpretation of the Peyote Cult. American Anthropologist 43 (4): 673–675.

Barber, Carroll G.
    1959 Peyote and the Definition of Narcotics. American Anthropologist 61 (4): 641–646.

Barnett, Homer G.
    1957 Indian Shakers: A Messianic Cult of the Pacific Northwest. Carbondale, Illinois: University of Southern Illinois Press.

Beals, Kenneth
    1971 The Dynamics of Kiowa Apache Peyotist. Papers in Anthropology of the University of Oklahoma 12 (1): 35–89.

Beals, Ralph L.
    1932 The Comparative Ethnology of Northern Mexico before 1750. Ibero-Americana 2. Berkeley.

Bean, Lowell J. and S. Brakke Vane
    1978 Cults and Their Transformations, pp. 662–672 in Handbook of North American Indians, ed. by William Sturtevant, vol. 8. Washington D.C.: Smithsonian Institution.

Bee, Robert L.
    1965 Peyotism in North American Indian Groups. Transactions of the Kansas Academy of Science 68 (1): 13–61.
    1966 Potawatomi Peyotism: the Influence of Traditional Patterns. Southwestern Journal of Anthropology 22 (2): 194–205.

Benedict, Ruth F.
    1922 The Vision in Plains Culture. American Anthropologist 24 (1): 1–23.
    1923 The Concept of the Guardian Spirit in North America. Memoirs of the American Anthropological Association 29. Menasha, Wis.
    1935 Patterns of Culture. London: Routledge.

Bennett, W. C., and R. M. Zingg
    1935 The Tarahumara: An Indian Tribe of Northern Mexico. Chicago: University of Chicago Press.

Benzi, Marino
    1972 Les derniers adorateurs du peyotl: croyances, coutumes et mythes des Indiens Huichol. Paris: Gallimard.

Bergman, Robert L.
    1971 Navajo Use of Peyote: Its Apparent Safety. American Journal of Psychiatry 128 (6): 695–699.

Berlandier, Jean Louis (ed. by John C. Ewers)
    1969 The Indians of Texas in 1830. Washington D.C.: Smithsonian Institution.

Berrin, Kathleen (ed.)
    1978 Art of the Huichol Indians. San Francisco: The Fine Arts Museums.

Bogoras, Waldemar
    1902 The Folklore of Northeastern Asia as Compared with that of Northwestern America. American Anthropologist 4 (4): 577–683.

Boyer, L. B., R. M. Boyer and H. W. Basehart
    1973 Shamanism and Peyote Use Among the Apaches of the Mescalero Indian Reservation, pp. 53–66 in Hallucinogens and Shamanism, ed. by Michael Harner. New York: Oxford University Press.

Brant, Charles S.
- 1950 Peyotism among the Kiowa-Apache and Neighboring Tribes. Southwestern Journal of Anthropology 6 (2): 212–222.
- 1963 Joe Blackbear's Story of the Origin of the Peyote Religion. Plains Anthropologist 8 (21): 180–181.

Broad, C. D.
- 1962 Lectures on Psychical Research. London: Routledge and Kegan Paul.

Bromberg, Walter and Charles L. Tranter
- 1943 Peyote Intoxication: Some Psychological Aspects of the Peyote Rite. Journal of Nervous and Mental Disease 97 (5): 518–527.

Budd, Susan
- 1974 Religion and Protest. Religion 4 (2): 156–159.

Burridge, Kenelm O. L.
- 1969 New Heaven, New Earth: A Study of Millenarian Activities. New York: Shocken Books; Oxford: Blackwell.

Campbell, T. N.
- 1958 Origin of the Mescal Bean Cult. American Anthropologist 60 (1): 156–160.

Catlin, George
- 1967 O-Kee-Pa, A Religious Ceremony and Other Customs of the Mandans. Ed. by John C. Ewers. New Haven: Yale University Press.

Clark, Walter H.
- 1969 Chemical Ecstasy. New York.

Clark, William P.
- 1885 The Indian Sign Language. Philadelphia: L. R. Hamersly.

Collins, John James
- 1967 Peyotism and Religious Membership at Taos Pueblo, New Mexico. Southwestern Social Science Quarterly 48: 183–191.

Collins, June McCormick
- 1950 The Indian Shaker Church: A Study of Continuity and Change in Religion. Southwestern Journal of Anthropology 6 (4): 399–411.

Colson, Elizabeth
- 1976 Culture and Progress. American Anthropologist 78 (2): 261–271.

Cooper, Guy H.
- 1984 Development and Stress in Navajo Religion. Stockholm Studies in Comparative Religion 23. Stockholm.

Couch, Carl J. and Joseph D. Marino
- 1979 Chippewa-Cree Peyotism at Rocky Boy's, pp. 7–15 in Lifeways of Intermontane and Plains Montana Indians, ed. by Leslie B. Davis. Museum of the Rockies Occasional Papers 1. Bozeman.

Curtis, Edward S.
- 1930 The North American Indian, vol. 19. Cambridge, Mass.: Harvard University Press.

Czaplicka, Marie Antoinette
- 1928 Siberia, Sibiriaks, Siberians. Encyclopaedia of Religion and Ethics, ed. by James Hastings, vol. XI, pp. 488–496. New York: Scribner.

Davenport, William
- 1969 The "Hawaiian Cultural Revolution": Some Political and Economic Considerations. American Anthropologist 71 (1): 1–20.

d'Azevedo, Warren L.
   1986 Washoe, pp. 466–498 in Handbook of North American Indians, ed. by William Sturtevant, vol. 11: Great Basin. Washington, D.C.: Smithsonian Institution.

Deardorff, Merle E.
   1951 The Religion of Handsome Lake. Bureau of American Ethnology, Bulletin 149, pp. 79–107. Washington.

Delay, J.
   1967 Psychopharmacology and Psychiatry: Towards a Classification of Psychotropic Drugs. Bulletin on Narcotics 19 (1): 1–6.

Deloria, Vine Jr.
   1970 Custer Died for Our Sins: An Indian Manifesto. New York: Avon Books.

Densmore, Frances
   1941 Native Songs of Two Hybrid Ceremonies among the American Indians. American Anthropologist 43 (1): 77–82.

Dittmann, A. T., and H. C. Moore
   1957 Disturbances in Dreams as Related to Peyotism among the Navaho. American Anthropologist 59 (4): 642–649.

Dixon, W. E.
   1899/1900 The Physiological Action of the Alkaloids Derived from Anhalonium Lewinii. Journal of Physiology 25: 69–86.

Dobkin de Rios, Marlene
   1976 The Wilderness of Mind: Sacred Plants in Cross-Cultural Perspective. Beverley Hills: Sage Publications.
   1977a Hallucinogenic Ritual as Theatre. Journal of Psychedelic Drugs 9 (3): 265–268.
   1977b Plant Hallucinogens and the Religion of the Mochica – an Ancient Peruvian People. Economic Botany 31 (2): 189–203.

Dobkin de Rios, Marlene, and Fred Katz
   1975 Some Relationships between Music and Hallucinogenic Ritual: The "Jungle Gym" in Consciousness. Ethos 3 (1): 64–76.

Dobkin de Rios, Marlene, and D. E. Smith
   1977 The Function of Drug Rituals in Human Society: Continuities and Changes. Journal of Psychedelic Drugs 9 (3): 269–275.

Dorsey, J. O.
   1884 Omaha Sociology. Third Annual Report of the Bureau of Ethnology. Washington.

Dorsinfang-Smets, A.
   1962 La recherche du salut chez les Indiens d'Amérique, pp. 113–125 in Religions de salut. Annales du centre d'étude des religions, vol. 2. Bruxelles.

Downs, James F.
   1966 The Two Worlds of the Washo. New York: Holt, Rinehart and Winston.

Dozier, Edward P.
   1962 Differing Reactions to Religious Contacts among North American Indian Societies, pp. 161–171 in Proceedings of the 34th International Congress of Americanists. Wien.

Driver, Harold E.
- 1939 The Measurement of Geographical Distribution Form. American Anthropologist 41 (6): 583–588.
- 1961 Indians of North America. Chicago: University of Chicago Press.

Driver, Harold E., and William C. Massey
- 1957 Comparative Studies of North American Indians. Transactions of the American Philosophical Society 47 (2). Philadelphia.

Drobin, Ulf
- 1982 Psychology, Philosophy, Theology, Epistemology – Some Reflections, pp. 263–274 in Religious Ecstasy, ed. by Nils G. Holm. Scripta Instituti Donneriani Aboensis XI. Stockholm.

DuBois, Constance Goddard
- 1908 The Religion of the Luiseño Indians of Southern California. University of California Publications in American Archaeology and Ethnology, vol. 8 (3), pp. 69–186. Berkeley.

Dusenberry, Verne
- 1962 The Montana Cree: A Study in Religious Persistence. Stockholm Studies in Comparative Religion 3. Stockholm.

Dustin, C. B.
- 1960 Peyotism and New Mexico. Farmington, New Mexico (privately printed).

Eliade, Mircea
- 1961 History of Religions and a New Humanism. History of Religions 1 (1): 1–8.

Elkin, Henry
- 1940 The Northern Arapaho of Wyoming, pp. 207–255 in Acculturation in Seven American Indian Tribes, ed. by Ralph Linton. New York: D. Appleton Century.

Euler, R. C.
- 1967 Ethnographic Methodology, pp. 61–67 in American Historic Anthropology, ed. by C. L. Riley and W. W. Taylor. Carbondale: Southern Illinois University Press.

Feinberg, Richard
- 1979 Shifting Residential and Subsistence Patterns in a Navajo Community. Ethnos 44 (3–4): 242–258.

Fernandez, J. W.
- 1965 Symbolic Consensus in a Fang Reformative Cult. American Anthropologist 67 (4): 902–910.

Fletcher, Alice C. and Francis La Flesche
- 1911 The Omaha Tribe. Twentyseventh Annual Report of the Bureau of American Ethnology. Washington.

Fortune, Reo F.
- 1932 Omaha Secret Societies. New York: Columbia University Press.

Furst, Peter T.
- 1972a Introduction, in Flash of the Gods: The Ritual Use of Hallucinogens, ed. by P. T. Furst. New York: Praeger.
- 1972b To Find Our Life: Peyote among the Huichol Indians of Mexico, pp. 136–184 in Flesh of the Gods: The Ritual Use of Hallucinogens, ed. by P. T. Furst. New York: Praeger.
- 1976 Hallucinogens and Culture. Novato, California: Chandler and Sharp.

Furst, Peter T. and Jill L. Furst
 1982 North American Indian Art. New York: Artpress Books (Rizzoli).
Geertz, Armin W.
 1992 The Invention of Prophecy: Continuity and Meaning in Hopi Indian Religion. Knebel: Brunbakke Publications.
Geertz, Clifford
 1966 Religion as a Cultural System, pp. 1–46 in Anthropological Approaches to the Study of Religion, ed. by Michael Banton. London: Tavistock Publications.
Gelpke, Rudolf
 1966 Vom Rausch im Orient und Okzident. Stuttgart.
Gerber, Peter
 1980 Die Peyote-Religion: Nordamerikanische Indianer auf der Suche nach einer Identität. Völkerkundemuseum der Universität Zürich.
 1982 Theoretical Explanations of the Peyote Religion. Abstracts, 44th International Congress of Americanists in Manchester, p. 302.
Gifford, Barry (ed.)
 1976 Selected Writings of Edward S. Curtis. Berkeley: Creative Arts Book Company.
Gill, Sam
 1979 Songs of Life: An Introduction to Navajo Religious Culture. Leiden: Brill.
Goddard, Ives
 1979 The Languages of South Texas and the Lower Rio Grande, pp. 355–389 in The Languages of Native America, ed. by Lyle Campbell and Marianne Mithun. Austin: University of Texas Press.
Grinspoon, Lester, and James B. Bakalar (eds.)
 1983 Psychedelic Reflections. New York: Human Sciences Press.
Guariglia, Guglielmo
 1959 Prophetismus und Heilserwartungs-Bewegungen als völkerkundliches und religionsgeschichtliches Problem. Wiener Beiträge zur Kulturgeschichte und Linguistik, vo. 13. Horn-Wien.
Gunther, Erna
 1949 The Shaker Religion of the Northwest, pp. 37–76 in Indians of the Urban Northwest, ed. by Marian W. Smith. New York: Columbia University Press.
 1950 The Westward Movement of Some Plains Traits. American Anthropologist 52 (2): 174–180.
Gurvich, I. S.
 1988 Ethnic Connections Across Bering Strait, pp. 17–21 in Crossroads of Continents: Cultures of Siberia and Alaska, ed. by William W. Fitzhugh and Aron Cromwell. Washington, D.C.: Smithsonian Institution Press.
Gusinde, Martin
 1939 Der Peyote-Kult, Entstehung und Verbreitung. St. Gabriel-Studien 8, pp. 401–499. Wien-Mödling.
Haile, Berard
 1940 A Note on the Navaho Visionary. American Anthropologist 42 (2): 359.
Hallowell, A. Irving
 1967 Culture and Experience. New York: Schocken Books.

Hamilton, Charles (ed.)
   1972 Cry of the Thunderbird. Norman: University of Oklahoma Press.
Harner, Michael (ed.)
   1973 Hallucinogens and Shamanism. New York: Oxford University Press.
Hartmann, Horst
   1973 Die Plains- und Prärieindianer Nordamerikas. Veröffentlichungen des Museums für Völkerkunde Berlin, Neue Folge 22. Berlin.
Hastings, Adrian
   1976 African Christianity: An Essay in Interpretation. London and Dublin: Geoffrey Chapman.
Heizer, R. F., and Theodora Kroeber
   1979 Ishi the Last Yahi: A Documentary History. Berkeley and Los Angeles: University of California Press.
Herskovits, Melville J.
   1948 Man and His Works. New York: Knopf.
Hertzberg, Hazel W.
   1971 The Search for an American Indian Identity: Modern Pan-Indian Movements. Syracuse: Syracuse University Press.
Hoebel, E. Adamson
   1949 The Wonderful Herb: An Indian Cult Vision Experience. Western Humanities Review 3: 126–130.
Hoffman, W. J.
   1891 The Midē'wiwin or "Grand Medicine Society" of the Ojibwa. Seventh Annual Report of the Bureau of Ethnology. Washington.
Holler, Clyde
   1984 Black Elk's Relationship to Christianity. American Indian Quarterly 8 (1): 37–49.
Howard, James H.
   1955 The Pan-Indian Culture of Oklahoma. The Scientific Monthly 18 (5): 215–220.
   1957 The Mescal Bean Cult of the Central and Southern Plains: An Ancestor of the Peyote Cult? American Anthropologist 59 (1): 75–87.
   1960 Mescalism and Peyotism Once Again. Plains Anthropologist 5 (10): 84–85.
   1962 Potawatomi Mescalism and Its Relationship to the Diffusion of the Peyote Cult. Plains Anthropologist 7 (16): 125–135.
   1967 Half Moon Way: The Peyote Ritual of Chief White Bear. University of South Dakota Museum News 28 (1–2): 1–24.
   1976 The Plains Gourd Dance as a Revitalization Movement. American Ethnologist 3 (2): 243–259.
   1981 Shawnee! The Ceremonialism of a Native American Tribe and Its Cultural Background. Athens, Ohio: Ohio University Press.
Hsu, F. L. K.
   1979 The Cultural Problem of the Cultural Anthropologist. American Anthropologist 81 (3): 517–532.
Hudson, Charles
   1976 The Southeastern Indians. Knoxville: University of Tennessee Press.

Hultkrantz, Åke
- 1956 Configurations of Religious Belief among the Wind River Shoshoni. Ethnos 21 (3–4): 194–215.
- 1960 General Ethnological Concepts. International Dictionary of Regional European Ethnology and Folklore, ed. by Åke Hultkrantz, Vol. 1. Copenhagen: Rosenkilde and Bagger.
- 1965 Type of Religion in the Arctic Hunting Cultures, pp. 265–318 in Hunting and Fishing, ed. by Harald Hvarfner. Luleå: Norrbottens Museum.
- 1968a "Miscellaneous Beliefs": Some Points of View concerning the Informal Religious Sayings. Temenos 3: 67–82.
- 1968b Natten tillhör den heliga peyote, pp. 57–67 in Stridsyxa och fredspipa, ed. by Erik U. Englund and Albin Widén. Stockholm: Norstedts.
- 1971 Review of La Barre, The Ghost Dance. Temenos 7: 137–144.
- 1973a A Definition of Shamanism. Temenos 9: 25–37.
- 1973b Metodvägar inom den jämförande religionsforskningen. Stockholm: Scandinavian University Books.
- 1975 Conditions for the Spread of the Peyote Cult in North America, pp. 70–83 in New Religions, ed. by Haralds Biezais. Scripta Instituti Donneriani Aboensis VII. Stockholm.
- 1976 Religion and Ecology among the Great Basin Indians, pp. 137–150 in The Realm of the Extra-Human, Ideas and Actions, ed. by A. Bharati. The Hague and Paris.
- 1977a Amerikanische Religionen, pp. 402–450 in Theologische Realenzyklopädie, vol. II. Berlin and New York: Walter de Gruyter.
- 1977b History of Religions in Anthropological Waters: Some Reflections against the Background of American Data. Temenos 13: 81–97.
- 1979a Naturkänsla, ekologi och religion i indianernas Nordamerika. Acta Societatis Anthropologicae Fennicae 5, pp. 109–117. Helsinki.
- 1979b The Religions of the American Indians. Berkeley and Los Angeles: University of California Press.
- 1981a Belief and Worship in Native North America. Ed. by Christopher Vecsey. Syracuse: Syracuse University Press.
- 1981b North American Indian Religions in a Circumpolar Perspective, pp. 11–28 in North American Indian Studies: European Contributions, ed. by Pieter Hovens. Göttingen: Edition Herodot.
- 1982 Religion and Experience of Nature among North American Hunting Indians, pp. 163–186 in The Hunters: their Culture and Way of Life, ed. by Åke Hultkrantz and Ørnulf Vorren. Tromsø: Universitetsforlaget.
- 1983a The Concept of the Supernatural in Primal Religion. History of Religions 22 (3): 231–253.
- 1983b The Study of American Indian Religions. New York and Chico, California: The Crossroad Publications Co. and Scholars Press.
- 1983c The Religion of the Goddess in North America, pp. 202–216 in The Book of the Goddess: Past and Present, ed. by Carl Olson. New York: Crossroad.
- 1984 The Myths of the Trickster and Culture Hero, pp. 113–126 in Anthropology as a Historical Science, ed. by M. Bhuriya and S. M. Michael. Indore.
- 1985 The Shaman and the Medicine-Man. Social Science & Medicine 20 (5): 511–515.

    1986a The American Indian Vision Quest: A Transition Ritual or a Device for Spiritual Aid? pp. 24–43 in Transition Rites: Cosmic, Social and Individual Order, ed. By Ugo Bianchi. Rome: L'Erma di Bretschneider.
    1986b The Peril of Visions. History of Religions 26 (1): 34–36.
    1987 Native Religions of North America. San Francisco: Harper & Row.
    1989 Health, Religion, and Medicine in Native North American Traditions, pp. 327–358 in Healing and Restoring: Health and Medicine in the World's Religious Traditions, ed. by Lawrence E. Sullivan. New York: Macmillan.
    1992 Shamanic Healing and Ritual Drama: Health and Medicine in Native North American Religious Traditions. New York: Crossroad.
    1993 Introductory Remarks on the Study of Shamanism. Shaman 1 (1): 3–14.
    1995 Some Viewpoints on the Peyote Religion in North America. Acta Americana 3 (2): 58–70.

Hurt, Wesley R.
    1960 Factors in the Persistence of Peyote in the Northern Plains. Plains Anthropologist 5 (9): 16–27.

Jackson, Barbara
    1980 Rice Village, in Anishinabe 6, Studies of Modern Chippewa, ed. by J. Anthony Paredes. Tallahassee: University Press of Florida.

Jackson, C. L., and G. Jackson
    1963 Quanah Parker: Last Chief of the Comanches. New York: Exposition Press.

James, William
    1902 The Varieties of Religious Experience. New York: University Books.

Janiger, Oscar and Marlene Dobkin de Rios
    1976 *Nicotiana:* An Hallucinogen? Economic Botany 30: 295–297.

Jennings, Jesse D.
    1964 The Desert West, pp. 149–174 in Prehistoric Man in the New World, ed. By J. D. Jennings and Edward Norbeck. Chicago: University of Chicago Press.

Jilek, Wolfgang G.
    1982 Indian Healing: Shamanic Ceremonialism in the Pacific Northwest Today. Washington: Hancock House.

Jones, J. A.
    1955 The Sun Dance of the Northern Ute. Bureau of American Ethnology, Bulletin 157 (47), pp. 203–263.

Jorgensen, Joseph G.
    1972 The Sun Dance Religion: Power for the Powerless. Chicago: University of Chicago Press.
    1986 Ghost Dance, Bear Dance, and Sun Dance, pp. 660–672 in Handbook of North American Indians, ed. by William Sturtevant, vol. 11. Washington D.C.: Smithsonian Institution.

Josephy, Alvin M.
    1962 The Patriot Chiefs. London: Eyre and Spottiswoode.

Kardiner, Abram
    1939 The Individual and His Society: the Psychodynamics of Primitive Social Organization. New York: Columbia University Press.

Kelley, J. Charles
    1966 Mesoamerica and the Southwestern United States, pp. 95–110 in Handbook of Middle American Indians, vol. 4. Washington, D.C.: Smithsonian Institution.

Kensinger, Kenneth M.
- 1973 Banisteriopsis Usage among the Peruvian Cashinahua, pp. 9–19 in Hallucinogens and Shamanism, ed. by Michael J. Harner. New York: Oxford University Press.

Kenton, Edna (ed.)
- 1954 The Jesuit Relations and Allied Documents. New York: The Vanguard Press.

Kluckhohn, Clyde
- 1967 (1944) Navaho Witchcraft. Boston: Beacon Press.

König, René
- 1983 Einige Bemerkungen zu Hans Peter Duerrs „Traumzeit", pp. 115–124 in Der gläserne Zaun, ed. by Rolf Gehlen and Bernd Wolf. Frankfurt am Main: Syndikat.

Kroeber, Alfred L.
- 1902–07 The Arapaho. Bulletins of the American Museum of Natural History, vol. XVIII. New York.
- 1925 Handbook of the Indians of California. Bureau of American Ethnology, Bulletin 78. Washington.
- 1948 Anthropology, second edition. New York: Harcourt, Brace and Co.
- 1952 The Nature of Culture. Chicago: University of Chicago Press.

La Barre, Weston
- 1938 The Peyote Cult. Yale University Publications in Anthropology 19. New Haven.
- 1939 Note on Richard Schultes' "The Appeal of Peyote". American Anthropologist 41 (2): 340–342.
- 1941 A Cultist Drug-Addicton in an Indian Alcoholic. Bulletin of the Menninger Clinic 5 (2), March 1941, pp. 40–46.
- 1946 Review of Omer Stewart, Washo-Northern Paiute Peyotism. American Anthropologist 48 (4): 633–634.
- 1947 Primitive Psychotherapy in Native American Cultures: Peyotism and Confession. Journal of Abnormal and Social Psychology 42 (3): 294–309.
- 1957 Mescalism and Peyotism. American Anthropologist 59 (4): 708–711.
- 1960 Twenty Years of Peyote Studies. Current Anthropology 1 (1): 45–60.
- 1964 The Narcotic Complex of the New World. Diogenes 48: 125–138.
- 1970a The Ghost Dance: Origins of Religion. Garden City, New York: Doubleday & Co.
- 1970b Old and New World Narcotics: A Statistical Question and an Ethnological Reply. Economic Botany 20 (1): 73–80.
- 1971 Materials for a History of Studies of Crisis Cults: A Bibliographic Essay. Current Anthropology 12 (1): 3–44.
- 1972 Hallucinogens and the Shamanic Origins of Religion, pp. 261–294 in Flesh of the Gods: The Ritual Use of Hallucinogens, ed. by Peter T. Furst. New York and Washington: Praeger.
- 1975a Anthropological Perspectives on Hallucination and Hallucinogens, pp. 9–52 in Hallucinations: Behavior, Experience and Theory, ed. by R. K. Siegel and L. J. West. New York: John Wiley.
- 1975b The Peyote Cult. Fourth edition enlarged. Hamden, Connecticut: Archon Books.

1979a Peyotl and Mescaline. Journal of Psychedelic Drugs 11 (1–2): 33–39.

1979b Shamanic Origins of Religion and Medicine. Journal of Psychedelic Drugs 11 (1–2): 7–11.

La Barre, Weston, *et alii*
1951 Statement on Peyote. Science 114: 2970, pp. 582–583.

La Farge, Oliver
1960 Defining Peyote as a Narcotic. American Anthropologist 62 (4): 687–689.

Lame Deer, John Fire and Richard Erdoes
1972 Lame Deer: Seeker of Visions. New York: Simon and Schuster.

Laird, Carobeth
1977 Encounter with an Angry God. New York: Ballantine Books.

Landes, Ruth
1970 The Prairie Potawatomi. Madison: University of Wisconsin Press.

Lanternari, Vittorio
1960 Movimenti religiosi di libertà e di salvezza dei popoli oppressi. Milano: Feltrinelli.

Lasswell, H. D.
1935 Collective Autism as a Consequence of Culture Contact: Notes on Religious Training and the Peyote Cult at Taos. Zeitschrift für Sozialforschung 4: 232–247.

Leary, Timothy, Ralph Metzner and Richard Alpert
1964 The Psychedelic Experience. New Jersey.

Levy, M.
1961 The Human Form in Art. London: Odhams Press.

Lewin, L.
1887/88 Über Anhalonium Lewinii. Archiv für experimentelle Pathologie und Pharmakologie 24: 401–411.

Liberty, Margot P.
1970 Priest and Shaman on the Plains: A False Dichotomy? Plains Anthropologist 15 (48): 73–79.

1980 The Sun Dance, pp. 164–178 in Anthropology of the Great Plains, ed. by W. Raymond Wood and Margot Liberty. Lincoln: University of Nebraska Press.

Lieber, M. D.
1972 Opposition to Peyotism among the Western Shoshone: The Message of Traditional Belief. Man 7 (3): 387–396.

Lindig, Wolfgang
1970 Geheimbünde und Männerbünde der Prärie- und der Waldlandindianer Nordamerikas. Wiesbaden: Franz Steiner.

Lindig, Wolfgang and A. M. Dauer
1961 Prophetismus und Geistertanz-Bewegung bei nordamerikanischen Eingeborenen, pp. 41–74 in Chiliasmus und Nativismus, ed. by W. E. Mühlmann. Berlin: Dietrich Reimer.

Lindblom, Johannes
1934 Profetismen i Israel. Stockholm: Diakonistyrelsen.

Linton, Ralph
1936 The Study of Man: An Introduction. New York and London: Appleton-Century Co.

    1943 Nativistic Movements. American Anthropologist 45 (2): 230–240.
    1945 The Cultural Background of Personality. New York: Appleton-Century-Crofts.
Ljungdahl, Axel
    1975 What We Can Learn from Non-Biblical Prophet Movements, pp. 84–91 in New Religions, ed. by Haralds Biezais. Scripta Instituti Donneriani Aboensis 7. Stockholm.
Loeb, E. M.
    1943 Primitive Intoxicants. Quarterly Journal of Studies on Alcohol 4 (2): 387–398.
Lowie, Robert H.
    1915 Psychology and Sociology. The American Journal of Sociology 21 (2): 217–229.
    1922 The Religion of the Crow Indians. Anthropological Papers of the American Museum of Natural History 25 (2). New York.
    1935 The Crow Indians. New York: Farrar & Rinehart.
    1960 Ceremonialism in North America, pp. 336–364 in Lowie's Selected Papers in Anthropology, ed. by Cora Du Bois. Berkeley and Los Angeles: University of California Press.
Lumholtz, Carl
    1900 Symbolism of the Huichol Indians. Memoirs of the American Museum of Natural History, vol. 3 (1). New York.
    1902 Unknown Mexico. 2 volumes. New York: Charles Scribner's Sons.
Lurie, Nancy O.
    1968 An American Indian Renascence? pp. 187–208 in The American Indian Today, ed. by Stuart Levine and Nancy O. Lurie. Deland, Florida: Everett and Edwards.
Lynch, John (ed.)
    1984 Past and Present in the Americas. Manchester: Manchester University Press.
McAllester, D. P.
    1949 Peyote Music. Viking Fund Publications in Anthropology 13. New York.
Malouf, Carling I.
    1942 Gosiute Peyotism. American Anthropologist 44 (1): 93–103.
Marriott, Alice and C. H. Rachlin
    1972 Peyote. New York: Mentor Books.
Marshall, C. R.
    1937 An Enquiry into the Causes of Mescal Visions. Journal of Neurology and Psychopathology 17: 289–304.
Martin, Calvin
    1978 Keepers of the Game: Indian-Animal relationships and the Fur Trade. Berkeley and Los Angeles: University of California Press.
Marty, Martin E.
    1960 Sects and Cults. Annals of the American Academy of Political and Social Sciences 332: 125–134.
Maurer, David W.
    1960 Peyote is not a Drug of Aiddiction. American Anthropologist 62 (4): 684–685.

Maurer, David W. and V. H. Vogel
  1954 Narcotics and Narcotic Addiction. Springfield: Ch. C. Thomas.
Medicine, Bea
  1981 Native American Resistance to Integration: Contemporary Confrontations and Religious Revitalization. Plains Anthropologist 26 (94): 277–286.
Merriam, A. P., and W. L. d'Azevedo
  1957 Washo Peyote Songs. American Anthropologist 59 (4): 615–641.
Merrill, W. L.
  1977 An Investigation of Ethnographic and Archaeological Specimens of Mescal-beans *(Sophora secundiflora)* in American Museums. Research Reports in Ethnobotany no. 1. Museum of Anthropology, Ann Arbor, Michigan.
Michaelsen, Robert S.
  1983 "We Also Have a Religion": The Free Exercise of Religion among Native Americans. The American Indian Quarterly 7 (3): 111–142.
Mooney, James
  1892 A Kiowa Mescal Rattle. American Anthropologist V: 64–65.
  1896a The Ghost-Dance Religion and the Sioux Outbreak of 1890. Fourteenth Annual Report of the Bureau of Ethnology, Part II. Washington.
  1896b The Mescal Plant and Ceremony. Therapeutic Gazette 12 (11): 7–11.
  1897 The Kiowa Peyote Rite. Der Urquell, no. 1, pp. 329–333. Leiden.
  1898 Calendar History of the Kiowa Indians. Seventeenth Annual Report of the Bureau of Ethnology, Part I. Washington.
  1907 The Cheyenne Indians. Memoirs of the American Anthropological Association, no. 1 (6), pp. 361–442. Menasha.
Moore, J., and B. Schroer
  1950 The Bitter Paste of Dom Apua. Rocky Mountain Empire Magazine. Denver April 30, 1950.
Morgan, George R.
  1976 Man, Plant and Religion: Peyote Trade on the Mustang Plains of Texas. Ph. D. Dissertation at the Department of Geography, University of Colorado. Boulder.
  1982 Hispanic-Indian Trade of an Indian Ceremonial Plant, Peyote, on the Mustang Plains of Texas. Abstracts, 44th International Congress of Americanists, p. 302. Manchester.
  1983 Recollections of the Peyote Road, pp. 91–99 in Psychedelic Reflections, ed. by L. Grinspoon and J. B. Bakalar. New York: Human Sciences Press.
Moses, L. G.
  1984 The Indian Man: A Biography of James Mooney. Urbana: University of Illinois Press.
Murie, James R.
  1914 Pawnee Indian Societies. Anthropological Papers of the Museum of Natural History, vol. 11 Part 7. New York.
Myerhoff, Barbara G.
  1974 Peyote Hunt: The Sacred Journey of the Huichol Indians. Ithaca, New York: Cornell University Press.
Müller, Werner
  1954 Die blaue Hütte. Wiesbaden: Franz Steiner.

Newberne, Robert E. L. and Charles Burke
- 1922 Peyote. An Abridged Compilation from the Files of the Bureau of Indian Affairs. Washington, D.C.: Government Printing Office.

Newcomb, W. W. Jr.
- 1955 A Note on Cherokee-Delaware Pan-Indianism. American Anthropologist 57 (5): 1041–1045.
- 1956 The Peyote Cult of the Delaware Indians. Texas Journal of Science 8 (2): 202–211.
- 1961 The Indians of Texas. Austin, Texas: University of Texas Press.

Norris, P. W.
- 1882 Annual Report of the Superintendent of the Yellowstone Park ... for the Year 1881. Washington.

Opler, Marvin K.
- 1940 The Character and History of the Southern Ute Peyote Rite. American Anthropologist 42 (3): 463–478.
- 1942 Fact and Fancy in Ute Peyotism. American Anthropologist 44 (1): 151–159.

Opler, Morris E.
- 1936 The Influence of Aboriginal Pattern and White Contact on a Recently Introduced Ceremony, the Mescalero Peyote Rite. Journal of American Folklore 49: 143–166.
- 1938 The Use of Peyote by the Carrizo and Lipan Apache Tribes. American Anthropologist 40 (2): 271–285.
- 1945 A Mescalero Apache Account of the Origin of the Peyote Ceremony. El Palacio 52 (10): 210–212.
- 1940 Myths and Legends of the Lipan Apache Indians. Memoirs of the American Folklore Society, vol. 36. New York.

Park, Willard Z.
- 1934 Paviotso Shamanism. American Anthropologist 36 (1): 98–113.
- 1938 Shamanism in Western North America. Northwestern University Studies in the Social Sciences 2. Evanston and Chicago.

Parsons, Elsie C.
- 1936 Taos Pueblo. General Series in Anthropology 2. Menasha, Wisconsin.

Pascarosa, P. and S. Futterman
- 1976 Ethnopsychedelic Therapy for Alcoholics: Observations in the Peyote Ritual of the Native American Church. Journal of Psychedelic Drugs 8 (3): 215–221.

Petrullo, Vincenzo
- 1934 The Diabolic Root: A Study of Peyotism, the New Indian Religion, among the Delawares. Philadelphia: University of Pennsylvania Press.

Pettazzoni, Raffaele
- 1931–1932 La confession des péchés. 2 volumes. Paris: Leroux.

Posern-Zielińska, Mirosława
- 1972 Peyotyzm Religia Indian Ameryki Północnej. Wrocław: Ossolineum.

Powell, Peter
- 1969 Sweet Medicine: The Continuing Role of the Sacred Arrows, the Sun Dance, and the Sacred Buffalo Hat in Northern Cheyenne History. 2 volumes. Norman: University of Oklahoma Press.

Powers, William K.
   1980 Plains Indian Music and Dance, pp. 212–229 in Anthropology on the Great Plains, ed. by W.R. Wood and Margot Liberty. Lincoln: University of Nebraska Press.

Rachlin, Carol K.
   1968 Tight Shoe Night: Oklahoma Indians Today, pp. 99–114 in The American Indian Today, ed. by Stuart Levine and Nancy O. Lurie. Deland, Florida: Everett and Edwards.

Radin, Paul
   1913 Personal Reminiscences of a Winnebago Indian. Journal of American Folklore 26: 293–318.
   1914 A Sketch of the Peyote Cult of the Winnebago: A Study in Borrowing. Journal of Religious Psychology 7: 1–22.
   1920 The Autobiography of a Winnebago Indian. University of California Publications in American Archaeology and Ethnology 16 (7). Berkeley: University of California Press.
   1923 The Winnebago Tribe. Thirtyseventh Annual Report of the Bureau of American Ethnology. Washington D.C.
   1926 Crashing Thunder. New York: D. Appleton.
   1933 The Method and Theory of Ethnology: An Essay in Criticism. New York and London: McGraw-Hill.
   1945 The Road of Life and Death. Bollingen Series. New:York: Pantheon Books.
   1950 The Religious Experiences of an American Indian. Eranos-Jahrbuch XVIII, pp. 249–290.
   1953 The World of Primitive Man. New York: Henry Schuman.
   1957 Primitive Religion: Its Nature and Origin. 2nd edition. New York: Dover Publications.

Redfield, Robert, Ralph Linton and Melville J. Herskovits
   1936 Memorandum on the Study of Acculturation. American Anthropologist 38 (1): 149–152.

Reichard, Gladys
   1949 The Navaho and Christianity. American Anthropologist 51 (1): 66–71.

Reichel-Dolmatoff, Gerardo
   1972 The Cultural Context of an Aboriginal Hallucinogen: Banisteriopsis Caapi, pp. 84–113 in Flesh of the Gods: The Ritual use of Hallucinogens, ed. by P. T. Furst. New York: Praeger.

Ripinsky-Naxon, Michael
   1993 The Nature of Shamanism: Substance and Function of a Religious Metaphor. Albany: State University of New York Press.

Roy, Chumilal, Adjit Chondhuri, and Donald Irvine
   1970 The Prevalence of Mental Disorders among Saskatchewan Indians. Journal of Cross-Cultural Psychology 1: 383–392.

Rudolph, Kurt
   1978 Die „ideologiekritische" Funktion der Religionswissenschaft. Numen 25 (1): 17–39.

Ruecking, F., Jr.
   1954 Ceremonies of the Coahuiltecan Indians of Southern Texas and Northeastern Mexico. Texas Journal of Science 6: 330–339.

Safford, William E.
   1915 An Aztec Narcotic. Journal of Heredity 6 (7): 291–311.

Sahagun, Fray Bernardino de
   1950–1969 The Florentine Codex: General History of the Things of New Spain, ed. by A. J. O. Anderson and Ch. E. Dibble. 12 Volumes. Santa Fe and Salt Lake City: School of American Research and University of Utah Press.

Sanford, Margaret
   1971 Pan-Indianism, Acculturation, and the American Ideal. Plains Anthropologist 16 (53): 222–227.

Sapir, Edward
   1949 The Meaning of Religion, pp. 346–356 in Selected Writings of Edward Sapir in Language, Culture, and Personality, ed. by D. G. Mandelbaum. Berkeley and Los Angeles: University of California Press.

Schaeffer, Claude E.
   1969 Blackfoot Shaking Tent. Glenbow-Alberta Institute, Occasional Paper 5. Calgary, Alberta.

Schultes, Richard E.
   1938 The Appeal of Peyote *(Lophophora Williamsii)* as a Medicine. American Anthropologist 40 (4): 698–715.
   1963 Botanical Sources of the New World Narcotics. Psychedelic Review 1: 145–166.
   1972 An Overview of Hallucinogens in the Western Hemisphere, pp. 3–54 in Flesh of the Gods, ed. by Peter T. Furst. New York: Praeger.

Schultes, Richard E. and Albert Hofmann
   1979 Plants of the Gods: Origins of Hallucinogenic Use. New York: McGraw-Hill.

Schuster, Meinhard
   1964 Zur Frage der Erste-Früchte-Riten in Nordamerika, pp. 611–619 in Festschrift für Ad. E. Jensen, ed. by Eike Haberland, Meinhard Schuster and Helmut Straube. München: Klaus Renner.

Shepardson, M., and B. Hammond
   1970 The Navajo Mountain Community. Berkeley and Los Angeles: University of California Press.

Shimkin, Dmetri B.
   1953 The Wind River Shoshone Sun Dance. Bureau of American Ethnology, Bulletin 151, pp. 397–484. Washington D.C.

Shonle, Ruth
   1925 Peyote: The Giver of Visions. American Anthropologist 27 (1): 53–75.

Siskin, Edgar E.
   1983 Washo Shamans and Peyotists: Religious Conflict in an American Indian Tribe. Salt Lake City: University of Utah Press.

Skinner, Alanson
   1915 Societies of the Iowa, Kansa, and Ponca Indians. Anthropological Papers of the American Museum of Natural History, vol. 11 (9). New York.
   1926 Ethnology of the Ioway Indians. Public Museum of the City of Milwaukee, Bulletin 5. Milwaukee.

Slotkin, James S.
   1951 Early Eighteenth Century Documents on Peyotism North of the Rio Grande. American Anthropologist 53 (3): 420–427.

1952 Menomini Peyotism. Transactions of the American Philosophical Society 42 (4). Philadelphia.
1955 Peyotism, 1521–1891. American Anthropologist 57 (2): 202–230.
1956a The Peyote Religion. Glencoe, Illinois: The Free Press.
1956b The Peyote Way. Tomorrow 4 (3): 64–70.

Smart, Ninian
1984 Eliade und die Analyse von Weltbildern, pp. 79–94 in Die Mitte der Welt: Aufsätze zu Mircea Eliade, ed. by Hans Peter Duerr. Frankfurt: Suhrkamp.

Smith, Anne M.
1974 Ethnography of the Northern Utes. Papers in Anthropology 17. Santa Fe: Museum of New Mexico Press.

Speck, Frank G.
1933 Notes on the Life of John Wilson, the Revealer of Peyote. General Magazine and Historical Chronicle 35: 539–556.

Spicer, E. H.
1954 Spanish-Indian Acculturation in the Southwest. American Anthropologist 56 (4): 663–684.
1961 (ed.) Perspectives in American Indian Culture Change. Chicago: The University of Chicago Press.

Spier, Leslie
1930 Klamath Ethnography. Berkeley: University of California Publications in American Archaeology and Ethnology, vol. 30.

Spindler, George D.
1952 Personality and Peyotism in Menomini Indian Acculturation. Psychiatry 15: 151–159.
1955 Sociocultural and Psychological Processes in Menomini Acculturation. University of California Publications in Culture and Society, vol. 5. Berkeley.

Spindler, George D. and Walter Goldschmidt
1952 Experimental Design in the Study of Culture Change. Southwestern Journal of Anthropology 8 (1): 68–83.

Spindler, George D. and Louise S. Spindler
1971 Dreamers without Power: The Menomini Indians. Case Studies in Anthropology. New York: Holt, Rinehart and Winston.

Spindler, Louise S.
1952 Witchcraft in Menomini Acculturation. American Anthropologist 54 (4): 593–602.

Spindler, Louise S. and George D. Spindler
1958 Male and Female Adaptations in Culture Change. American Anthropologist 60 (2): 217–233.

Spiro, Melford E.
1966 Religion: Problems of Definition and Explanation, pp. 85–126 in Anthropological Approaches to the Study of Religion, ed. by Michael Banton. London: Tavistock Publications.

Steinmetz, Paul B., SJ
1980 Pipe, Bible and Peyote among the Oglala Lakota. Stockholm Studies in Comparative Religion 19. Stockholm.

Steltenkamp, Michael F.
   1982 The Sacred Vision: Native American Religion and Its Practice Today. New York: Paulist Press.

Stenberg, Molly P.
   1946 The Peyote Culture among Wyoming Indians. University of Wyoming Publications 12 (4): 85–156. Laramie.

Stewart, Omer C.
   1938 Cactus Christianity. Broadcast no. 1934, University of California Radio Service, March 13, 1938.
   1939 Washo-Northern Paiute Peyotism: A Study of Acculturation. Proceedings of the Sixth Pacific Science Congress, vol. 4, pp. 65–68.
   1941a Culture Element Distributions: XIV, Northern Paiute. Anthropological Records 4 (3). Berkeley and Los Angeles.
   1941b The Southern Ute Peyote Cult. American Anthropologist 43 (2): 303–308.
   1944 Washo-Northern Paiute Peyotism: A Study in Acculturation. University of California Publications in American Archaeology and Ethnology 40 (3), pp. 63–142. Berkeley and Los Angeles.
   1948 Ute Peyotism. University of Colorado Studies, Series in Anthropology, vol. 1. Boulder, Colorado.
   1956 Three Gods for Joe. Tomorrow, Quarterly Review of Psychical Research 4 (3): 71–76.
   1961a Peyote and the Arizona Court Decision. American Anthropologist 63 (6): 1334–1335.
   1961b The Native American Church and the Law with Description of Peyote Religious Services. Westerners Brand Book 17, pp. 5–47.
   1970 Peyotism. Encyclopaedia Britannica, fourteenth edition, vol. 1, pp. 790–791. Chicago.
   1972 The Peyote Religion and the Ghost Dance. The Indian Historian 5 (4): 27–30.
   1973 Anthropologists as Expert Witnesses for Indians: Claims and Peyote Cases, pp. 35–43 in Anthropology and the American Indian: A Symposium, ed. by James Officer. San Francisco: The Indian Historian Press.
   1974 Origin of the Peyote Religion in the United States. Plains Anthropologist 19 (65): 211–223.
   1979 A New Look at Cree Peyotism, pp. 151–155 in Lifeways of Intermontane and Plains Montana Indians, ed. by Leslie H. Davis. Museum of the Rockies Occasional Papers no. 1. Bozeman.
   1979/1980 Ethnohistorical Aspects of Peyotism and Mescalism. Journal of Altered States of Consciousness 5 (4): 277–296.
   1980a Peyotism and Mescalism. Plains Anthropologist 25 (90): 297–309.
   1980b The Ghost Dance, pp. 179–187 in Anthropology on the Great Plains, ed. by W. Raymond Wood and Margot Liberty. Lincoln: University of Nebraska Press.
   1980c The Native American Church, pp. 188–196 in Anthropology on the Great Plains, ed. by W. Raymond Wood and Margot Liberty. Lincoln: University of Nebraska Press.
   1980d American Indian Religion: Past, Present, Future. Wassaja, The Indian Historian 13 (1): 15–18.

1982 The History of Peyotism in Nevada. Nevada Historical Society Quarterly 25 (3): 197–209.

1986 The Peyote Religion, pp. 673–681 in Handbook of North American Indians, ed. by William Sturtevant, vol. 11: Great Basin. Washington, D.C.: Smithsonian Institution.

1987 Peyote Religion: A History. Norman: University of Oklahoma Press.

1991 Peyote and the Law, pp. 44–62 in Handbook of American Indian Religious Freedom, ed. by Christopher Vecsey. New York: Crossroad.

Stewart, Omer C., and David F. Aberle
1984 Peyotism in the West: A Historical and Cultural Perspective. Salt Lake City: University of Utah Press.

Stone, Lyle M., and Donald Chaput
1978 History of the Upper Great Lakes Area, pp. 602–609 in Handbook of North American Indians, ed. by William Sturtevant, vol. 15: Northeast. Wahington: Smithsonian Institution.

Sundkler, Bengt
1976 Zulu Zion and some Swazi Zionists. Studia Missionalia Upsaliensia XXIX. Uppsala.

Swanson, Guy E.
1960 The Birth of the Gods: The Origin of Primitive Beliefs. Ann Arbor: University of Michigan Press.

Swiderski, S.
1975 Notions théologiques dans la religion syncrétique Bouiti au Gabon. Église et théologie 6, pp. 319–364.

Tax, Sol
1937 The Social Organization of the Fox Indians, pp. 241–282 in Social Anthropology of North American Tribes, ed. by Fred Eggan. Chicago: University of Chicago Press.

Thomas, Robert K.
1968 Pan-Indianism, pp. 77–85 in The American Indian Today, ed. by Stuart Levine and Nancy O. Lurie. Deland, Florida: Everett and Edwards.

Thurman, M. D.
1973 Supplementary Material on the Life of John Wilson, "The Revealer of Peyote." Ethnohistory 20 (3): 279–287.

Troike, Rudolph C.
1962 The Origins of Plains Mescalism. American Anthropologist 64 (5): 946–963.

Turner, H. W.
1978 Bibliography of New Religious Movements in Primal Societies, vol. II: North America. Boston: G. K. Hall & Co.

Tylor, Edward Burnett
1891 Primitive Culture. 2 volumes. Third Edition. London: John Murray.

Underhill, Ruth M.
1948 Ceremonial Patterns in the Greater Southwest. Monographs of the American Ethnological Society 13. New York.

1952 Peyote, pp. 143–148 in Proceedings of the 30th International Congress of Americanists in Cambridge. London: Royal Anthropological Institute.

1956 The Navajos. Norman: University of Oklahoma Press.

1957 Religion among American Indians. Annals of the American Academy of Political and Social Science 311, pp. 127–136.
1965 Red Man's Religion. Chicago: University of Chicago Press.

Vecsey, Christopher
1983 Traditional Ojibwa Religion and Its Historical Changes. Philadelphia: The American Philosophical Society.
1988 Imagine Ourselves Richly: Mythic Narratives of North American Indians. New York: Crossroad.

Voget, Fred
1956 The American Indian in Transition: Reformation and Accommodation. American Anthropologist 58 (2): 249–263.
1984 The Shoshoni-Crow Sun Dance. Norman: University of Oklahoma Press.

Vogt, Evon Z.
1957 The Acculturation of American Indians. Annals of the American Academy of Political and Social Sciences 311, pp. 137–146.
1961 Navaho, pp. 278–336 in Perspectives in American Indian Culture Change, ed. by E. H. Spicer. Chicago: University of Chicago Press.

Wach, Joachim
1947 Sociology of Religion. London: Kegan Paul.

Wagner, Günter
1932 Die Entwicklung und Verbreitung des Peyote Kultes: ein Beitrag zum Problem der Akkulturation. Baessler-Archiv 15, pp. 59–141. Berlin.

Wagner, Roland M.
1974 Western Navajo Peyotism: A Case Analysis. Ph.D. thesis, University of Oregon.
1975a Pattern and Process in Ritual Syncretism: The Case of Peyotism among the Navajo. Journal of Anthropological Research 31 (2): 162–181.
1975b Some Pragmatic Aspects of Navaho Peyotism. Plains Anthropologist 20 (69): 197–205.

Wallace, Anthony F. C.
1956 Revitalization Movements. American Anthropologist 58 (2): 264–281.
1959 Cultural Determinants of Response to Hallucinatory Experience. A.M.A. Archives of General Psychiatry 1: 58–69.
1966 Religion: An Anthropological View. New York: Random House.

Wallace, Ernest and E. Adamson Hoebel
1952 The Comanches: Lords of the South Plains. Norman: University of Oklahoma Press.

Washburn, Wilcomb E.
1975 The Indian in America. New York: Harper and Row.

Webb, Walter P.
1931 The Great Plains. New York: Grosset and Dunlap.

Wheeler, Geoffrey E.
1974 Salvation, pp. 201–204 in Encyclopaedia Britannica, Vol. 16.

Whitman, William
1937 The Oto. Columbia University Contributions to Anthropology 28. New York: Columbia University Press.

Wilson, Bryan R.
    1969 A Typology of Sects, pp. 361–383 in Sociology of Religion, ed. by R. Robertson. Harmondsworth.
    1973 Magic and the Millennium. New York: Harper and Row.

Wilson, John
    1977 Making Inferences about Religious Movements. Religion 7 (2): 149–166.

Winick, Charles
    1956 Dictionary of Anthropology. New York: Philosophical Library.

Wissler, Clark
    1918 The Sun Dance of the Blackfoot Indians. Anthropological Papers of the American Museum of Natural History 16 (3). New York.
    1941 North American Indians of the Plains. Third edition. New York: American Museum of Natural History.

Witherspoon, Gary
    1973 Sheep in Navajo Culture and Social Organization. American Anthropologist 75 (5): 1441–1447.

Wood, W. Raymond
    1974 Northern Plains Village Cultures: Internal Stability and External Relationships. Journal of Anthropological Research 30 (1): 1–16.

Wright, Muriel E.
    1951 A Guide to the Indian Tribes of Oklahoma. Norman: University of Oklahoma Press.

Yinger, Milton
    1957 Religion, Society, and the Individual. NewYork: Macmillan.

Index

Acculturation 7, 16, 17, 85 ff., 99, 128, 191
  cultural deprivation 17, 92 f., 190
  cultural disintegration theory 92
  economic deprivation 91 f., 190
  economic drives 142, 144, 190
  loss of religious values 97 f.
  syncretism 126, 151 ff., 155; cf. Process: assimilation
  messianistic movements 13, 15
  millenarian movements 13, 15
  prophetic movements 13
  revivalistic movements 13, 15
African Bwiti "cult" 42
Agnosticism, atheism 188
Anti-White ideology 145 ff.
Appeal of Peyote 115, 203 ff.

Basic motivation and cultural causes 179 f., 187 f.

Christian impact
  Christian ideas in Peyotism 16, 17, 39–42, 45, 46 f., 74, 85, 122, 136, 139 f., 145, 147 ff., 151 f., 153 ff., 175 ff., 182, 186 f., 188, 194 f., 203
  Christianity and ritual 155
  Church organization as model 194
  difficulties to adopt Christianity 175 f.
  growth of Christian elements 155 ff.
Chungichnish religion 15 note
Community religion 17
Confession of sins 49, 95 f., 176 f., 190
Conservatism 196 f., 198
Conversion 167 f., 177
Crisis religions 13, 83 ff., 190
  Peyote as a crisis religion 83 ff., 182

Datura 15, 15 note, 119, 170, 199
Declination of Peyote religion 205

Diffusion of Peyote
  diffusion of Peyote 14, 18, 31 ff., 78 ff., 169, 181 ff., 190, 203 f.
  external factors in Peyote diffusion 84 f., 174
Disregard of religious factors 91, 92
Doctrine 43 ff., 134

Ecstasy, cf. trance 166, 168 f., 207
Eschatology 15, 95, 145
Ethics 44, 135
  dualism, ethical 95, 145
Escapism 93
Factionalism and mutual distrust 55 f., 196
Feeling of harmony 59

Harmony 175, 176 f.
Hunting culture 172, 203

Indianness 123 note, 127, 151 f.
Indoctrination 175
Intertribal religion 128

Leaders of Peyote Movement
  Daveko 138
  Hensley, Albert 141, 152
  Koshiway, Jonathan 41, 139, 195
  Lancaster, Ben 141
  Lone Bear, Sam 102
  Lopez, Walter 138
  Murdock, Henry 140 f.
  Parker, Quanah 44, 139, 140 f., 150, 163, 185
  Personality types 163
  Prophets in Peyotism 15, 17, 136, 145
  Rave, John 107, 124, 141, 143 f., 152, 156, 163, 167, 197
  S. B. Winnebago Peyotist 163, 167, 168
  Setkopti 100, 139

Stacher, Herbert 138
Tenskwatawa 197
Washakie, Charlie 51, 58, 139
Wesaw, George 54, 56, 57
Wesaw, Tom 53f., 56f.
Wilson, John 39, 118 note, 138, 141f., 194

Medical aspects
  curative functions 38, 99ff., 104f., 175, 191f.
  health and Peyote 58, 80
  medicine for health improvement 58, 79, 91, 99ff.
  medicine in a supernatural context 103ff., 108
  Peyote as doctor 101ff.
Magic 173, 174
Medicine men 30, 32, 100ff, 136, 198
Medicine power 117
Mescalism 109ff.
  Mescal 109
  Mescal bean cult 15, 21, 38, 108ff., 113, 184, 203
  Mescal bean medicine society 110f.
  Red bean cult, see mescal bean cult
Mexican ideas in Peyotism 16, 17, 29f., 35ff., 80, 108f., 110, 137f., 183, 191
Mysticism 167, 169

New World narcotic complex 171

Origin tales 74–78

Pan-Indianism 14, 37, 123ff., 128ff., 195, 204
Personal Motivation
  aims of Peyote taking 58f.
  anxiety as impetus 98f.
  causes of taking Peyote 47, 57, 81ff., 164, 166, 174, 179f.
  individualistic choices 80f., 161 note, 179, 184
Peyotism, Peyote religion
  blessings in Peyotism 94, 143
  future of Peyotism 205ff.

growth of Peyote religion 181ff.
Huichol Peyotism 30
ideological clashes between Peyotists and non-Peyotists 134f., 138
midnight song 49, 66f.
missionary activity 144f.
missionary religion 140, 151, 155f.
Native American Church 14, 15, 29, 118, 136, 139, 151, 195f., 204
Navajo deprivation and Peyote 86ff.
perceptive approach to religion 165
Peyote adaptations 183, 185
Peyote as an alternative to Christianity 148f
Peyote as a model 177f.
Peyote as a religion 174, 182
Peyote as the middle way 189
Peyote as pan-Indian 123ff., 131f.
Peyote's best mark: it is Indian 123
Peyote's blessings 73
Peyote experiences 168
Peyote in tribal groups 8, 18f.
Peyote lodge 59
Peyotism 14, 29, passim
Peyote personalities 136ff., 139
Peyote symbolism 60, 183
Peyote way 15
Plains area as a Peyote centre 198f.
Prayer meetings 48f., 52
Priests in Peyotism 136ff., 139
Proselytizing 33, 39, 136ff.
rejections of Peyote 201f.
Reservation system as cause 84
Sacred morning meal 61
simplicity of Peyote religion 132ff.
smoking 61, 63
sources of Peyotism 18
traditionalism among Peyotists 197f.
transport system as cause 84f.
vomiting 31, 49, 109
Peyotism as pan-Indian 123ff., 131f., 192, 203f.
Peyote as a crisis religion 83ff., 182
Peyote as pan-Indian 123ff., 131f.
Peyote bulb
  legality of Peyote 25f.
  Peyote as narcotic 79f.

231

Peyote: botany and chemistry 29, 79f., 170ff.
Peyote trigger to Peyotism 165
Peyote personalities 136ff., 139
Peyoteros 30
Pilgrimage 30
Plains Peyotism 31, 108, 128f., 182f., 184ff., 192, 203f.
Possession 168f.
Power loss 91, 92
Pre-Christian religion 176
Process
   acculturation 7, 16, 17, 85ff., 99, 128, 191
   assimilation 151ff.
   nativistic movements 13, 15f.
   nativism 126
   personal adjustment 97ff.
   revitalization movement 15
   revivalistic movements 13, 15
Prophetism and Peyotism 15, 17, 136, 145
Psychoactive agents
   alcoholism 107f., 167
   Ayahuasca 7
   Black drink 31 note, 33, 96, 110
   cactus religion 16, 17, 29, 170
   drug religion 15, 172, 184
   hallucinogenic drugs 7, 165, 170f.
   narcotic drugs 23
   psychotropic drugs 24, 172
   psychoactive 25, passim
   tobacco 22f., 168, 197, 200
Psychoanalytic explanation 164
Psychedelic 24f.
Pueblo Indians 34f., 120, 182, 201f.

Redemptive movements 16
Reductionism 166
Reformative nativism 16, 16 note, 126
Reliability of oral information 177, 179f.
Religious origins 170ff., 181ff., 203
Religion
   charismatic religion 151
   compartments of religion 149ff., 168, 181f.
   cultural identity and religion 127f.
   definition of Peyote religion 15, 17

   definition of religion 13, 164f.
   existential concerns 165, 169
   pharmacological theory of religion 172f.
   religion of faction 17
   religious motivation 164, 169, 175
   religious experience 28, 143f.
   religious frame 177, 190, 191
   religious tolerance 149f., 181
   sects 17
   symbolic dimension of religion 166
   transitional religion 87ff., 97f., 194f.
   tribal intercommunication 195
   tribal religion 125ff., 182f., 189, 196f.
Ritualism
   annual thanksgiving ritual 31, passim
   altar forms 39, 48f., 59f.
   cult 13f., 42, 184
   ceremonialism 194, 197
   death and resuscitation rite 14f.
   drum 60
   feathers 60f.
   Ghost dance 17, 17 note, 84, 94, 130f., 158ff., 189
   Midewiwin society 111f.
   prayers 63f.
   rattles 60
   ritual continuity 108ff., 192f.
   ritual development 35ff.
   ritual functionaries 49, 62f.
   ritual Peyotism 29, 47, 48
   ritual attraction 133ff.
   shooting ritual 110ff.
   Shoshoni ritual meeting 61–71
   staff 61
   Sun Dance 186f., 189, 197
   Sun Dance renewal 132, 189

Salvation 94f., 145, 161 note
Shakerism 14 note, 168, 199f.
Shamanism 7, 30f., 38, 62, 101ff., 136ff., 171ff., 183, 200, 203
   democratization of shamanism 174, 183f.
Sin 176
Social prestige 142f.
Sociological view of religion 166f.

Suffering 89ff., 166
Supernatural beings
   eagle 49, 60, 121 note
   guardian spirits 7, 38, 91, 101, 134, 167f., 173, 193
   Mother Earth 46, 64
   pantheon 44–47
   Peyote spirit 45f.
   supernatural 165, 172
   supernatural plants 106f.
   supernatural power 92, 105f., 115ff., 120, 122, 172, 175, 200
   Supreme Being 45, 55, 63, 121f., 126, 154, 168, 175, 181, 197
   thunderbird 46
   waterbird 46, 49
   water woman 47
   white buffalo calf woman 47
Symbolism of Peyote and its ritual instruments 59ff., 152f.

Taboo in connection with menstruation 197f.
Time perspective 19
Trance 28, 165f., 168

Universalism 145

Visions and hallucinations
   hallucinations, auditory 68, 70f., 117
   hallucinatory experiences, structuring of 173
   hallucinations in Peyotism 21f., 27f., 165f.
   visions 26f., 58, 78, 105f., 108, 113ff., 117ff., 121ff., 151, 163, 171f., 174f., 183f., 186, 189, 193f., 198f., 203f.

Washakie family religion 57 note
Witchcraft 200